VOICES FROM
THE WORLD OF
Samuel Pepys

D1490759

CONTENTS

Samuel Pepys
and *his World*

It is more than 300 years since Samuel Pepys walked the streets of London. But if he were to come back today to the city where he was born, he would have no trouble getting his bearings. There are buildings enough that date back to his time, and the vast majority of street names are unchanged.

He might begin a tour of the modern city at the most enduring landmark of all – the Tower of London. The fortress is a thousand years old now, and it was venerably ancient then. Pepys would have walked under the shadow of its thick Norman battlements almost every day. He was just as familiar with the view of the Tower from the water. On hundreds of occasions he passed by Traitor's Gate as he was rowed up and down the River Thames on official business. He knew the inside of the Tower too: for a short, unhappy spell he was a political prisoner inside its walls.

Close by the Tower is the Church of All Hallows, from the spire of which Pepys looked out on the smoking debris of London after the Great Fire. The church itself was only slightly damaged, and is much as Pepys would remember it. After crossing Great Tower Street (stopping only to wonder at the endless river of traffic and the infernal din it makes) Pepys, or his ghost, would come to the foot of Seething Lane. This is the street where he lived during the ten years he kept his famed diary. His workplace, the Navy Office, was here too.

The home that Pepys knew has long since disappeared: the site is now occupied by a disappointingly anonymous office block. But halfway up the road the ethereal Pepys would be gratified to come across a bust of his own self, standing on a pedestal in a narrow urban garden. A little further on he would encounter another flattering surprise: the dead end he knew as Catherine Court, just down the road from his apartments, is now a cut-through called Pepys Street.

Across the way from the site of the Navy Office stands Pepys's parish church, St Olave's. This is where Pepys worshipped most Sundays, and where he buried his wife Elizabeth. The memorial he had made for her is still there, to the north side of the altar. High on the wall of the church's south aisle, close to the spot where he was wont to sit in the Navy Office gallery, is a large plaque dedicated to Pepys himself. It was erected there more than a century ago by one of his Victorian editors. Like Elizabeth's monument, it takes the form of a life-sized carving of its subject's head. So the stone likenesses of man and wife gaze affectionately and eternally at each other across the empty pews.

As he wandered the streets close to his old office, Pepys would be pleased to see that this part of town is still dedicated to the sea and to nautical endeavour. The grand Edwardian massif of the Port of London Authority dominates the area; Trinity House, the organization that maintains Britain's lighthouses, is just around the corner. On Pepys Street there is a 1960s block called Mariner House, and the old pub nearby on Hart Street is called The Ship. All this would make Pepys feel very much at home: in many ways, he would be no stranger in today's London.

But there would be much that struck him as odd or baffling. Since he was intensely interested in money he would, for example, be intrigued by what has become of the national currency. In his day, and for generations after, the English pound was divided into 20 shillings and each shilling into 12 pennies. It follows that there were 240 pence in a pound, and that an old shilling is equivalent to 5p in modern-day terms.

The decimal currency would seem bizarre to Pepys, but he would be much more astonished by the devaluing effect of three centuries' inflation. The prices of everyday things would stagger him. In his day, a loaf of bread cost a penny. A domestic servant could expect to earn a pound a year; and Pepys, at the outset of his naval career in 1660, knew that he could live very comfortably on a government pay-packet of

£250 pounds per annum. In fact he raked in much more than his official salary. By the end of the diary period he had savings in the region of £10,000, and could count himself a very wealthy man.

The altered state of the English language would fascinate Pepys as much as the changes in the English coinage. From a linguistic point of view, Pepys lived on the cusp of the modern era, when the norms of what we now think of as 'Standard English' were beginning to emerge. So while Pepys's writing is unquestionably modern, he does use some redundant forms. Among them are contracted adverbs such as 'mighty' ('I was mighty pleased ...'), which was a particular affectation of the time. The old third person singular of the verb to do – 'doth' – crops up often, as do obsolescent past tenses such as 'ketched' for 'caught' and 'durst' for 'dared'.

Pepys's orthography is unpredictable. Dr Johnson's English dictionary was still a century away, and in Pepys's day a man's spelling was almost as much a matter of personal idiosyncracy as his handwriting. Pepys habitually writes 'then' for 'than', and often spells the same word different ways in the space of a few lines. The rendering of proper names was particularly unstable. Pepys had an actress friend to whom he refers as Mrs Knipp or Mrs Knepp, apparently without knowing or caring which was right. And take Pepys's own surname, though Pepys always spelled it in the odd manner that we now know him by, his contemporaries noted it variously as Peps, Peyps, Peeps, Peypes and Pippis. No one, not even Pepys, could tell them they were wrong. Occasionally the spelling or meaning of a word in the diary, or in some other text, is so arcane or archaic that it is hard for a modern reader to understand. So in this book, any word that is likely to confuse is explained in square brackets at the point where it occurs.

But generally speaking, the English of the mid-17th century, even with its peculiar locutions and conventions, is not difficult for a 21st-century English-speaker to follow. Some of the people whose voices are heard in this book are naturally harder to make sense of than others. For example John Evelyn, the other great diarist of the Restoration period, is fond of forms of expression so extravagant and complex that they must occasionally have taxed his own contemporaries: he is not a straightforward writer. Pepys, on the other hand, wrote his diary in a style that is spontaneous, vivid, almost chatty. His words are generally a pleasure to read because his affability, his democratic instincts and his *joie de vivre* shine through in every paragraph.

Herein lies another reason that Pepys would be at home in our times: he is really not very different from the people who, centuries later, still crowd the streets he knew so well. He desperately wanted to succeed in life; he worried about his health; he argued with his wife though he loved her dearly; he liked a drink and sometimes drank too much; he did his best to live up to the standards he set for himself, and usually failed. This most important part of Pepys world – his interior world – is exactly like yours and mine. He provided posterity with the chance to share in it, and that is his unique achievement.

The World Turned

Upside Down

At the time of his birth, Samuel Pepys seemed destined for ordinariness. There was nothing in the least bit remarkable about the time or the circumstances of his arrival. His father, John, was a jobbing tailor who had done his apprenticeship in Cambridgeshire, and had come to work in London as a young man. It was in the city that he met and married Margaret Kite. She was from a family of butchers, and had been a washerwoman until her marriage. Now her job was managing the busy household and the almost annual round of childbirth. Sam was the fifth of her eleven children, most of whom – and this was depressingly normal – did not survive to adulthood.

The couple lived in tall tottering house at Salisbury Court, a ramshackle square located between Fleet Street and the slow, smelly highway of the River Thames. Salisbury Court had once been a bishop's palace – Salisbury House. Over the course of the previous century, the palace and the surrounding buildings had been subdivided and extended to make homes for artisans such as John Pepys. Sam was born above his father's cutting shop on 23 February 1633.

The 1630s were a brief interlude of relative quiet in England's history. The glorious, martial era of 'Good Queen Bess' had come to an end a generation before. Only a few very aged men could now remember how, as small boys, they heard the news of the defeat of the Spanish Armada. As for the other great glory of the Elizabethan age, William Shakespeare, there were still a good few people around who could recall seeing him and his players fret and strut their hour upon the stage. But his unique genius was as yet unrecognized, and the stage itself – the

Globe across the river in Southwark – had burned down 20 years before in the time of James I. The reigning monarch, Charles I, had been on the throne for eight years. He had been ruling without parliament for the past four, and this was the cause of grumbling discontent in political circles. But the kingdom was – albeit a little uneasily – at peace.

The most exciting thing about the world of the young Samuel Pepys was the city in which he found himself. More than half a million people lived in London, by far the largest city in the kingdom. But though London was immense by contemporary standards, it was not so large that one person – one curious and streetwise boy – could not get to know its byways and bailiwicks in their entirety. It was an easy walk to the open fields of Islington and Hackney, a rather longer hike through the separate conurbation of Westminster and beyond that, to the little village of Chelsea. On the streets outside Pepys's father's house there were fascinating things to be seen: that new-fangled invention, the sedan chair; a sailor with a live and comical dodo tucked under his arm; the cock-fights in Shoe Lane; the fish-market at Billingsgate; the jugglers and the puppet-shows at St Bartholomew's Fair in Smithfield.

But the many pleasures and possibilities of metropolitan life were suddenly denied to the boy Samuel when, at around the age of nine, he was sent to live with his uncle Robert at Brampton in Cambridgeshire. It is not clear what prompted Samuel's parents to send him away. Perhaps it was anxiety brought on by the successive deaths of many siblings. Samuel was already troubled by pain in his kidneys – so possibly it was thought that removing him from the crowded streets and polluted air of London might do his health some good. Or maybe John and Margaret saw some spark of talent in their young son, and thought it might best be nurtured in the provincial homeland of the Pepyses, where they had one slightly distant but highly placed relative. Samuel's great aunt Paulina had in 1618 made an astonishingly good marriage to Sir Sidney Montagu, brother of the Earl of Manchester. The Montagus held estates in Cambridgeshire, and were socially and politically very well-connected both in the provinces and in London.

The Montagus were also patrons of the university at Cambridge, and it may have been that Samuel's educational prospects were at the forefront of his parents' mind when they packed him off to the flat, bleak fen country. Uncle Robert's house was a short hike from Huntingdon Grammar School, a good place of learning for a small boy like Samuel, whose main assets were his appetite for knowledge and his sharp mind. So it was that Sam Pepys joined his new classmates at Huntingdon Grammar in 1642. This was a momentous year in the life of the country, because the long-standing antagonism between king and parliament burst into flame that summer – and England went to war against itself.

For King or for Parliament

The conflict had been brewing for at least a decade. The king's insistence on 'personal rule' – without recourse to parliament – allowed long-standing resentments to build up. Parliament was summoned as seldom as possible, and then only for the purpose of authorizing taxes. So when Charles called parliament in 1640, the members used the opportunity to air their grievances and to undermine Charles's autocratic methods. Many members of parliament were alarmed by Charles's flirtation with Catholicism; they, like the vast majority of the population, were staunchly Protestant or else fiercely Puritan, and were worried that the king was leading the country back into the embrace of Rome. To this extent the struggle between king and parliament was religious, but there was also a political element to it. Charles believed utterly in his divine right to rule: since he was king with God's blessing, it was at best impious and at worst downright blasphemous for his subjects to oppose him. Parliament and its supporters, on the other hand, were feeling their way towards a new definition of their role. They began to see themselves not so much as a committee of humble subjects at the beck and call of the monarch, but as sovereign representatives of the English people, charged to defend the people's ancient freedoms and rights.

The parliament summoned in the spring of 1640 flexed its muscle by refusing to vote the king any money until its grievances were addressed. Charles responded by dissolving it straight away, earning it the name of the Short Parliament. But the need to raise revenue did not go away; indeed it became more acute, and so a new parliament was called in the autumn. This one was here to stay, and so came to be called the Long Parliament. The make-up of the Long Parliament was even more radical than the one that had been dismissed six months before, and it had an eloquent and fiery spokesman in John Pym, a country squire who articulated brilliantly the role of parliament in English polity. He, perhaps more than any other individual, laid the foundations of modern parliamentary democracy. 'Parliament,' he said 'is the soul of the commonwealth.'

The newly assembled MPs knew they had the king in a financial stranglehold, and they used this circumstance to vote through some downright revolutionary reforms. The king's main advisers, the Earl of Strafford and Archbishop Laud, were impeached and imprisoned in the Tower; a bill was passed requiring the summoning of parliament every three years even without the initiative of the king; and the present parliament was not to be dismissed without its own consent. Little by little, they were dismantling the throne of England – or at least the authority that went with it. At the end of the year, Pym and his associates drew up the Grand Remonstrance, a long and rambling list of complaints against the king and his advisers going back to the beginning of the reign. The Remonstrance also demanded reform of the Anglican Church, and the right for parliament to appoint the king's ministers. The document was the subject of a long and angry debate in parliament, but it was passed with a narrow majority. One of the MPs who voted in favour of it was a former pupil of the school where Pepys had just begun his formal education; his name was Oliver Cromwell, and after the vote was passed he was heard to say that if it had been rejected, 'he would have sold all he had next morning and never have seen England more.'

The Grand Remonstrance set the ideological battle lines of the coming war. Those who were for it tended to support the roundheads (so called for the pudding-bowl haircuts favoured by militant Puritans); those who were against it rallied to the king. Charles's immediate response to it was to make conciliatory noises, while at the same time plotting to arrest the most radical parliamentarians. He decided that he would make the arrests in person. It was to be a pivotal moment in Charles's reign, and in British history.

On 4 January 1641, the king walked from Whitehall to Westminster at the head of his troops to take Pym and four of his associates. Pym and his comrades had received word that the king was on his way, and slipped out of the Commons to the watergate that led to the river. By the time the king arrived at Westminster Hall, they were in a boat en route to a safehouse in the City. Sir Ralph Verney was on the benches of the House of Commons when the king arrived.

A little after, the King came with all his guard, and all his pensioners, and two or three hundred soldiers and gentlemen. The King commanded the soldiers to stay in the hall and sent us word that he was at the door. The Speaker was commanded to sit still, with the mace lying before him, and then the King came to the door ... and commanded all that came with him – upon their lives – not to come in. So the doors were kept open, and the Earl of Roxburgh stood within the door, leaning upon it.

Then the King came upwards, towards the chair, with his hat off, and the Speaker stepped out to meet him. Then the King stepped up to his place and stood upon the step, but sat not down in the chair. And, after he had looked a great while, he told us he would not break our privileges, but treason had no privilege. He came for those five gentlemen, for he expected obedience yesterday and not an answer. Then he called Mr Pym and Mr Holles by name, and no answer was made. Then he asked the Speaker if they were here, or where they were.

Upon that the Speaker fell on his knees and desired his excuse, for he was a servant of the House and had neither eyes nor tongue to see or say anything but what they commanded. Then the King told him he thought his eyes were as good as his, and then said his birds were flown but he did expect the House would send them to him. And if they did not he would seek them himself, for their treason was foul and such a one as they would

**thank him to discover. Then he assured us they should have
a fair trial, and so went out, putting off his hat till he came
to the door.**

The speaker's declaration of his first loyalty, though expressed in
somewhat craven terms, has gone down in parliamentary history. As for
the king, he suffered a loss of face from which he never recovered. His
humiliation was compounded the next day when he went to the City in
search of his 'birds', and again came away empty-handed. He then lost
his nerve completely and withdrew to Hampton Court, allowing Pym
and the others to return to Westminster in triumph. Parliament saw
the king's incursion into their territory as an act of war and responded
accordingly. They decreed that the local militias should answer to them
rather than the king and that the commanders of all forts and other
strongholds should be parliament appointees. They created a committee
of public safety, and appointed the Earl of Essex commander of a force
of 20,000 infantrymen and 4,000 cavalry. There were those in
parliament who thought these preparations for war had gone too far.
Thirty-two peers and 65 members of the Commons went north to join
the king at York, where he was rallying his own forces. In August 1642
he marched south and raised the royal standard at Nottingham, and the
military phase of the war began.

Brother Against Brother

The lines that divided England into cavalier and roundhead were
twisted and blurred. Geographically, the north and west of England
(along with Wales) was broadly royalist; while London, the south,
and East Anglia were for parliament. Socially, the landed gentry,
the peasants who worked for them, the hierarchy of the Anglican
Church and England's Catholic minority were for the king; the urban
middle-classes (such as the Pepys family), the self-made men of the
merchant class, and the highest-ranking aristocrats gravitated to
the parliamentary cause. But, as is always the case in civil wars, the
ideological lines often cut through blood ties, and members of the same

family found themselves on opposite sides. Sir Ralph Verney, the MP who witnessed the king's trespass on the Commons received this rebuke from his brother Edmund when he declared his allegiance:

> Brother, what I feared is proved too true, which is your being against the King. Give me leave to tell you in my opinion 'tis most unhandsomely done, and it grieves my heart to think that my father already and I, who so dearly love and esteem you, should be bound in consequence (because in duty to our King) to be your enemy. I hear 'tis a great grief to my father. I beseech you to consider that Majesty is sacred ... I believe you will say you intend not to hurt the King, but can any of you warrant any one shot to say it shall not endanger his very person? I am so much troubled to think of your being of the side you are that I can write no more. Only I shall pray for peace.

The parliamentarian Bulstrode Whitelocke remarked mournfully that, 'All were Englishmen, and the pity of it was that such courage should be spent in the blood of each other.' Similar sentiments were expressed by a royalist officer, Sir John Oglander: 'Thou wouldst think it strange if I should tell thee there was a time in England when brothers killed brothers, cousins cousins, and friends their friends.' The wistful tone of these two pronouncements suggests that the line that separated a roundhead from a cavalier sometimes passed through the heart of individuals. There were dozens of men who fought as royalists but had sat in parliament until war became inevitable. And there were roundheads who never dreamed that the war would overthrow the monarchy, still less end in regicide. Sir Edmund Verney, father of the brothers Ralph and Edmund, found his loyalties split almost equally between the two sides and his two sons, though in the end the balance of his sympathies tipped marginally in the king's favour:

> I do not like the quarrel, he said, and do heartily wish that the King would yield and consent to what they desire ... My conscience is only concerned in honour and in gratitude to

follow my master. I have eaten his bread and served him near thirty years, and will not do so base a thing as to forsake him; and choose rather to lose my life (which I am sure I shall do) than to preserve and defend those things that are against my conscience to protect and defend.

Old men who knew what war was tended to agree that the situation represented, as one pamphlet put it, 'the world turn'd upside down'. For younger men, the martial preparations now being made were a source of excitement rather than a cause of sorrow. Thomas Wood was in his teens in 1642, so he was some years older than Sam Pepys. But like Pepys, he was hard at his studies in the parliamentary heartland as the war began. Thomas (who in this reminiscence refers to himself in the third person as 'Mr Wood') had just gone up to college at Oxford:

Mr Wood's father had then armour or furniture for one man, namely a helmet, a back and breastpiece, a pike and a musket, and other appurtenances; and the eldest of his men-servants (for he had then three at least) named Thomas Burnham did appear in those arms, when the scholars and privileged men trained; and when he could not train, as being taken up with business, the next servant did train: and much ado there was to keep Thomas Wood, the eldest son, then a student of Christ Church and a youth of about 18 years of age, from putting on the said armour and to train among the scholars. The said scholars and privileged men did sometimes train in New College quadrangle, in the eye of Dr Robert Pink, the deputy Vice-Chancellor, then Warden of the said college. And it being a novel matter, there was no holding of the school-boys in their school in the cloister from seeing and following them. And Mr Wood remembered well, that some of them were so besotted with the training and activity and gaiety therein of some young scholars, as being in a longing condition to be one of the train, that they could never be brought to their books again. It was a great disturbance to the youth of the city, and Mr Wood's father foresaw that if his sons were not removed from Oxford they would be spoil'd.

Over in Huntingdonshire, Samuel's well-to-do cousin, Edward Montagu, had nailed his colours to the mast. He was only 18 and had not long since left the school where Sam was now ensconced. But he was old enough and precocious enough to raise a troop to fight for parliament. In neighbouring Cambridgeshire, 43-year-old Oliver Cromwell was gathering a cavalry regiment. Cromwell, like Montagu, had very little military experience at this point. But he was a born fighter, and he had just found his metier.

His body was well compact and strong, said his steward, John Maidston. **His stature was under six foot, I believe about two inches, his head so shaped as you might see it a storehouse and shop both of a vast treasury of natural parts. His temper exceeding fiery, as I have known, but the flame of it kept down for the most part or soon allayed with those moral endowments he had. He was naturally compassionate towards objects in distress, even to an effeminate measure. Though God had made him a heart wherein there was left little room for any fear ... yet did he exceed in tenderness towards sufferers. A larger soul, I think, hath seldom dwelt in a house of clay than his was ... He lived and died in comfortable communion with God, as judicious persons near him well observed.**

That phrase, 'he lived and died in comfortable communion with God', would make a fitting epitaph for any number of history's tyrants. But Cromwell the dictator was still in the future. For now he was a God-fearing roundhead officer, no more no less. Sir William Waller, a general in the parliamentary army, characterized the future Lord Protector as follows:

At this time he had never shown extraordinary parts, nor do I think he did himself believe that he had them. For although he

was blunt he did not bear himself with pride or disdain. As an officer he was obedient, and did never dispute my orders or argue upon them.

Cromwell's own instincts as a soldier were meritocratic, and rooted in the rightness of the cause he served. He was criticized for recruiting men of low birth as officers, to which he replied:

If you choose godly honest men to be captains of horse, honest men will follow them. I had rather have a plain russet-coated captain that knows what he fights for, and loves what he knows, than what you call a gentleman and is nothing else. I honour a gentleman that is so in deed. No man swears but that he pays his twelve pence; if he is in drink he is set in the stocks or worse. The countries where they come leap for joy at them.

This morally driven military code would eventually be applied not just to the army, but to the country at large. That was the essence of the despotism that descended on England during the years of the Republic, and it is what made the people discard the Commonwealth in the end. But at the time Cromwell was merely making a tactical point about the value of commitment combined with strict discipline. His troops were popular with the civilian masses not just because he forbade them to get drunk or swear, but also because they did not indulge in loot and pillage. So the Cromwellian way furthered the parliamentary cause by winning hearts and minds.

But they also needed to win the war. Cromwell fought at Edgehill, the first pitched battle of the war. Here is one royalist's account of the day:

On Sunday last I saw the battle which was the bloodiest I believe the oldest soldiers in the field ever saw. We have routed utterly their horse and slain and chased away so considerable a part of their foot that the enemy is very weak. The Earl of Lindsey, Willoughby and Colonel Luston, the Lord St John with the Lord Fielding are slain, with many others. My Lord Essex [commander-in-chief of the parliamentary forces] **escaped us by being in an alehouse. We have his coach and much money in it. At the beginning of the fight two double troops came over to the King's party, commanded by Sir Faithfull Fortescue, and fought on our side. Marquis Hertford is now on the march with ten thousand men armed out of Wales and intends to meet the King at Oxford. Sir R Hopton and Mr Rogers bring as many from the West Country.**

This partisan account gives the impression that the battle ended in total victory for the royalists. In fact it was a hard-fought draw. Each side lost about 3,000 men. The last-minute defection of a section of the cavalry was a blow to the parliamentary side, but the royalists lost valuable people too. Sir Edmund Verney, the reluctant royalist, was killed defending the king's standard.

The indecisive outcome of the Battle of Edgehill made a long war inevitable. Having failed to destroy the parliamentary army with one blow, the king moved his base to Oxford and dug in for the winter. The university city in effect became the royalist capital. Parliament's stronghold, London, was never in any danger of capture. And so both sides had a firm base from which to operate. In the first phase of the war, the royalists won more victories, but the parliamentarians learned more lessons. Cromwell's cavalrymen in particular became a stronger and more fearsome fighting force the longer the war went one. They became known as 'Ironsides' – a nickname none of them objected to. They were a crucial factor at the Battle of Marston Moor in 1644, where the royalist armies in the north were destroyed. It had appeared that the battle was going the king's way, but late in the day, the Ironsides smashed the opposing cavalry under the command of Charles's nephew Prince Rupert, and so swung it in their favour.

We came down in the bravest order and with the greatest resolution that ever was seen, said one of Cromwell's infantrymen. **In a moment we were past the ditch and into the moor, upon equal grounds with the enemy, our men into a running march.**

> The enemy seeing us coming in such a gallant posture to charge
> them, left all thought of pursuit and began to think that they
> must fight again for that victory which they had already got.
> Here the business of the day, nay of the kingdom, came to be
> determined. Cromwell's own division had a hard pull of it; for
> they were charged by Rupert's bravest men both in front and
> flank. They stood at sword's point a pretty while, hacking one
> another, but at last he [Cromwell] brake through them, scattering
> them like a little dust.

The following year the parliamentary forces were re-organized into
a New Model Army. This new force was to be well-paid, thoroughly
drilled, well-equipped and ideologically committed – like the 'plain
russet-coated captains' that Cromwell so admired. Cromwell himself
was appointed second-in-command and Lieutenant-General of the
Horse. It was this army that won the decisive victory at Naseby in
1645, where the royalist armies in the Midlands gave up the fight.
Cromwell was triumphant. 'Sir, this is none other but the hand of
God, and to him alone belongs the glory ...' he said, addressing the
Speaker in parliament.

> ... honest men served you faithfully in this action. They are
> trusty. I beseech you in the name of God not to discourage
> them. He that ventures his life for the liberty of his country,
> I wish he trust God for the liberty of his conscience, and you
> for the liberty he fights for.

The king surrendered to a Scottish army fighting on the parliamentary
side the following year, but that was not the end of the war. Royalists
carried on fighting throughout England, though many had given their
word not to take up arms again against parliament. There were local
uprisings in Kent, Essex and Cumberland, and in Wales unpaid
parliamentary troops mutinied. The leaders of parliament were not
inclined to show mercy to those who had broken their word and
rekindled the war. They included the captive king in this reckoning,

for they knew very well that he was orchestrating this second conflict. Nevertheless, some moderates in parliament were still hoping that the king would be returned to the throne, and said so in debate. The very idea of reinstating the king outraged the bruised and exhausted men of the parliamentary army. In December 1648 they carried out a military coup to prevent it. A force of soldiers marched on the House of Commons and arrested the moderates, leaving just the hardliners to decide what should be done with the king. In the hands of this so-called 'Rump Parliament', a new and vengeful plan took shape. Shortly before Christmas, the remaining members of the Commons voted to put the king on trial as a traitor.

Death of a King

The men who wrote the indictment against Charles did their best to explain how a king could be guilty of treason, given that the definition of treason was rebellion against the king: they simply ruled retrospectively that parliament, not the crown, was the highest authority in the land.

> **That the said Charles Stuart,** ran the indictment, **being admitted King of England ... out of a wicked design to uphold in himself an unlimited power to rule according to his will and to overthrow the rights and liberties of the people ... hath traitorously and maliciously levied war against the present Parliament and the people therein represented.**

It followed from this piece of legal casuistry that all depredations of the civil war years were the king's fault. The dates and places of battles were listed as if each one were a separate offence on the charge sheet:

> **Upon or about 30th June 1642 at Beverley in the county of York; 24th August at the county of the town of Nottingham, where and when he set up his standard of war; also on 23rd October at Edgehill or Keynton-field in the county of Warwick;**

30th November at Brentford ... 30th August 1643 at Caversham
Bridge near Reading; 30th October upon the city of Gloucester;
30th November at Newbury; 31 July 1644 at Copredy Bridge,
Oxon; 30th September at Bodmin and other places adjacent in
the county of Cornwall; 30th September at Newbury; 8th June
1645 at Leicester; also on 14th of the same month at Naseby-
field ...

[He] hath also renewed the said war against the parliament and
good people of this nation in 1648 in the counties of Kent, Essex,
Surrey, Sussex, Middlesex and many other counties.

The said Charles Stuart hath been the occasioner, author, and
continuer of the said unnatural, cruel and bloody war and therein
guilty of all the treasons, murders, rapines, burnings, spoils,
desolations, damages and mischiefs to this nation, acted and
committed in the said wars.

This indictment was read out in full on the first day of the trial, 20
January 1649. The proceedings were held in Westminster Hall. Tickets
were sold for the event, so the galleries were packed with spectators.
Serried ranks of pikemen guarded the accused. Charles listened to the
indictment without removing his hat for the judges. This small piece of
effrontery symbolized his entire attitude to the court: for him it did not
exist, or at least it had no right to exist, which legally amounted to the
same thing. After the reading of the indictment Charles was asked by
the Lord President, John Bradshaw, how he pleaded. He cleared his
throat and seemed to chuckle. Then he said:

I would know by what power I am called hither. I would know
by what authority – I mean *lawful*. There are many *unlawful*
authorities in the world: thieves and robbers by the highway.
Remember I am your king, your *lawful* king, and what sins you
bring upon your hand, and the judgment of God upon this land ...

Bradshaw, riled by being compared to a highwayman, interrupted at this
point and peevishly asserted that Charles was brought to trial 'in the

name of the people of England, of which you are elected king'. Charles leapt on the crass error in Bradshaw's outburst. England was not an elective kingdom, he pointed out, 'but a hereditary kingdom for these thousand years. I do stand more for the liberty of my people than any here that come to be my pretended judges'.

The first day of the trial ended in a confused stand-off: Bradshaw seemed uncertain how to proceed without a plea having been entered by the accused. So on the second day he went over the same ground. Charles continued to run legal rings round his accusers.

Having already made my protestations not only against the illegality of this pretended court, but also that no earthly power can justly call me, who am your king, in question as a delinquent. I do not know how a king may become a delinquent. But how the House of Commons can erect a Court of Judicature, which was never one itself, I leave to God and the world to judge. And it were full as strange that they should pretend to make laws without King or Lords' House to any that have heard speak of the laws of England.

Charles's cool disdain was winning him the respect of the gallery, but it infuriated the judges. One of them, Colonel Hewson, rushed forward from his judgely seat and crying 'Justice!' spat in the face of the king. 'Well, sir,' said Charles, wiping his face, 'God has justice in store for both you and me.' Bradshaw was still trying in vain to persuade Charles to enter a plea. Charles steadfastly refused, and instead made a counterdemand of his own: 'I do require you give me my reasons,' he said to Bradshaw. 'Sir, it is not for prisoners to require,' replied the prosecutor. 'Prisoner, sir?' responded Charles, imperiously raising his voice, '*I am no ordinary prisoner.*'

On the third day, the duelling between Charles and Bradshaw resumed. Sympathy for the deposed king was still growing among the spectators, and even some of the soldiers set to guard him were heard to mutter, 'God bless you, sir.' In desperation, Bradshaw ruled that the trial would now be held behind closed doors, without the presence of the accused. For three days the judges met in the Painted Chamber and listened to evidence from roundhead veterans who had seen the king on the battlefield urging his cavaliers to kill his own subjects.

On Saturday the court reconvened in Westminster Hall. The pause had done Bradshaw some good. Amid occasional interruptions from the gallery (one woman shouted 'Oliver Cromwell is a traitor'), he finally made an eloquent statement of parliament's case, answering the legal points that Charles had raised on the first two days.

> **There is a contract and a bargain between the King and his people,** said Bradshaw. **And certainly the bond is reciprocal, for as you are the liege lord, so they are liege subjects. The one tie, the one bond, is the bond of protection that is due from the sovereign; the other is the bond of subjection that is due from the subject. Sir, if this bond be once broken, farewell sovereignty … Whether you have been, as by your office you ought to be, a Protector of England – or the Destroyer of England – let all England judge, or all the world that have looked upon it.**

Charles tried to answer this point, but this time Bradshaw refused him leave. The time for discussion was over, in any case. A verdict had been reached, and Bradshaw was ready to pronounce sentence: 'Charles Stuart as tyrant, traitor, murderer and public enemy to the good people of this nation shall be put to death by the severing of his head from his body.'

Charles was led away. Many people – and not just ardent royalists – were outraged by the conduct and the verdict of this show-trial.

> **Never was such a damnable doctrine vented before in the world,** wrote one contemporary, **for the persons of sovereign princes have ever been held sacred even among the most barbarous nations. In many kingdoms Kings have been regulated by force of arms and afterwards deposed and sometimes murdered, but in no history can we find a parallel for this, that ever the rage of rebels extended so far to bring their sovereign lord to public trial and execution.**

Even the judges were wavering. One of them, John Downes, had begun to voice doubts almost before the king was out of the courtroom. 'Have we hearts of stone? Are we men?' said Downes out loud; he had to be shushed by Oliver Cromwell himself, who was sitting nearby.

But the sentence stood. The death warrant – signed by Bradshaw, Cromwell and 57 others (including John Downes) – was delivered two days later to St James's Palace, where Charles was being held. It restated the verdict, and said that sentence was to be carried out 'in the open street before Whitehall on the morrow ... between the hours of ten in the morning and five in the afternoon.'

After the delivery of the warrant, Charles was permitted a visit from his two younger children, 13-year-old Princess Elizabeth and nine-year-old Henry, Duke of Gloucester (the two older sons, Charles and James, were in France, beyond the reach of parliament). Elizabeth was distraught. 'Sweet heart,' said her father, 'You will forget this.' 'No,' swore the princess, 'I will never forget it while I live.' For Henry, Charles had some stern political advice. Sitting the boy on his knee he said:

Now they will cut off thy father's head. Mark what I say: you must not be a king so long as your brothers Charles and James live, for they will cut off your brothers' heads, when they catch them, and cut off thy head too at last. And therefore I charge thee do not be made a king by them.

'I will be torn in pieces first,' said the stone-faced boy, then burst into tears. By all accounts, the guards were in tears too.

Charles was up before dawn the next morning, 30 January 1649.

This day his Majesty was brought from St James's, about ten in the morning, says one eyewitness account to the day's events. **Walking on foot through the Park, with a regiment of foot for his guard, with colours flying, drums beating, his private guard of partisans with some of his gentlemen before and some behind, bareheaded: Dr Juxon, late Bishop of London, next behind him**

and Colonel Thomlinson (who had charge of him) to the gallery in Whitehall, and so into the cabinet chamber where he used to lie, where he continued at his devotion, refusing to dine (having before taken the Sacrament), only at about twelve noon he drank a glass of claret wine and ate a piece of bread.

It was a long wait in the room that used to be his bedroom. The scaffold was not yet complete. It was under construction outside a first-floor window on a turn in the staircase. When the time came, Charles was to be led to the staircase and asked to step through the window on to the wooden platform, where he would be in full view of the assembled crowd. Somewhere in that waiting crowd was 16-year-old Samuel Pepys, who had sneaked away from school to be there.

They came for the king just after two o'clock.

He was accompanied by Dr Juxon, Colonel Thomlinson, Colonel Hacker and the guards before-mentioned through the Banqueting House, adjoining to which the scaffold was erected, between Whitehall Gate and the gate leading into the Gallery from St James's. The scaffold was hung round with black; and the floor covered with black, and the axe and block laid in the middle of the scaffold. There were divers companies of foot and horse on every side of the scaffold, and the multitudes of people that came to be spectators were very great. The King, making a pass upon the scaffold, look'd very earnestly on the block and asked Colonel Hacker if there were no higher; and then spoke thus, directing his speech to the gentlemen on the scaffold ...

'I shall be very little heard of anybody here,' began the King, speaking from notes on a small piece of paper he had taken from his pocket, 'I shall therefore speak a word unto you here. Indeed, I could hold my peace very well, if I did not submit to the guilt as well as to the punishment.' He protested his innocence of beginning the war against the two Houses of Parliament and of any intention to encroach upon their privileges. 'If anybody will look upon the dates of the commissions, they will see clearly that they began these unhappy troubles, not I.' But he did not lay the guilt on Parliament, 'for I believe that ill instruments between them and me has been the chief cause of all this bloodshed.' ... He professed his forgiveness now for all men, even the chief causers of his death.

'Now, Sirs, I must show you both how you are out of your way and I will put you in that way.' Conquest in an unjust cause would avail them nothing. 'You will never do right, nor God will never prosper you, until you give God his due, the King his due (that is, my successors) and the people their due. I am as much for them as any of you. You must give God his due by regulating rightly his Church (according to his Scriptures) which is now out of order ... A national synod, freely called, freely debating among yourselves, must settle this, when that every opinion is freely and clearly heard. For the King indeed I will not –' Charles suddenly stopped and turning to a gentleman who was fingering the axe he said, 'Hurt not the axe that may hurt me.' Then he continued. The laws of the land would clearly instruct them as to their duty to the King. 'For the people truly I desire their liberty and freedom as much as anybody whatsoever; but I must tell you their liberty and freedom consists in having government, those laws by which their lives and their goods may be most their own. It is not their having a share in government; that is nothing appertaining to them. A subject and a sovereign are clean different things ... Sirs, it was for this that I am now come here. If I would have given way to an arbitrary way, for to have all laws changed according to the power of the sword, I needed not to have come here. And therefore I tell you I am the martyr of the people. In truth, Sirs, I shall not hold you much longer ...'

Dr Juxon prompted him to add something about religion, and Charles at once declared: 'I die a Christian according to the profession of the Church of England as I found it left to me by my father.' Then, looking towards the Army officers, he said, 'Sirs, excuse me for this same. I have a good cause and I have a gracious God. I will say no more.'

Then, turning to Colonel Hacker, he asked, 'Take care that they do not put me to any pain ...' But then a gentleman coming near the axe again, the King said 'Take heed of the axe! Pray take heed of the axe!' Then the King, speaking to the executioner, said, 'I shall say but very short prayers, and then thrust out my hands.' Then the King called to Dr Juxon for his nightcap; and having put it on, he said to the executioner, 'Does my hair trouble you?' who desired him to put it all under his cap, which the King did accordingly by the help of the executioner and the Bishop. Then the King, turning to Dr Juxon, said, 'I have a good cause and a gracious God on my side.'

Dr Juxon: 'There is but one stage more. This stage is turbulent and troublesome. It is a short one. But you may consider it, it will soon carry you a very great way. It will carry you from earth to heaven, and there you shall find your great joy the prize. You haste to a crown of glory.'

King: 'I go from a corruptible to an incorruptible crown, where no disturbance can be.'

Dr Juxon: 'You are exchanged from a temporal to an eternal crown, a good exchange.'

Then the King took off his cloak and his George [the Order of St George], giving his George to Dr Juxon saying, 'Remember!' (it is thought for the Prince), and some other small ceremonies passed. After a while the King, stooping down, laid his neck upon the block; and after a little pause, stretching forth his hands, the executioner at one blow severed his head from his body.

Philip Henry, a student at Oxford University, had somehow managed to get close enough to see the king's last moment.

The blow I saw given, and can truly say with a sad heart, at the instant whereof, I remember well, there was such a Grone by the Thousands then present as I never heard before and desire I may never hear again.

The axeman lifted the king's bleeding head by its hair and pronounced the customary words: 'Behold the head of a traitor.' Some people managed to rush forward and dip cloths or handkerchiefs in the royal blood before the troops began the rough business of dispersing the assembled spectators. The gruesome show was at an end, and so, it appeared, was the English monarchy. A new Commonwealth, an English Republic, was about to be born.

Life in the Republic

For more than a decade England was ruled by radicals and extremists. Parallels can be drawn between Cromwell's regime and many later revolutionary states. In its insistence that its authority came from God and in its determination to impose its own strict morality on the masses, Puritan-ruled England stands comparison with the theocratic government of the ayatollahs in Iran. And in its single-minded persecution of the established church, England under the Puritans was like Bolshevik Russia in the 1920s and 1930s. Smashing up churches, with a view to removing idolatrous images, became the professional pastime of a particular cast of godly zealot.

One of the most notorious iconoclasts was a man named William Dowsing. In the 1640s, during the war, he toured Cambridgeshire, Suffolk and Norfolk, and with his team of workmen systematically defaced or destroyed graven images – stained-glass madonnas, wooden cherubs, plaster saints, brass crucifixes – in more than 250 churches. Sometimes he smashed up four churches in day – all in the name of God and for the good of the Puritan cause. He did great damage to the college chapels of Cambridge University. And as his vandalism was official in nature, he kept bureaucratically precise records of every destructive act. Here are some entries from his meticulous journal:

Suffolk. At Haveril [Haverhill] Jan 6 1644. We brake down about a hundred superstitious pictures, and 7 fryers [friars] hugging a nun; and the picture of God, and Christ; and divers others very superstitious. And 200 had been broke down afore

I came. We took away 2 popish inscriptions with *Ora pro nobis*; and we beat down a great stoning cross on top of the church.

At Clare, Jan 6. We brake down a 1000 pictures superstitious; and brake down 200, 3 of God the Father, and 3 of Christ, and the Holy Lamb, and 3 of the Holy Ghost like a dove with wings; and the 12 apostles were carved in wood on the top of the roof, which we gave order have taken down; and 20 cherubims to be taken down. And the sun and moon in the east window, by the King's Arms, to be taken down.

The Latin phrase *Ora pro nobis* – pray for us – was objectionable to Puritans when used on gravestones and memorials because praying for the dead was seen as an unbiblical Roman Catholic practice. And so to smash such monuments was to strike a blow for good theology. Dowsing's activities, though carried out in wartime, were not acts of war. They were a natural and central part of the philosophy of the eventual victors, the men who ten years later were at the peak of power.

But in peacetime as well as war, the main source of political power in the Commonwealth was the army. The country was divided into 15 regions, each one under the governance of a Major-General. The functions of these local military commanders were not unlike those of Hitler's provincial *gauleiters*: to enforce centrally approved patterns of behaviour on the people, in both their private and public lives, and to suppress or excise known opponents of the regime – 'malignants' as they were known in the damning political jargon of the time. Like all dictatorships, Cromwell's government aimed to take control of the media. In 1655 an order of the Protector and Council declared that no one was 'to presume to publish in print any matter of public news, or intelligence, without leave and approbation of the Secretary of State.' Total state censorship, in other words.

The remit of the Major-Generals extended to the sexual morality of English citizens. The Adultery Act of 1650 made marital unfaithfulness a capital offence for both parties. It was a lesser offence for unmarried people to sleep with each other: the crime of fornication was punishable by three months' imprisonment at the first offence. 'Drunkeness,

swering and all other kindes of lowness and debauchery' could lead
to arrest, and sometimes did. But these more public sins were easier to
prove in a court of law. Very few prosecutions for sexual immorality
were ever brought to court, and most of those accused were acquitted.
On a legal level, the crimes of adultery and fornication were hard to
prove. And English juries, much to their credit, were unwilling to bring
back guilty verdicts when the penalties were so severe, the offence
entirely victimless, and the jurors themselves no doubt aware that some
of their own number might just as easily be seated in the dock as sitting
in judgment.

The Major-Generals were more successful when it came to regulating
public behaviour. They closed the theatres; they forbade May Day
celebrations – in particular the suggestive pagan practice of dancing
round the maypole; they put a stop to bear-baiting and cock-fighting
(the poor tormented bears that were a major draw on the south bank
of the Thames were – perhaps mercifully – shot dead). They cracked
down on brothels and unlicensed alehouses.

To the great resentment of the populace at large, the regime made a
concerted effort to prevent the celebration of Christmas. In June 1647
parliament announced that the feast of the Nativity of Christ, along
with all other religious festivals, must no longer be observed. That
December, town-criers tramped the streets of many towns and repeated
the order, just in case it had slipped people's minds. In many places, of
course, that was the first the common folk had heard of the new law,
and they were outraged. Christmas was, after all, the only holiday of
the year for many working people. In Canterbury, on Wednesday 22
December, pro-Christmas riots broke out when the local crier ...

... by the appointment of Master Major [Mayor], openly
proclaimed that Christmas Day and all other superstitious
festivals should be put downe, and that a Market should be kept
upon Christmas Day ... They continued in arms till Tuesday
morning; there are none as yet dead, but diverse dangerously
hurt. Master Sheriffe ... striving to keep the Peace, was knockt
down, and his head fearfully broke; it was God's mercy his

braines were not beat out, but it should seem he has a clung pate [hard head] of his own.

They also went without St George's Gate, and did much injury to Mr Lee. As I am credibly informed, the injuries done are these. They have beat down all the windows of Mr Major's house, burnt the stoups [steps] at the comming in of his dore, Master Reeves' windows were broke, Master Page, and Master Pollen, one Buchurst, Captaine Bridge, Thomas Harris, a busie prating fellow, and others were sorely wounded.

Parliament tried to set a good example by ignoring Christmas and sitting on December 25. Local officials and ministers ordered shopkeepers to open up as usual, but were often ignored, or even defied: many shops in the City of London remained closed, and there was a lively black market in holly and other winter greenery. The government bolstered its judicial efforts with propaganda. Puritan newspapers printed anti-Christmas tracts making the point that the true date of Christ's birth was not known, that in any case it had most likely occurred some time in September, and claiming that God had deliberately concealed the exact date precisely in order to prevent it becoming a day of celebration. One newspaper cheerlessly suggested that if people had to have a holiday then why not give thanks instead on 5 November, the day that parliament was delivered from Guy Fawkes and his Romish plot. 'Many people in these times,' said the article, 'are too much addicted to the superstitious observance of this day, December 25th. The state hath done well to null it, as Moses did the brazen serpent.'

In 1645 a strange pamphlet was published in London. Its title, 133 words long, was as follows:

The Arraignment, Conviction and Imprisonment of CHRISTMAS on St. Thomas Day last. And How he broke out of Prison in the Holidayes and got away, onely Left his hoary hair and gray beard, sticking between two Iron Bars of a Window. With an Hue and Cry after Christmas, and a Letter from Mr

> Woodcock, a Fellow in Oxford, to a Malignant Lady in London. And divers passages between the Lady and the Cryer, about Old Christmas: And what shift he was fain to make to save his life, and great stir to fetch him back again. With divers other Witty Passages. Printed by Simon Minc'd Pye, for Cissely Plum-Porridge; and are to be sold out by Ralph Fidler, Chandler at the signe of the Pack of Cards, in Mustard-Alley, in Brawn Street, 1645.

This rather leaden humour is carried through to the body of the text, which describes Father Christmas in the manner of a 'wanted' poster, saying that:

> The wanton Women dote after him; he helped them to so many new Gownes, Hatts and Hankerches, and other fine knacks, of which he hath a pack on his back, in which is good store of all sorts, besides the fine knacks that he got out of husband's pockets for household provisions for him. Whosoever can tel what is become of [Christmas], or where he may be found, let them bring him back againe into England, to the Crier, and they shall have a Benediction from the Pope, an hundred oaths from the Cavaliers, 40 kisses from the Wanton Wenches, and be made Pursevant to the next Archbishop. Malignants will send him a piece of Braune, and every Prentice boy will give him his point; next Holy Thursday the good Wives will keepe him in some corner of their mince pies, and the new Nuncio in Ireland will return him to be canonised the next Reformation of the Calender. And so Pope save Christmas.

The surprising thing about this pamphlet is that it was published with the approval of the government. Its intention was to pour scorn on the nostalgic yearning for Christmas, but it might just as easily be understood as a satire on the futile attempt to abolish it. It must surely often have been read in that spirit. As a piece of propaganda it is very lame, and cannot have discouraged any determined person from celebrating the day of Jesus's birth. Certainly Pepys, in the diary, never mentions having gone without Christmas in the Interregnum years.

The heavy-handed methods of the police state were a more effective deterrent than propaganda. On Christmas Day 1657, the last winter of Cromwell's reign, John Evelyn, a lifelong churchman, was caught red-handed attending a clandestine nativity service in the chapel at Exeter House, a known venue for illegal Anglican worship. He and the rest of the congregation were arrested. This is his personal account of a Christmas spoiled:

> I went to London with my wife to celebrate Christmas-day, Mr Gunning preaching in Exeter chapel on Micah ... Sermon ended, and as he was giving us the Holy Sacrament the chapel was surrounded with soldiers, and all the communicants and assembled surprised and kept prisoners by them, some in the house, others carried away. It fell to my share to be confined to a room in the house, where yet I was permitted to dine with the master of it, the Countess of Dorset, Lady Hatton, and some others of quality who invited me. In the afternoon came Colonel Whalley, Goffe, and others from Whitehall, to examine us one by one. Some they committed to the marshall, some to prison. When I came before them they took my name and abode, examined me why, contrary to the ordinance made that none should any longer observe the superstitious time of the Nativity (so esteemed by them), I durst offend, and particularly be at Common Prayers, which they told me was but the mass in English, and particularly pray for Charles Stuart, for which we had no Scripture. I told them we did not pray for Charles Stuart, but for all Christian Kings, Princes and Governors. They replied in so doing we prayed for the King of Spain, too, who was their enemy and a Papist, with other frivolous and ensnaring questions and much threatening. And finding no colour to detain me, they dismissed me with much pity of my ignorance. These were men of high flight and above ordinances, and spake spiteful things of our Lord's Nativity. As we went up to receive the Sacrament, the

miscreants held their muskets against us, as if they would have shot us at the altar. But yet suffering us to finish the office of Communion, as perhaps not having instructions what to do in case they found us in that action.

So I got home late the next day, blessed be God!

The Rising Mr Pepys

This was the dour world in which the young Pepys grew to manhood. In 1645, at the end of the first phase of the war, he had come back from Huntingdon and gone to St Paul's – a respectable school in the shadow of the cathedral, and just a hop and a skip from the house where he was born. St Paul's was a seedbed of Puritanism, and its grimly pious ethos seems to have seeped into Samuel along with the Latin, the Greek and the Hebrew. One former schoolmate described him as a 'great roundhead'. Years later, much to his own embarrassment, Pepys recalled 'the words that I said the day that the king was beheaded – that were I to preach upon him my text should be: "The memory of the wicked shall rot."' He seems to have grown out of this rather pompous religiosity soon after going up to Magdalen College, Cambridge, in 1651. In his university days he was, by all accounts, a typical student. He took time off from his books to frequent taverns, flirt with barmaids and sing bawdy songs. Once he was given an official dressing-down by the college authorities for drunken behaviour.

Pepys graduated in 1653, the year in which Cromwell forcibly dissolved the Rump Parliament. An 'Instrument of Government', a kind of republican constitution, was drawn up to define a new political reality. It stated that, 'Oliver Cromwell, Captain-General of the forces of England, Scotland and Ireland, shall be, and is hereby declared to be, Lord Protector of the Commonwealth of England, Scotland and Ireland, and the dominions thereto belonging, for his life.' England was finally a one-man dictatorship. The revolutionary who had fought in the name of liberty now gathered all political power to himself, in the pattern that was to become familiar in other countries and later centuries: Napoleon in France, Stalin in Russia, Mao in China, Castro in Cuba, and so on down the ages. Here in England, under the world's first written constitution, the Lord Protector had more powers at his disposal than could have been claimed by the royal personage he had replaced. Cromwell could not legally be removed from office, and he could name his own successor. He was, in all but name, an autocratic monarch. The irony of this was lost on no one; but no one spoke of it above a whisper. If they used the mocking words 'King Oliver the First', they made very sure that they were not overheard.

But it was this entrenchment of the republican system that set Pepys on his career path. His cousin Edward Montagu was now a 28-year-old colonel and a trusted lieutenant of Cromwell. He had been troubled by the execution of the king and retired to his estates, but now, as the machinery of the Protectorate was put in place, Cromwell took the younger man into his inner circle, appointing him in quick succession a member of the Council of State, commissioner of the Treasury, and then lord president of the Council of State. Montagu was suddenly an important political figure, and he needed staff. So he took on his younger cousin, recently graduated from Magdalen College, as a kind of personal assistant. It was a lowly but glamorous job – rather like being an MP's researcher today. For the first time, Samuel was moving in the corridors of power. He listened to the gossip and saw the great men of state almost every day. It was the first manifestation of his lifelong knack for putting himself where the action was. This is a properly journalistic talent for a man born on Fleet Street, but it is almost uncanny all the same. And it is what makes his diary not just an intimate autobiography of a rising man, but also a fabulous piece of reportage.

But the diary was still some years off. For now, Pepys was busy with his incipient career – and with momentous events in his private life. In 1655, Pepys married Elizabeth St Michel, the 15-year-old daughter of a French Huguenot living in London. It was a strange match, for their union made no sense as a step up the social ladder – and Pepys was generally very well-attuned to such things. Elizabeth's father, though of noble descent, was practically penniless. Though her family had declared themselves to be Protestant through and through, Elizabeth herself had received some of her early education in a French convent – something that could easily have put her beyond the pale in Puritan England. But Elizabeth was exotic, pretty, vivacious and funny. Pepys later recalled that he was so passionately in love with her he made himself ill.

Their marriage was conducted by a magistrate according the civil rite then in force; the Anglican Church had been disestablished by the republican government. That ceremony was held on 1 December 1555. But the day they always marked as their anniversary was 10 October, and it seems likely that they underwent an illegal religious wedding three months before their 'official' wedding. Clandestine Anglican services were a feature of life under the roundheads, and it is known that Pepys occasionally attended 'underground' sermons during these years. At any rate, a public celebration of their nuptials was held at a tavern in Old Fish Street, close to the house where Pepys grew up.

At the time of his marriage, Pepys was living in one room in the extensive apartments of 'my Lord Montagu' in Whitehall. It appears that Elizabeth waited a few months before moving in with him, perhaps because she was so young. These must have been difficult days for a man like Pepys – to be married but living the celibate life of a bachelor cannot have come easily to him. Perhaps these tensions were too much for the young couple, because their life as a married couple soon ran into trouble. Within a few months of moving in with him, Elizabeth had moved back out and went to stay with friends at Charing Cross. The cause of this rift can only be guessed at. Given his later sexual conduct, it is not beyond the bounds of possibility that Pepys broke his marriage vows in the weeks or months before Elizabeth came to live with him. That would certainly have provided Elizabeth with cause for walking out, had she suspected it. Or perhaps one or other, or both, of them simply found that the reality of living together was a comedown after the excitement of courtship. Samuel would have been away at work for long hours; Elizabeth would have been bored and lonely in their single room; he would often have come home late, perhaps having first spent an hour or two in the tavern, to a meal prepared by an inexperienced and unpractised cook ... Both of them had fiery tempers, after all. It is not difficult to see how, after yet another blazing row, they could start believing that they had made a dreadful mistake. Whatever the cause of their differences, a trial separation did the trick. By December 1657 they were back together. The following year they moved to a house in Axe Yard, a street in Whitehall now disappeared. Here they had a number of rooms to themselves – what luxury that must have seemed – and Pepys went so far as to employ a maid.

But no sooner had Pepys ironed out his marital troubles than he had to face another, even graver crisis. The terrible pain that he had been experiencing in his kidneys since childhood had grown worse in recent years. Since his university days, the agony of the stone had been an intermittent but ever-present burden. One day when he was 20 years old,

> upon drinking an extraordinary quantity of conduit-water out of Aristotle's Well near Cambridge ... the weight of the said water carried after some days' pain the stone out of the kidneys more sensibly [agonizingly] through the urater [ureter] into my bladder, till I was about 26 years of age when the pain growing insupportable I was delivered both of it and the stone by cutting.

Being 'cut for the stone' was a common enough operation, but it was also quite often fatal. It was performed without anaesthetic, so the speed at which the surgeon operated was an important consideration. Thomas Hollier of St Thomas's Hospital, the man whom Pepys chose for the task, was known to have performed 30 such operations in one year without a single death.

So the omens were good when, on 26 March 1658, Samuel Pepys submitted himself to the horror of a 17th-century lithotomy. He left no account of the experience, but the writer John Evelyn saw one performed in Paris in 1650. This is his unflinching description:

> The sick creature was strip'd to his shirt, & bound armes and thighes to an high Chaire, 2 men holding his shoulders fast down: then the Chirurgion [surgeon] with a crooked Instrument

prob'd til he hit on the stone, then without stirring the probe which had a small channell in it, for the Edge of the Lancet to run in, without wounding any other part, he made Incision thro the Scrotum about an Inch in length, then he put in his forefingers to get the stone as neere the orifice of the wound as he could, then with another Instrument like a Cranes neck he pull'd it out with incredible torture to the Patient, especially at his after raking so unmercifully up & downe the bladder with a 3rd Instrument, to find any other Stones that may possibly be left behind: The effusion of blood is greate. Then was the patient carried to bed, & dress'd with a silver pipe accommodated to the orifice for the urine to pass, when the wound is sowed up: The danger is feavor, & Gangreene, some Wounds never closing.

Pepys kept the stone that was removed from his bladder as a keepsake. Years later he showed it to John Evelyn, who in the interval had become a firm friend. It was, said Evelyn admiringly 'the size of a tennis ball'. Every year Pepys would lay on a feast on 26 March, the anniversary of his operation, as if it were a second birth. He knew that he was lucky to have survived (even the dexterous Doctor Hollier went on to lose four patients in a row). But one unhappy consequence of the operation was that it apparently rendered Pepys sterile – though he was always far from impotent. It is highly likely that his sperm ducts were severed in the course of the procedure. Samuel and Elizabeth kept a room in their house that they called the 'nursery', but it became increasingly clear over the years that no child would every occupy it. This was a source of occasional bouts of melancholy for Pepys; we can only wonder how Elizabeth felt about it.

Samuel's career, meanwhile, was progressing nicely. He had made himself an indispensable asset to his important cousin. He ran Montagu's household and dealt with all his business when he was away. And Montagu was absent for long periods, since in 1656 he was appointed General-at-Sea, in effect second-in-command of the Navy. He was abroad for four successive summers, during which time Pepys inevitably extended his range of responsibilities to cover his employer's absence. It was in these years, and in this relatively small and self-contained arena, that he taught himself the techniques of management, accountancy and record-keeping.

With Montagu's sponsorship, Pepys obtained his first official civil service job. In 1656, he was given the post of clerk to George Downing, Teller of the Receipt in the Exchequer. Downing was a formidable personality and an expert in the machinery of government (he is the man in whose honour Downing Street is named). Pepys had been apprenticed to a grand master in the art of civil administration. The part-time job at the Exchequer provided an extra salary, which was itself supplemented by gratuities and kickbacks from the contractors whose moneys he paid out. Pepys's presence on Downing's staff was also advantageous for Montagu. He knew that his trusted right-hand man was curious, observant and a good judge of the political currents. Montagu needed eyes and ears in Whitehall, because the times were looking ever more turbulent. So Pepys, while working for Downing, was in effect a low-level spy for the General-at-Sea.

In September 1658, while Pepys was still arranging the furniture in his new house at Axe Yard, Oliver Cromwell died. He had appointed his son Richard to succeed him as Lord Protector, but Richard Cromwell, though no fool, did not have the hard-earned authority or the political nous to hold the fissiparous republic together. He was overthrown in April 1659. In the summer there was a half-baked and entirely ineffectual uprising by royalists. In October, the generals of the army carried out a coup and dismissed the Rump Parliament. Anarchy loomed – or worse, a new civil war. There were calls for a restored parliament. Everyone knew (though none could say it out loud just yet) that such a parliament would surely vote for the restoration of the monarchy, because that was the outcome that promised most stability. December of that year was a month of intense manoeuvring. General Monck, commander of the army in Scotland, declared his disapproval of the coup and moved his troops to the border. Montagu secretly entered discussions with Charles Stuart, the exiled son of Charles I; the rank and file of the army was in favour of whichever party seemed most likely to pay their back-wages. The London apprentices marched en masse through the streets, and there they clashed with soldiers sent to pacify and disperse them. The scuffle turned into a riot and Pepys was there to see it. He dutifully reported the violence in a letter to Edward Montagu:

> Some young men in the name of the City apprentices presented their petition to the Lord Mayor and Common Council. This meeting of the Youth was interpreted as the forerunner of an insurrection, and to prevent that the soldiers were all (horse and foot) drawn into the City, which the apprentices by another mistake thought to be done on purpose to prevent the delivery of their petition. Hence rose jealousies on both sides so far that the shops throughout London were shut up, the soldiers as they marched were hooted all along the streets, and where any straggled from the whole body the boys flung stones, tiles, turnips, &c ... at [them] with all the affronts they could give them. Some they disarmed and kicked; others abused the horses with stones and rubbish they flung at them ... In some places the apprentices would get a football (it being a hard frost) and drive it among the soldiers on purpose, and they either darst not (or prudently would not) interrupt them. *In fine* [at last], many soldiers were hurt with stones, and one I see was very near having his brains knocked out with a brickbat flung from the top of an house at him. On the other side, the solders proclaimed the proclamation against any subscriptions, which the boys shouted at in contempt, which some could not bear but let their muskets fly and killed in several places (whereof I see one in Cornhill shot through the head) 6 or 7, and several wounded.

Revolutions have been ignited by smaller sparks than this. Pepys added in a despatch a day or two later that 'never was there, my lord, so universal a fear and despair as now.' But what one detects in Pepys's description is the adrenalin rush that is so familiar to the front-line newsman, and the heightened eye for detail that makes him not just a good reporter but a great one. The grammar and the syntax are faulty,

and words are left out, but that is because these notes are the first
rushed draft of history; one can imagine his hand shaking as he wrote.
It must have been some time soon after this dangerous and exciting day
that an idea long in his head took definite form. A few days later Pepys
was back in Cornhill – peaceful now – to buy a thick notebook from
a stationer named John Cade. He took it home and over the course
of several days ruled margins on each of the 282 pages.

Architects *of* Fortune

Pepys sat down to write the first entry in his diary on 1 January 1660. Taking his pen in hand, he made the following opening statement – writing, as he always would, in the Sheltonian shorthand script he had learned at Cambridge:

Blessed be God, at the end of the last year I was in very good health, without any sense of my old pain but upon taking of cold.

I lived in Axe Yard, having my wife and servant Jane, and no more in family than us three.

My wife, after the absence of her terms for seven weeks, gave me hopes of her being with child, but on the last day of the year she hath them again. The condition of the State was thus. Viz. the Rump, after being disturbed by my Lord Lambert, was lately returned to sit again. The officer of the army all forced to yield. Lawson lies still in the River and Monke is with his army in Scotland. Only my Lord Lambert is not yet come in to the Parliament; nor is it expected that he will without being forced to it.

The new Common Council of the City doth speak very high; and hath sent to Monke their sword-bearer to acquaint him with their desire for a free and full Parliament, which is at present the desires and the hopes and the expectation of all – 22 of the old secluded members having been at the House door the last week to demand entrance; but it was denied them, and it is believed that they nor the people will not be satisfied till the House be filled.

> **My own private condition very handsome; and esteemed rich,
> but indeed very poor, besides my goods of my house and my
> office, which at present is somewhat uncertain. Mr Downing
> master of my office.**

It is an intriguing beginning. The telling use of the past tense in the
second paragraph – 'I lived in Axe Yard' – suggests that from the outset
Pepys hoped that he might be writing for posterity. And perhaps it was
a sense of obligation before history that made him attempt a summary
of the political situation. This overview is unsatisfying, partly because
Pepys is not yet an insider and so has no special insight, and partly
because, with the country in crisis, the details he records are of only
fleeting importance. The effect is like reading the breathless headlines
of a very old newspaper.

It is the personal details that make the first page of Pepy's *magnum
opus* so engaging. We at once get a glimpse of his almost obsessive
concern with his health and his wealth – themes that run right through
the diary to the last page. The understated melancholy of his remark
about having hoped to become a father that year suggests that here is a
man who finds his private world as worthy a subject of contemplation as
the wider universe. Pepys's almost forensic interest in his own emotions
and motives is one of the things that makes the diary rather not just a
priceless historical sourcebook, but also a fine work of art.

And then there is the surprising intimacy of the reference to
Elizabeth's menstrual cycle – a detail that was excised for reasons of
decency from every published edition of the diary before 1971. The
openness of it prefigures the appealing frankness of Pepys's account of
his home and his marriage, the self-imposed glasnost about the good and
the bad in his domestic life. This candour is both one of the glories of
the finished work and the most attractive personality trait of its author.

The Return of the King

As Pepys suspected, the year 1660 turned out to be a momentous one
both in his own life and in the life of the nation. Events moved very

quickly in those first months of the new decade. General Monck came down from Scotland with his troops. At first it looked as if he might support the Rump Parliament, that supine creature of the Commonwealth. That would have been a deeply unpopular move: 'Boys do now cry "Kiss my Parliament" instead of "Kiss my arse", so great and general a contempt is the Rump come to among all men, good and bad,' wrote Pepys. Monck had the military muscle to uphold the Rump Parliament and even to head a new regime, if he so chose. Instead, he came out in favour of new elections to a full parliament.

This decision of Monck's set in motion the events that led to the restoration of the Stuart dynasty, and it was greeted with rejoicing on the streets of London. Pepys, naturally, was in the crowd, soaking up the atmosphere and the detail, and enjoying the spontaneous and ironic feasting on rumps of beef on every corner.

And endeed I saw many people give the soldiers drink and money, and all along in the streets cried, 'God bless them' and extraordinary good words. Hence ... to the Star taverne ... where we drank and I wrote a letter to my Lord from thence. In Cheapside there was a great many bonefires, and Bow-bells and all the bells in all the churches as we went home were a-ringing. Hence we went homewards, it being about 10 a'clock. But the common joy that was everywhere to be seen! The number of bonefires, there being fourteen between St. Dunstans and Temple-bar. And at Strand bridge I could at one view tell 31 fires. In King-streete, seven or eight; and all along burning and roasting and drinking for rumps – there being rumps tied upon sticks and carried up and down. The butchers at the maypole in the Strand rang a peal with knifes when they were going to sacrifice their rump. On Ludgate-hill there was one turning of the spit, that had a rump tied upon it, and another basting of it. Indeed, it was past imagination, both the greatness and the suddenness of it. At one end of the street, you would think there was a whole lane of fire, and so hot that we were fain to keep still on the further side merely for heat.

It was only a week or two later that Pepys ceased to be just an observer of the great changes, and became a minor player. Pepys's kinsman and patron, Montagu, had been biding his time. Having been promoted to General-at-Sea by Cromwell, he was now looking to make sure that he remained a man of influence under Cromwell's successors – whoever they might turn out to be. Now he came to the capital to play his part in the drama, and while he was there he met with Pepys. It was Shrove Tuesday, 6 March, and it was a day that was to change the course of Samuel Pepys's life.

> He called me by himself to go along with him into the garden, where he asked me how things were with me ... He likewise bade me look out now, at this turn, some good place; and he would use all his own and all the interest of his friends that he hath in England to do me good. And asked me whether I could without too much inconvenience go to sea as his Secretary, and bade me think of it. He also began to speak of things of state, and told me that he should now want one in that capacity at sea that he might trust in. And therefore he would have me to go.
>
> My Lord told me that there was great endeavours to bring in the Protector again; but he told me too, that he did believe it would not last long if he were brought in; no, nor the king neither (though he seems to think that he will come in) unless he carry himself very soberly and well. Everybody now drink the King's health without any fear, whereas before it was very private that a man dare do it.
>
> My mind, I must needs remember, hath been very much eased and joyed in my Lord's great expression of kindness this day; and in discourse there upon, my wife and I lay awake an hour or two in our bed.

So once again, Pepys was given a hand up by his influential relative. Here began his lifelong association with the Navy; soon after his talk with Montagu, he began to make preparations for going to sea. He resigned his job at the Exchequer – he would have no more need of it –

and he arranged for Elizabeth to go and stay with a colleague (at which she was not best pleased). He prudently made a will, and he engaged a servant boy and a clerk. He joined his cousin's flagship, the *Swiftsure*, on 23 March and was immediately surprised and delighted by the pleasant little cabin he was assigned to, and by the respect that was shown to him by the captains of the fleet. They understood – and Pepys very quickly learned – that his position as gatekeeper to the General-at-Sea gave him a very particular form of power. Many people who were more powerful than Pepys wanted to keep in with him, and so the general's secretary found himself on the receiving end of all manner of gifts – barrels of oysters, bottles of wine, bags of money …

The nature of the fleet's mission soon became clear. Montagu's errand was to loiter at sea between England and Holland – where Charles Stuart was now waiting in Schevelingen – until a new parliament could be elected and take a vote on reinstating the monarchy. That process took a matter of weeks, during which time Pepys was kept busy drafting letters, sending out commissions and orders, and generally regulating the flow of correspondence between London, Montagu, and the soon-to-be king. For the first time in his life he was at the political epicentre of things. It was a glorious, exciting place to be and he enjoyed it immensely.

On May Day 1660 the king was proclaimed in London. Almost two weeks later the flagship weighed anchor and set out for the Hague, where the fleet was to pick up Charles and his brother James. On 14 May, Pepys woke up to find that the Dutch coast was in sight. Later that day he went ashore and spent a happy couple of days as a tourist. He marked the pleasing habit of Dutch women to kiss complete strangers in greeting; he had a disappointing mutton dinner and was generally snooty about the taverns, where he saw, 'Duch boores eating of fish in a boorish manner'; gallingly, he lost his 'Copenhagen knife', but he bought a Dutch basket as a souvenir for his wife. He found it surprisingly easy to come into the presence of the nine-year-old Prince of Orange, 'a very pretty boy' who – did Pepys but know it – would one day become king of England and put paid to the career that was just now beginning. He also kissed the hand of the new king, who struck him – quite wrongly for once – as 'a very sober man'.

The king was carried back to England on a ship with the unfortunate name of *The Naseby*; it was hastily rechristened *The Royal Charles* for the crossing. Pepys spent some time on board, and accompanied the king as he strode up and down the deck and told the story of his escape from England. 'It made me ready to weep to hear the stories that he told of his difficulties that he had passed through,' wrote the man who had, not so long before, taken grim satisfaction in the execution of the raconteur's father.

As his travelling four days and three nights, every step up to the knees in dirt, with nothing but a green coat and a pair of country breeches on and a pair of country shoes, that made him so sore all over his feet that he could scarce stir.

Yet he was forced to run away from a miller and other company that took them for rogues.

His sitting at table at one place, where the master of the house that had not seen him in eight years, did know him but kept it private; when at the same table there was one that had been of his own Regiment at Worcester, could not know him but made him drink the Kings health and said that the King was at least four fingers higher than he.

Another place, he was by some servants of the house made to drink, that they might know him not to be a Roundhead, which they swore he was.

The tale (which Charles never tired of telling) made a fitting contrast to the present situation. His reception on his return was rapturous. Charles's arrival at Dover, and his first steps in English soil as king, were marked with 'infinite shooting off of the guns'. Pepys missed Charles's royal progress through the countryside and triumphal entry into London as he was still with ship. But there were compensations. The Duke of York had spoken to him, 'called me Pepys by name, and upon my desire did promise me his future favour'. More encouraging still were the parting words of Montagu, who said that 'we must have a little patience, and we will rise together. In the meantime I will do you all the good Jobbs I can.' Even if those assurances turned out to be empty, there was the comfort to be taken in the hard cash that had accrued to Pepys like barnacles to a wooden keel. He had made more money during his two months away than he had been able to put by during his five years of stewardship for his high-flying cousin.

In the event, Montagu was as good as his word. He himself was rapidly created Lord Sandwich, then made a Knight of the Order of the Garter, then given the lucrative and prestigious post in the royal household of Master of the Great Wardrobe. In his continuing capacity as General-at-Sea he now made good his promise to Pepys by appointing him Clerk of the Acts to the Navy Board. Pepys knew nothing about the navy apart from what he had gleaned during his recent adventure. But this was the job he was to fulfil for decades to come, enlarging its scope, transforming its significance, and in the process making himself England's leading expert on naval affairs.

So it was that Pepys installed himself in his new job (and in a grand new house on Seething Lane) during the same months that Charles was settling himself on the throne. But in those topsy-turvy days as many people were cast down as were raised up like Pepys and Lord Sandwich. The chief losers in the regime change were, of course, the rulers of the old order. The men who had signed the old king's death warrant were singled out for retribution, which was swift in coming. In October Pepys 'went out to Charing-cross to see Major-Generall Harrison hanged, drawn, and quartered – which was done there'. In one of his wryest moments, Pepys adds that Harrison was ...

... looking as cheerfully as any man could do in that condition. He was presently cut down and his head and his heart shown to the people, at which there was great shouts of joy. It is said that he said that he was sure to come shortly at the right hand of Christ to judge them that now have judged him. And that his wife doth expect his coming again.

Thus it was my chance to see the King beheaded at White-hall and to see the first blood shed in revenge for the blood of the King at Charing-cross.

It was Harrison's misfortune not to have died sooner, but then the dead enemies of the monarchy were not spared either. In January 1661, the bodies of Oliver Cromwell, his son-in-law Henry Ireton, and the trial judge John Bradshaw were exhumed. On the 12th anniversary of the old king's execution the cadavers were dragged to Tyburn, where, according to one witness, a merchant named Samuel Sainthill,

> **They were hanged by the neck from morning till four in the afternoon. Cromwell in a green seare cloth, very fresh embalmed; Ireton, having been buried long, hung like a dried rat, yet corrupted about the fundament. Bradshaw, in his winding sheet, the fingers of his right hand and nose perished, having wet the sheet through. The rest very perfect, insomuch that I knew his face, when the hangman, after cutting it off, held it up; of his toes I had five or six in my hand, which the prentices had cut off. Their bodies were thrown into an hole under the gallows, with their seare-cloth and sheet. Cromwell had eight cuts [to sever his head], Ireton four, and their heads were set up on the south end of Westminster Hall.**

Cromwell's shrivelled, traitorous head remained on a pole in Westminster for more than 20 years, until it blew down in a storm.

The world turned upside down seemed to have righted itself, after a fashion. And the chief beneficiary of the turnaround was of course the king himself. He went from a time of personal and financial insecurity to a life of indulgence and luxury. His lavish coronation was a taste of the excesses to come, and it was an event that Pepys was not about to miss. His description of it is one of his magnificent set pieces. In the manner of a great storyteller – Tolstoy comes to mind – he zooms cinematically in and out, focusing at one moment one the grand pageantry, the wide canvas, and at the next on minutiae, some of it distinctly sordid, such as his own sorry, hungover state the next morning. Here is Pepys's vivid account of a royal coronation that was also a celebration of the passing-away of the joyless Puritan tyranny.

About 4 in the morning I rose. And got to the abby, where I fallowed Sir J. Denham the surveyour with some company that he was leading in. And with much ado, by the favour of Mr. Cooper his man, did get up into a great scaffold across the north end of the abby – where with a great deal of patience I sat from past 4 till 11 before the King came in. And a pleasure it was to see the Abbey raised in the middle, all covered with red and a throne (that is a chaire) and footstoole on the top of it. And all the officers of all kinds, so much as the very fidlers, in red vests.

At last comes in the Deane and prebends of Westminster with the Bishops (many of them in cloth-of-gold Copes); and after them the nobility all in their parliament-robes, which was a most magnificent sight. Then the Duke and the King with a scepter (carried by my Lord of Sandwich) and Sword and mond [orb] before him, and the crowne too.

The King in his robes, bare-headed, which was very fine. And after all had placed themselves – there was a sermon and the service. And then in the Quire at the high altar he passed all the ceremonies of the Coronacion – which, to my very great grief, I and most in the Abbey could not see. The crowne being put upon his head, a great shout begun. And he came forth to the Throne and there passed more ceremonies: as, taking the oath and having things read to him by the Bishopp, and his lords (who put on their capps as soon as the King put on his Crowne) and Bishopps came and kneeled before him.

And three times the King-at-armes went to the three open places on the scaffold and proclaimed that if any one could show any reason why Ch. Steward should not be King of England, that now he should come and speak.

And a Generall pardon also was read by the Lord Chancellor; and meddalls flung up and down by my Lord Cornwallis – of silver; but I could not come by any.

But so great a noise that I could make but little of the Musique; and endeed, it was lost to everybody. But I had so great a list to pisse, that I went out a little while before the King had done all his ceremonies and went round the abby to Westminster-hall, all the way within rayles, and 10000 people, with the ground coverd with blue cloth – and Scaffolds all the way. Into the hall I got – where it was very fine with hangings and scaffolds, one upon another, full of brave ladies. And my wife in one little one on the right hand.

Here I stayed walking up and down; and at last, upon one of the side-stalls, I stood and saw the King come in with all the persons (but the Souldiers) that were yesterday in the cavalcade; and a most pleasant sight it was to see them in their several robes. And the King came in with his Crowne on and his sceptre in his hand – under a Canopy borne up by six silver staves, carried by Barons of the Cinqueports – and little bells at every end.

And after a long time he got up to the farther end, and set themselves down at their several tables – and that was also a rare sight. And the King's first Course carried up by the Knights of the Bath. And many fine ceremonies there was of the Heralds leading up people before him and bowing; and my Lord of Albimarles going up to the Kitchin and eat a bit of the first dish that was to go to the King's table.

But above all was these three Lords, Northumberland and Suffolke and the Duke of Ormond, coming before the Courses on horseback and staying so all dinner-time; and at last, to bring up (Dymock) the King's Champion, all in armor on horseback, with his Speare and targett carried before him. And a herald proclaim that if any dare deny Ch. Steward to be lawful King of England, here was a Champion that would fight with him; and with those words the Champion flings down his gantlet; and all this he doth three times in his going up toward the King's table. At last, when he is come. The King drinks to him and then sends him the Cup, which is of gold; and he drinks it off and then rides back again with the cup in his hand.

I went from table to table to see the Bishops and all others at their dinner, and was infinite pleased with it. And at the Lords' table I met with Will. Howe and he spoke to my Lord for me and

he did give him four rabbits and a pullet; and so I got it, and Mr.
Creed and I got Mr. Michell to give us some bread and so we at
a Stall eat it, as everybody else did what they could get.

I took a great deal of pleasure to go up and down and look upon
the ladies – and to hear the Musique of all sorts; but above all,
the 24 viollins.

About 6 at night they had dined; and I went up to my wife and
there met with a pretty lady (Mrs. Frankelyn, a Doctor's wife, a
friend of Mr. Bowyers) and kissed them both – and by and by
took them down to Mr. Bowyers. And strange it is, to think that
these two days have held up fair till now that all is done and the
King gone out of the hall; and then it fell a-raining and
thundering and lightening as I have not seen it do some years –
which people did take great notice of God's blessing of the work
of these two days – which is a foolery, to take too much notice
of such things.

I observed little disorder in all this; but only the King's
Footmen had got hold of the Canopy and would keep it from the
barons of the Cinqueports; which they endeavoured to force from
them again but could not do it till my Lord Duke of Albermarle
caused it to be put into Sir R. Pye's hand till tomorrow to be
decided.

At Mr. Bowyers, a great deal of company; some I knew, others
I did not. Here we stayed upon the leads and below till it was
late, expecting to see the Fireworkes; but they were not performd
tonight. Only, the City had a light like a glory round about it,
with bonefyres.

At last I went to Kingstreete; and there sent Crockford to
my father's and my house to tell them I could not come home
tonight, because of the dirt and a coach could not be had.

And so after drinking a pot of ale alone at Mrs. Harpers, I
returned to Mr Bowyers; and after a little stay more, I took my
wife and Mrs Frankelyn (who I proferred the civility of lying
with my wife at Mrs. Hunts tonight) to Axe yard. In which, at
the further end, there was three great bonefyres and a great many

great gallants, men and women; and they laid hold of us and would have us drink the King's health upon our knee, kneeling upon a fagott; which we all did, they drinking to us one after another – which we thought a strange Frolique. But these gallants continued thus a great while, and I wondered to see how the ladies did tiple.

At last I sent my wife and her bedfellow to bed, and Mr. Hunt and I went in with Mr. Thornbury (who did give the company all their wines, he being yeoman of the wine-cellar to the King) to his house; and there, with his wife and two of his sisters and some gallant sparks that were there, we drank the King's health and nothing else, till one of the genlemen fell down stark drunk and there lay speweing. And I went to my Lord's pretty well. But no sooner a-bed with Mr. Sheply but my head begun to turne and I to vomitt, and if ever I was foxed it was now – which I cannot say yet, because I fell asleep and sleep till morning – only, when I waked I found myself wet with my spewing. Thus did the day end, with joy everywhere; and blessed be God, I have not heard of any mischance to anybody through it all, but only to Serjeant Glynne, whose Horse fell upon him yesterday and is like to kill him; which people do please themselves with, to see how just God is to punish that rogue at such a time as this – he being now one of the King's Serjeants and rode in the Cavalcade with Maynard, to who people wished the same fortune.

There was also this night, in Kingstreet, [a woman] had her eye put out by a boy's flinging of a firebrand into the coach.

Now after all this, I can say that besides the pleasure of the sight of these glorious things, I may now shut my eyes against any other objects, or for the future trouble myself to see things of state and shewe, as being sure never to see the like again in this world.

Charles II, and his brother James, the Duke of York, both came to know Pepys better in later years, and he gives a thoughtful and rounded account of their personalities. Though he did not always approve of their behaviour, Pepys was a unquestioning monarchist from this time on. It was not just that, for a man like Pepys, life was more congenial under them than under the lugubrious Puritans. There was also the fact that his fate seemed to be running in parallel with Charles's. He found his rightful place in the world at the same time as the king regained his throne. Both spent the first half of the decade making themselves masters of their sometimes unmanageable realms. The king's realm was his government and his subjects, his court, his coterie of mistresses. Pepys's realm was his native city, his job at the Navy Board, his household and servants, and his wife.

A Great Beauty to his Wife

Of all the vast cast of characters who move through the pages of the diary, the warmest, most real and most constant presence is Elizabeth – 'my wife' as Pepys unchangingly refers to her. The diary contains many verbal snapshots of their life together. One lazy Sunday in 1662 finds Samuel …

> … talking long in bed with my wife about our frugall life for the time to come, proposing to her what I would do if I were worth 2000 pounds; that is, be a Knight and keep my coach – which pleased her; and so I do hope we shall hereafter live to save something, for I am resolved to keep myself by rules from expences.

This endearing sketch of a young couple planning their future is recognizable in any age. But the Pepyses home life was not always so peaceful and idyllic. Their relationship had been rocky from the start. And though they never again separated from each other as they did temporarily in the days before the diary, they quarrelled often. Elizabeth could give as good as she got. On one occasion he called her a 'beggar' because she had come to him with no dowry. This was an insult deliberately calculated to hurt a woman so proud of her family links to the Angevin dynasty of France. She retorted by calling him a 'pricklouse', a condescending term for a common tailor such as his father. This was hitting the snobbish careerist in Pepys exactly where it hurt. Shamefully, he sometimes resorted to physical violence when they argued – or rather, when he was losing an argument. On the day that he witnessed the torture of the unfortunate Major-General Harrison, he came home and in a fit of temper at Elizabeth's slovenliness broke the basket he had brought her from Holland. Rather more reprehensibly by modern standards (though not unusually for the age), he was wont to pinch her by the nose as a form of reproof. Elizabeth was not one to submit to this humiliating punishment, and she found a way to make Samuel think twice before using it again:

> This evening I observed my wife mighty dull; and I myself was not mighty fond, because of some hard words she did give me at noon, out of a jealousy at my being abroad this morning; when, God knows, it was upon the business of the office unexpectedly; but I to bed, not thinking but she would come after me; but waking by and by out of a slumber, which I usually fall into presently after my coming into the bed, I found she did not prepare to come to bed, but got fresh candles and more wood for her fire, it being mighty cold too. At this being troubled, I after a while prayed her to come to bed, all my people being gone to bed; so after an hour or two, she silent, and I now and then praying her to come to bed, she fell out into a fury, that I was a rogue and false to her ...
>
> At last, about one a-clock, she came to my side of the bed and drow my curtaine open, and with the tongs, red hot at the ends, made as if she did design to pinch me with them; at which dismay I rose up, and with a few words she laid them down and did by little and little, very sillily, let all the discourse fall.

Most of their quarrels were trivial, and there were recurring themes. One of them, as in many a marriage, was money. Pepys loved money and could be downright Scrooge-like at times. Elizabeth, with no income of her own, had constantly to beg him for an allowance and for housekeeping money. At the beginning of the diary period, five years into their marriage and when they were still relatively poor, he was willing to indulge his wife with little fripperies. 'This morning I took my wife toward Westminster by water ...' he wrote in August 1660,

> ... and landed her at White-Friars with 50 shillings to buy her a petticoat. And I to the Privy Seale. By and by comes my wife to tell me that my father hath persuaded her to buy a most fine cloth of 26 shillings per yard and a rich lace, that the petticoat will come to 5 pounds, at which I was somewhat troubled. But she doing it very innocently I could not be angry.

It is amazing that Pepys did not blame his father, the tailor, for talking his daughter-in-law into handing over to him twice as much money as Pepys had budgeted. They must have caught him on a very good day. But Pepys was always happier when the price of his wife's coquetry was negligible. That winter the fashion for beauty spots – fake moles – made itself felt in the Pepys household. 'My wife seemed very pretty today,' wrote Pepys, 'It being the first time that I have given her leave to weare a black patch.' But later in their marriage Pepys was reluctant to pay for his wife's finery. At the same time he never ceased to want her to dress impressively, to bathe in the reflected glory of her beauty. Elizabeth's vanity put two of his deepest social impulses at odds with each other. On the one hand he wanted to hoard money and so become a man of substance; on the other he wanted to spend it conspicuously, to show off his wife at her best so that all the world could see the material trappings of his success. As a result, Elizabeth was forced to go to theatrical lengths in her plea for new clothes.

> So home to dinner, where my wife having dressed herself in a silly dress, of a blue petticoat uppermost and a white satin waistcoat and white hood (though I think she did it because her gown is gone to the tailor's) did, together with my being hungry (which always makes me peevish), make me angry. But when my belly was full, was friends again.

A few weeks' later he was complaining to the diary about Elizabeth's inclination to follow the vogue for white wigs:

> In my way home discovered my trouble to my wife for her white locks, swearing to God several times (which I pray God forgive me for) and behind my fist, that I would not endure it. She poor wretch, was surprized with it, and made me no answer all the way home. But there we parted, and I to the office late; and then home, and without supper to bed, vexed.

But on this occasion, Elizabeth shrewdly saw an opportunity in her husband's sudden outburst.

> Up, and to my chamber to settle some accounts there; and by and down comes my wife to me in her nightgown: and we begun calmly, that upon having money to lace her gown, she would promise to wear white locks no more in my sight; which I, like a severe fool, thinking not enough, begun to except against and made her fly out to very high terms, and cry; and in her heat told me of keeping company with Mrs. Knipp, saying that if I would promise never to see her more (of whom she hath more reason to suspect then I had heretofore of Pembleton), she would never wear white locks more. This vexed me, but I restrained myself from saying anything; but do think never to see this woman; at least, to have her here more. But by and by I did give her money to buy lace, and she promised to wear no more white locks while I lived; and so all very good friends as ever, and I to my business and she to dress herself.

The Mr Pembleton whom Pepys mentions was Elizabeth's dance teacher. He was the blameless cause of some bitter strife between Samuel and Elizabeth. Pepys had decided that dancing lessons would give Elizabeth a socially useful accomplishment while at the same time mitigating the boredom of her days at home. He took on Pembleton in April 1663, and for months to come was by turns convinced that

Pembleton and Elizabeth were having an affair, or else wracked with guilt for having suspected them. Pembleton riled Pepys early on by showing him a few dance steps one day when he came home early from the office, and then implying that Pepys owed him for his services. 'I did begin, and then was obliged to give him entry-money, 10 shillings, and am become his Scholler,' wrote Pepys ruefully.

For Pepys it was quite a short subconscious step from feeling he had been robbed of his money to suspecting he was being robbed of his wife. On 12 May he noted that he was 'a little angry with my wife for minding nothing now but the dancing-maister, having him come twice a day, which is a folly,' but he does not spell out why it troubles him. Perhaps he did not yet know. At any rate, his first attack of jealousy came on him like a fever four days later.

Home, where I find it almost night and my wife and the Dancing Maister alone above, not dancing but walking. Now, so deadly full of jealousy I am, that my heart and head did cast about and fret, that I could not do any business possibly, but went out to my office; and anon late home again, and ready to chide at everything; and then suddenly to bed and could hardly sleep, yet durst not say anything; but was forced to say that I had bad news from the Duke concerning Tom Hater as an excuse to my wife – who by my folly hath too much opportunity given her with that man; who is a pretty neat black man [dark-haired], but married. But it is a deadly folly and a plague that I bring upon myself to be so jealous; and by giving myself such an occasion, more than my wife desired, of giving her another month's dancing – which however shall be ended as soon as I can possibly.

The restless prose of this paragraph is a terrific evocation of a suspicious mind. It darts from one uneasy thought to another, just as Pepys shuttles back and forth from his house to his office in search of some mental ease. This is Pepys as a kind of small-minded, bourgeois Othello. But later Pepys added another small incident to this day's diary entry, squeezing it into a gap on the page. It is a tiny episode, but so

psychologically revealing that any modern novelist would be proud
to have dreamed it up.

> But I am ashamed to think what a course I did take by lying to
> see whether my wife did wear drawers today as she used to do,
> and other things to raise my suspicion of her. But I found no true
> cause of doing it.

So Pepys found some way of getting his wife to show him that she was
still in her underwear, knowing all along that it would prove nothing
one way or the other. The unseemly subterfuge was available to him
only because his wife was French; English women of the day did not
wear drawers at all.

The next day, unsurprisingly, Pepys was full of remorse.

> Up, with my mind disturbed and with my last night's doubts upon
> me. For which I deserve to be beaten, if not really served as I am
> fearful of being. Especially since, God knows, that I do not find
> honesty enough in my own mind but that upon a small
> temptation I could be false to her, and therefore ought not to
> expect any more justice from her – but God pardon both my sin
> and my folly herein.

But the sickness would not go away so long as the dancing lessons
continued. There were several occasions when Pepys came home to find
his wife dining alone with Pembleton. It was merely the courteous thing
to do, but it added to the growing catalogue of circumstantial evidence
in Pepys's mind. One Sunday soon after he 'espied Pembleton' at
church, and thought he saw him 'leer upon my wife all the sermon'.
The following Tuesday started well for Pepys, but soon descended into
a torment of doubt and mistrust that carried on well into the following
night. Pepys, by his own account, was close to being unhinged:

> Lay long in bed, talking and pleasing myself with my wife. So up
> and to my office a while and then home, where I find Pembleton;

and by many circumstances I am led to conclude that there is something more then ordinary between my wife and him; which doth so trouble me that I know not, at this very minute that I now write this almost, what either I write or am doing nor how to carry myself to my wife in it, being unwilling to speak of it to her for making of any breach and other inconveniences, nor let it pass for fear of her continuing to offend me and the matter grow worse thereby. So that I am grieved at the very heart, but I am very unwise in being so.

There dined with me Mr Creed and Captain Gove; and before dinner, I had much discourse in my chamber with Mr. Deane, the Builder of Woolwich, about building of ships. But nothing could get the business out of my head, I fearing that this afternoon, by my wife's sending every[one] abroad and knowing that I must be at the office, she hath appointed him to come. This is my devilish jealousy; which I pray God may be false, but it makes a very hell in my mind; which the God of heaven remove, or I shall be very unhappy. So to the office, where we sat a while.

By and by, my mind being in great trouble, I went home to see how things were; and there I find as I doubted, Mr. Pembleton with my wife and nobody else in the house, which made me almost mad; and going up to chamber, after a turn or two I went out again and called somebody, upon pretence of business, and left him in my little room at the door (it was the Duchman, commander of one of the King's pleasure-boats; who having been beat by one of his men sadly, was come to the office today to complain), telling him I would come again to him to speak with him about his business; so in great trouble and doubt to the office; and Mr. Coventry nor Sir G. Carteret being there, I made a quick end of our business and desired leave to be gone, pretending to go to the Temple, but it was home; and so up to my chamber and, as I think, if they had any intentions of hurt, I did prevent doing anything at that time; but I continued in my chamber vexed and angry till he went away, pretending aloud, that I might hear, that he could not stay, and Mrs. Ashwell not being within they would

not dance. And Lord, to see how my jealousy wrought so far, that I went saftly up to see whether any of the beds were out of order or no, which I found not; but that did not content me, but I stayed all the evening walking, and though anon my wife came up to me and would have spoke of business to me, yet I construed it to be but impudence; and though my heart was full, yet I did say nothing, being in a great doubt what to do. So at night suffered them to go all to bed, and late put myself to bed in great discontent.

The dancing lessons ended soon after, but this did not immediately put Pepys's mind at rest. Now he suspected his wife of sending messages to Pembleton via the errand-boy. He was not happy until the time came for Elizabeth to go off on her summer break to the country. As soon as she was gone his mood changed. He was, he said, 'sad for want of my wife, whom I love with all my heart, though of late she hath given me some troubled thoughts.'

The day after Elizabeth went away, Pepys had dinner with Sir John Mennes (a colleague from the office who lived close by on Seething Lane) and his mentor, Lord Sandwich. The talk turned to pretty women, and Sandwich said to Mennes, 'Why sir, what do you think of your neighbour's wife? Do you not think that he hath a great beauty to his wife? Upon my word he hath.' It was an unexpected compliment to Elizabeth and, by extension, to Pepys himself. And it came just at the right moment. Pepys was, he confided to the diary, 'not a little proud'.

The Food on the Table

Both Samuel and Elizabeth took pride in their house on Seething Lane. The diary is full of accounts of good times spent there. Taken together, these passages are a rich source of information about the domestic life of a middle-class 17th-century family. Pepys's taste in food, books and music (all of which he was very fond of) seem to be typical of the age.

It was commonly said in the 17th century that, 'the Spaniard eats, the German drinks, and the Englishman exceeds in both.' Breakfast usually consisted of cold meat or fish, cheese and beer. Pepys, who was regularly up at four or five in the morning during the summer months, often ate the remains of last night's dinner for breakfast, or went to a tavern after an hour or two at the office. It was also possible to buy fast food on the street. M Misson, a French visitor to London, described the 'cookshops' near the river:

> Generally, four spits, one over the other, carry round each five or six pieces of butcher's meat – beef, mutton, veal, pork and lamb; you have what quantity you please cut off, fat, lean, much or little done; with this, a little salt and mustard upon the side of the plate, a bottle of beer and a roll; there is your whole feast.

Dinner, taken around midday, was the main meal. Towards the end of the century dinner started to drift towards evening. This shift was probably a consequence of a new fashion for a late breakfast of coffee with bread rolls. Noontime was now too early for the main meal of the day. But Pepys – in the diary years at least – always ate early. 'The English eat a great deal at dinner,' wrote Misson. 'They rest a while, and to it again, till they have quite stuffed their paunch. Their supper is moderate; gluttons at noon, and abstinent at night.' This generalization seems to fit Pepys's dietary habits.

Meat was central to most English meals, a fact that foreigners often remarked on. Meat predominates in all Pepys's descriptions of meals, partly because its presence on the table was a marker of affluence: the poor subsisted on bread and cheese. Pepys ate 'surloyne of beef' at home for the first time in November 1661, and records the fact as a milestone in his growing prosperity. Thereafter beef appears on his table more and more frequently. Chicken was an expensive delicacy, and venison a very rare treat. At least it ought to have been a treat. Pepys had this slightly disappointing experience with a side of venison soon after he started at the Navy Board:

> To my Lord about business; and being in talk, in comes one with half a Bucke from Hinchingbrooke, and it smelling a little strong,

> my Lord did give it me, though it was as good as any could be.
> I did carry it to my mother (where I had not been a great while)
> ...and did leave the venison with her to dispose of as she pleased.

It is typical of Pepys's stream-of-consciousness method that, in this account, the reeking venison was perfectly fine in the moment that it was a gift from his patron.

Vegetables are rarely mentioned in the diary, but probably because they were taken for granted. Fruit and vegetables were certainly available in the London markets. Cabbages, carrots and onions were commonplace; peas and asparagus were eaten in season. But there were no potatoes as we know them. The white-fleshed Virginian variety was already cultivated in Ireland, but it was unknown in England, which had only the sweet potato (brought back from the Caribbean by Sir Walter Raleigh). Native fruits such as apples and pears were available at some times of year, but Pepys usually only ate them cooked. More exotic fruits such as melons and peaches were grown in the hothouses and orchards of the well-to-do, who kept them to themselves. 'China oranges' – actually imported from Spain and Portugal – were a theatre-goers' snack. Pineapples were a royal monopoly.

Pepys was fond of giving the occasional dinner party, and his annual feast to mark his 'cutting of the stone' was always a sumptuous occasion. In 1663 the anniversary fell in the middle of Lent, but Pepys was not going to let a religious fast stand in the way of a good party:

> By and by comes Roger Pepys, Mrs Turner, her daughter, Joyce
> Norton and a young lady, a daughter of Collonell Cockes – my
> Uncle Wight – his wife and Mrs Anne Wight ... Very merry
> before, at, and after dinner, and the more for that my dinner was
> great and most neatly dressed by our own only mayde. We had
> a Fricasse of rabbets and chicken, a leg of mutton boiled – three
> carps in a dish – a great dish of a side of lamb – a dish of roasted
> pigeons – a dish of four lobsters – three tarts – a Lampry pie, a
> most rare dish – a dish of anchovies – good wine of several sorts;
> and all things mighty noble and to my great content.

A less successful meal was had the previous June, when Pepys invited
his senior colleague back to his house at midday. He asked the maid to
serve up a pickled sturgeon which he had been given the previous
month (Pepys's bribes often took edible form):

> Took Commissioner Pett home with me to dinner, where my
> stomach was turned when my sturgeon came to table, upon which
> I saw very many little worms creeping, which I suppose was
> through the staleness of the pickle.

The commissioner seems to have made his excuses and left rather rapidly.
Pett was also present, along with Pepys, at the wedding anniversary of
Sir William Batten – where this surprising dish was served.

> Among other Froliques, it being their third year, they had three
> pyes, whereof the middlemost was made of an ovall form in an
> Ovall hole with the other, which made much mirth and was called
> the middle peace; and above all the rest, we had great striving to
> steal a spoonefull out of it; and I remember Mrs Mills the
> minister's wife did steal one for me and give it to me; and to end
> all Mrs Shippman did fill the pie full of white wine (it holding at
> least a pint and a half) and did drink it off for a health to Sir Wm.
> and my Lady, it being the greatest draught that I ever did see a
> woman drink in my life.

This name for this pie within a pie within a pie was 'a bride pie'. Such
flamboyantly inedible dishes, sometimes termed 'subtleties', had been
a common feature of wedding celebrations a generation or two before
in Queen Elizabeth's day, but were falling out of fashion by the time
of the Restoration. One recipe published in 1660 in a book called
The Accomplisht Cook, recommended this variant on a bride pie 'for
a wedding, to pass away the time.'

> *To make an extraordinary Pie, or a Bride Pye of several*
> *Compound, being several distinct Pies on one bottom.* You

> may bake the middle one full of flour, it being baked and cold,
> take out the flour in the bottom, and put in live birds, or a
> snake, which will seem strange to the beholders, which cut
> up the pie at the Table.

Such confections are of course the inspiration for the scenario in the
nursery rhyme: 'Four and twenty blackbirds baked in a pie/When the
pie was opened the birds began to sing.' But the formula for the
ultimate bride pie, the *ne plus ultra* of a dainty dish to set before a king,
can be found in that same 1660 recipe book, which was written by a
cook named Robert May. The method is so fraught with culinary
dangers and presentational pitfalls, that it is worth quoting in full.

> Make the likeness of a ship in paste-board and cover it with
> paste, with Flags and Streamers, the guns belonging to it of
> Kickses [marzipan or almond paste], with such holes and trains of
> powder that they may all take Fire; place your ship firm in a great
> Charger; then make a salt round about it, and stick therein egg
> shells filled with rose-water.
> Then in another Charger have the proportion of a stag made
> of coarse paste, with a broad arrow in the side of him and his
> body filled with claret wine.
> In another Charger have the proportion of a Castle with
> Battlements, Percullises, Gates and Drawbridges made of paste-
> board, the guns of Kickses, and covered with coarse paste as the
> former; place it at a distance from the Ship, to fire at each other,
> the Stag being placed between ... At each end of the Charger,
> wherein is the Stag, place a Pie made of coarse paste in one of
> which let there be live Frogs, in the other live Birds. Make these
> Pies of coarse paste filled with Bran, and yellowed over with
> Saffron or Yolks of Eggs, gild them over in spots, as also the Stag,
> the Ship and the Castle; bake them and place them with gilt bay-
> leaves on the turrets and tunnels of the Castle and Pies; being
> baked make a hole in the bottom, take out the bran, put in your
> Frogs and Birds and close up with coarse paste.

Fire the trains of powder, order it so that some of the Ladies may be persuaded to pluck the Arrow out of the Stag, then will the claret follow as blood running from a wound. This being done with admiration to the beholders, after some short pause, fire the train of the Castle, that the pieces all of one side may go off; then fire the trains of one side of the Ship, as in a battle, and by degrees fire the trains of each other side, as before. This done, to sweeten the stink of the powder, let the Ladies take the eggshells full of sweet waters, and throw them at each other. All dangers being over, by this time you may suppose they will desire to see what is in the Pies; where, lifting off the lid of one pie, out skips some Frogs, which makes the Ladies to skip and shreek; next after the other Pie, whence comes out the Birds, who by a natural instinct flying at the light, will put out the Candles, so that what with the flying Birds, and skipping Frogs, the one above, the other beneath, will cause much delight and pleasure to the company: at length the candles are lighted and a banquet brought in, the music sounds, and everyone with much delight and content rehearses their actions in the former passages. These were formerly the delights of Nobility, before good-housekeeping had left England.

Words and Music

Pepys had a number of cookery books in his collection, but since he never cooked a meal himself he may have bought them just because he liked the look of them. Books were his lifelong passion. Many of his purchases were made at the booksellers' shops in St Paul's Churchyard, where there were at least a couple of dozen separate establishments. Other centres of the book trade were the Temple and Westminster Hall. Pepys spent many a happy hour in these places, and many a golden guinea too. This was one area of his life where his innate stinginess could not win out. He bought books for the knowledge they contained, but he also loved them as objects. Unlike bibliophiles of later ages, he could decisively influence the appearance and desirability of his purchases, as most books were sold in loose quires, and it was down to the buyer to provide the binding. (Herein lies the origin of the 'half-title' – the first page of a book showing the title and nothing else: it allowed buyers and sellers easily to identify a book before it had acquired a cover.) Pepys gave a great deal of thought to the bindings of his books. In the mid-1660s, by which time he must have had a least a couple of hundred volumes clogging up his home office at Seething Lane, he went to Joseph Kirton, a bookseller at St Paul's, 'and there did give thorough direction for the new binding of a great many of my old books, to make my whole study of the same binding, within a few.'

In the course of the 1660s he acquired about 500 volumes, all of which he lovingly catalogued and re-catalogued according to size (which dictated their place on the shelf) subject and alphabetical sequence. He had had a ship's carpenter build two fine bookcases for his collection, and resolved to have no more books than would fit in them. This self-imposed limitation appealed to his sense of neatness, and also allowed him the exquisite pleasure, known only to obsessive collectors, of weeding out items that had dropped out of favour or fallen foul of his ever stricter criteria for inclusion.

Pepys's reading, like his eating, is an instructive guide to the tastes of the age. But his library in its totality is also a register of his interests over the course of a lifetime. It is the very map of his curious mind. So what did he read? Some of his favourite texts seem extremely high-brow by modern standards. In June 1662 we find that he was …

… up by 4 o'clock in the morning, and read Cicero's Second Oracion against Cataline, which pleased me exceedingly; and more I discern therein than ever I thought was to be found in him. But I perceive it was my ignorance, and that he is as good a writer as ever I read in my life.

Pepys happily read Latin for pleasure – not only the classics, but also modern works written in what was still the common tongue of scholarship throughout Europe (Pepys occasionally spoke Latin to foreigners when neither spoke the other's native tongue – just as today a Spaniard and a Korean, say, would naturally resort to English in the first instance). He was fond of the works of the Elizabethan thinker Francis Bacon, and once speaks of reading his *Faber Fortunae* ('Architect of Fortune') as he walked from the office to Woolwich. It is not surprising that Bacon's views on providence appealed to Pepys. He was deeply interested in his own fortune in both senses of the word. The first paragraph of Bacon's essay *De Fortunae* ('On Fortune') could easily serve as a the moral of Pepys's whole life story:

It cannot be denied but outward accidents conduce much to fortune; favour, opportunity, death of others, occasion fitting virtue: but chiefly the mould of a man's fortune is in his own hands. 'Every man is the architect of his own fortune', saith the poet ... Overt and apparent virtues bring forth praise; but there be secret and hidden virtues that bring forth fortune.

The practical social climber in Pepys enjoyed manuals of correct conduct and books of improving advice – including the occasional sermon. He read a great deal of history, especially recent history. Naturally enough, a great deal of royalist revisionism found its way into print after the restoration, and it was consumed with the same kind of avidity that Russians evinced for critiques of communism in the years after its fall. The high-point of this genre was Clarendon's *History of the Great Rebellion*, which was published in 1702, a few months before Pepys died. In his old age, he must surely have got much pleasure from a book in which so many of the protagonists were known to him personally.

Pepys, ever the autodidact, tried to keep abreast of the latest scientific advances. He was acquainted with Robert Boyle, and so it was probably with some sense of obligation that he tackled the great chemist's *Experiments and Considerations Touching Colours*. But he found it very hard going, and was easily distracted.

After dinner by water, the day being mighty pleasant and the tide serving finely – I up (reading in Boyles book of Colours)

> as high as Barne Elmes; and there took one turn alone and then
> back to Putny church, where I saw the girls of the schools, few
> of which pretty.

Later that night he wrote that he was 'mightily pleased with my reading
Boyles book of Colours today; only troubled that some part of it, indeed
the greatest part, I am not able to understand.' A month and a half later
he limped to the end of the book, which had once again blighted an
otherwise enjoyable boat trip to Putney.

> Being weary and almost blind with writing and reading so much
> today, I took boat at the Old Swan, and there up river all alone,
> as high as Puttny almost; and then back again, all the way
> reading and finishing Mr Boyle's book of Colours, which is so
> Chymicall that I can understand but little of it, but understand
> enough to see that he is a most excellent man.

Pepys found comical books almost as much of a struggle as chemical
ones. For such a convivial and clubbable man, he is strangely lacking
in an individual sense of humour. There are very few consciously funny
anecdotes in the diary, and most of the amusing episodes are
unintentionally so. One such is Pepys's doomed attempt to see the point
of Samuel Butler's *Hudibras*. This long poem is a kind of slapstick
version of *Don Quixote* in which a Puritan knight and his squire journey
through a series of brawls and romantic assignations. It is a satire on
many things, including the various religious sects of the day (the
Puritans in particular), as well as pedants and politicians, marriage,
witchcraft and astrology. Pepys was one of the first to buy it, but he
didn't like it at all:

> Hither came Mr Battersby; and we falling into a discourse of a
> new book of Droller in verse called *Hudebras*, I would needs go
> find it out; and met with it at the Temple, cost me two shillings
> and sixpence. But when I came to read it, it is so silly an abuse
> of the Presbyter-Knight going to the warrs that I am ashamed of

> it; and by and by meeting at Mr Townsends at dinner, I sold it
> to him for 18 pence.

In the course of the next month or two, Butler's book became the talk
of the town. According to Evelyn, the king carried a copy in his pocket.
Pepys, a conformist at heart, felt he had to give it a second chance.

> So to a bookseller's in the Strand, and there bought *Hudibras*
> again, it being certainly some ill humour to be so set against that
> which all the world cries up to be the example of wit – for which
> I am resolved once again to read him and see where I can find it
> or no.

In the end Pepys was reduced to asking older colleagues over dinner
what it is that makes some books funny. He got a long answer which,
judging by his attempt to summarize it, left him none the wiser.

> Up and to the office; and at noon to the Coffee-house, where I
> sat with Sir G Asckue and Sir Wm. Petty, who in discourse is
> methinks one of the most rational men that ever I heard speak
> with a tongue, having all his notions the most distinct and clear;
> and did among other things (saying that in all his life these three
> books were the most esteemed and generally cried up for wit in
> the world – *Religio Medici*, Osborne's *Advice to a Son*, and
> *Hudibras*) did say that in these, in the two first principally, the
> wit lie in confirming some pretty sayings, which are generally
> like paradoxes, by some argument smartly and pleasantly urged
> – which takes with people who do not trouble themselves to
> examine the force of an argument which pleases them in the
> delivery, upon a subject which they like; whereas (as by many
> perticular instances of mine and others out of Osborne) he did
> really find fault and weaken the strength of many of Osbornes
> arguments, so as that in downright disputation they would not
> bear weight; at least, so far but that they might be weakened,
> and better found in their rooms to confirm what is there said.

> He showed finely whence it happens that good writers are not
> admired by the present age; because there are but few in any age
> that do mind anything that is abstruce and curious; and so, longer
> before anybody doth put the true praise and set it on foot in the
> world – the generality of making pleasing themselves in the easy
> delights of the world, as eating, drinking, dancing, hunting,
> fencing, which we see the meanest men do the best, those that
> profess it. A gentleman never dances so well as the dancing-
> master and an ordinary fiddler makes better music for a shilling
> then a gentleman will do after spending forty. And so in all the
> delights of the world almost.

Pepys hung on to his second copy of *Hudibras*. But whether he ever got
the joke, he doesn't say.

He was on firmer ground with music – which, he said, 'is the thing
of the world that I love most, and almost all the pleasure that I can
now take.' Pepys was a very fine amateur musician. He played the viol,
the violin, the lute and the flageolet (a kind of early recorder). He was
confident enough in his abilities to show off a little when the
opportunity presented itself.

> At night to my viallin (the first time that I have played on it since
> I came to this house) in my dining roome; and afterwards to my
> Lute there – and I took much pleasure to have the neighbours
> come forth into the yard to hear me.

Pepys love of music may have been heightened by the fact that it was
a commodity in short supply during the Republic. The Puritans had no
objection to music per se, but they banned its use in church (even going
so far as to destroy some church organs); they closed the theatres where
'popular' music was performed; and they dispersed the large contingent
of court musicians. The effect of these rules was to turn music-making
into a largely amateur, home-based activity, and it was in this context
that Pepys excelled. Pepys also fancied himself as a composer, and set
two passages from John Davenant to music. 'A very fine song it seems

to be,' was his own assessment of one of these tunes. So proud of it was he that he posed for a portrait holding his own musical composition, as if this was the achievement he wished to be remembered for.

The diary is full of his reactions to music, some of them more positive than others. One evening he spent the evening with some 'Scotch people', and was unimpressed by their music.

> At supper there played one of their servants upon the viallin some Scotch tunes only – several – and of the best of their country, as they seemed to esteem they by their praising and admiring them; but Lord, the strangest ayre that ever I heard in my life, and all of one cast. But strange to hear my Lord Lauderdale say himself that he had rather hear a Catt mew than the best Musique in the world ... and that of all instrument he hates the Lute most; and next to that, the Baggpipe.

It is possible that Lauderdale was exaggerating the case, having been as bored and irritated by the Scottish airs as his guest was. But for Pepys, this was a shocking statement nevertheless. A life without music was unthinkable to him – all the more so when he began to have trouble with his eyesight and could not enjoy reading or writing. On one occasion at the theatre in 1667 he had a musical experience that was so intense it was a kind of epiphany. As an encounter with a piece of art, it is the polar opposite of his unsatisfactory experience with *Hudibras*. And his description of it is so fluent and so joyous that it makes one long to hear or feel for oneself what Pepys heard and felt that night:

> To the King's House to see *Virgin Martyr*, the first time it hath been acted a great while and it is mighty pleasant; not that the play is worth much, but it is finely Acted by Becke Marshall; but that which did please me beyond anything in the whole world was the wind-musique when the Angell comes down, which is so sweet that it ravished me; and endeed, in a word, did wrap up my soul so that it made me really sick, just as I have formerly been

when in love with my wife; that neither then, nor all the evening going home and at home, I was able to think of anything, but remained all night transported, so as I could not believe that ever any music hath real command over the soul of a man as this did upon me.

After the diary years, Pepys combined his love of books and his passion for music by making a large and scholary collection of ballads. They are one of the treasures of the Pepys Library, which at the time of his death ran to 3,000 volumes and filled 12 bookcases – the latter ten all built to match the first two. Pepys bequeathed them all to Magdalen College, Cambridge, where they are still housed today in the original cases. It is here that the true intellectual breadth of Pepys can be seen. Besides the many works of literature and song, there are books on naval matters, on theology and religion, on topography and travel, on language and philology – to name but a few of the areas that interested him. There are books in English, French, Latin, Greek and Spanish. And of course there are the six volumes containing the diary itself, which Pepys (modestly or immodestly) had bound and placed on his shelves alongside all the rest.

The Pleasures *of* Love

Hidden away among Pepys's books was a volume to which, when it was bound, he gave the innocent title *Rochester's Life*. It was written by John Wilmot, 2nd Earl of Rochester, who was a courtier of King Charles II. He was the perfect companion for a pleasure-seeker like Charles. Boredom was the mental state that Charles feared above all, and Rochester was never dull. He was sharp and witty, and he knew how to keep the king amused.

But he was also decadent and dangerous, drunken and dissolute. The earl lived a life of spectacular appetite-driven excess. He was a rock star 300 years before that profession was invented – and as is the case with some rock stars, his unbridled hedonism existed side by side with genuine creativity. For Rochester had a gift for poetry that was even more prodigious that his talent for dissipation. He combined these skills to write some of the most jaw-droppingly obscene verse ever penned in the English language. None of it was published under his name in his lifetime; his works circulated anonymously in broadsheets, and found their way into the booksellers around St Paul's. Pepys's *Rochester's Life* was his copy of the poetry, and he guarded it almost as closely as his beloved diary.

The odes and epigrams that Rochester turned out were often politically charged. This self-destructive little ditty got him sent to prison.

We have a pretty witty king,
Whose word no man relies on;

He never said a foolish thing,
Nor ever did a wise one.

Such impertinence would have cost a less entertaining man everything,
but the king was loath to lose the company of such an inventive court
jester. He is said to have commented on the poem: 'It is true; for my
words are my own, but my actions are those of my ministers.' This was
a magnanimous reaction on the king's part; it amounted to a royal
pardon. Rochester was out of his prison cell and back at the king's
side before long.

The earl remained a fixture at court throughout the 1660s. But by
the time he turned 30 he had burned himself out. He was crippled by
alcoholism and riddled with syphilis. He took to wearing a silver nose-
piece to hide his rotting nostrils. In a kind of final bilious flourish he
wrote an utterly pornographic satire on the king and his many
mistresses. Somehow, by accident, he managed to send it to the king
himself, and had to flee for his life. A single couplet will suffice to give
the flavour of the piece:

His sceptre and his prick are of a length;
And she may sway the one who plays with th'other ...

As was the case with Rochester's earlier jibe, the judgment was harsh
but true. If Charles did not this time admit it, then everybody else in
the kingdom knew it. The Marquis of Halifax, one of the intelligent
men in Charles's immediate circle, had this to say of the king's love life.

Mistresses were recommended to him, which is no small matter in
a court. A mistress either dexterous in herself, or well-instructed
by those that are so, may be very useful to her friends, not only
in the immediate hours of her ministry, but by her influences and
insinuations at other times. It was resolved generally by others
whom he should have in his arms, as well as whom he should
have in his councils. Of a man who was so capable of choosing,
he chose as seldom as any man that ever lived.

This is essentially the same point as Rochester was making – with the additional insight that Charles's mistresses were not so much players in the political game as part of the sporting paraphernalia. Courtesans were launched in Charles's direction like bowling balls on a green. The team that won was the team that positioned its piece closest to the royal jack.

The Illustrious Lady of Pleasure

Barbara Villiers was the first and in many ways the most successful of Charles's royal mistresses. She was, it was agreed by everyone who ever saw her, quite fabulously beautiful. Pepys went into raptures every time he laid eyes on her. She was born in 1640, the only daughter of Viscount Grandison, an impoverished royalist general. At the age of 17 she embarked on an affair with the dashing Philip Stanhope, 2nd Earl of Chesterfield. The liaison was not interrupted by her marriage in 1659, at the age of 19, to a young man named Roger Palmer. Palmer was an active royalist, closely involved in the plan to bring Charles back from exile. Through him, Barbara found herself involved with the royal cause. In the spring of 1660 she was asked by some of Palmer's associates to carry messages across the sea to Charles, now watching and waiting in Brussels. She gladly undertook this little adventure, and embarked on one of her own when she got there. In Belgium she became the lover of the king-in-waiting.

She was back in England before the restored king arrived there in triumph in May 1660. Some accounts say that Charles spent his first night on English soil in her bed. It is more than likely that he did, since the king had granted to Palmer a house on King Street, ostensibly as a mark of gratitude for his clandestine services. Mrs Palmer would now be living conveniently close to the palace at Whitehall. She was practically Charles's next-door neighbour.

It so happened that the Palmers' house was literally next door to the home of Pepys's patron Lord Sandwich. One night in July, Pepys was there with employer and his young protégé, Will Howe. There he got a hint of things to come.

> **Late writing letters; and great doings of music at the next house,**
> **which was Whally's; the King and Dukes there with Madame**
> **Palmer, a pretty woman that they have a fancy to, to make her**
> **husband a cuckold. Here at the old door that did go into his**
> **lodgings, my Lord, I, and W. Howe, did stand listening a great**
> **while to the music.**

As he eavesdropped on the king, Pepys was not yet aware that he was
a long way behind the news. Barbara was already pregnant with the
king's child. She gave birth to a daughter the following February. In
1662 Roger Palmer was created Earl of Castlemaine. The title, said
the warrant, was 'to him and the heirs of his body gotten on Barbara
Palmer, his now wife', a condition, as Pepys remarked 'the reason
whereof everybody knows'. The rumour that Pepys had heard in
Sandwich's house in July 1660 had become a scandal for all the world
to talk about.

The king married Catherine of Braganza, the Portuguese infanta,
in 1662. Like Barbara three years before, he saw no reason why he
should give up his lover just because he was to have a spouse. Lady
Castlemaine, as she now had the right to call herself, was in any case
far more beautiful that the queen, who was not only rather plain, but
also humourlessly pious. Her retinue consisted mostly of dour
Portuguese matrons dressed entirely in black. Barbara kept tactfully in
the background during the early days of the king's marriage, but soon
re-emerged as the most important woman in his household. He insisted
on installing her as a lady-in-waiting to his wife, an arrangement to
which the queen naturally objected. But Charles was adamant, and
chose what seemed to him like a good moment to introduce his mistress
to his wife. As soon as the queen learned the identity of the tall lady
standing before her she blushed crimson, blood gushed from her nose,
and she fell into a faint. It was the only means she had of upstaging
her vampish rival.

Such instances outraged and titillated everybody at court and
beyond. Pepys jotted down every bit of tittle-tattle and rumour that
came his way.

> This day I was told that my Lady Castlemayne (being quite fallen
> out with her husband) did yesterday go away from him, with all
> her plate, jewels, and other best things; he wrote in July 1662.
> And is gone to Richmond to a brother of hers; which, I am apt to
> think, was a design to get out of town, that the King might come
> at her the better. But strange it is how for her beauty I am willing
> to conster [construe] all this to the best, and to pity her wherein it
> is to her hurt, though I know well enough she is a whore.

That dismissive judgment evaporated whenever he found himself
physically close enough to her to come under her bewitching spell.
When the king and the new queen arrived in London from Hampton
Court that August, Pepys had eyes only for Lady Castlemaine.

> I glutted myself with looking on her. But methought it was
> strange to see her Lord [Roger Palmer] and her upon the same
> place, walking up and down without taking notice one of another;
> only at first entry he put off his hat, and she made him a very
> civil salute, but afterwards took no notice one of another; but
> both of them now and then would take their child, which the
> nurse held in her armes, and dandle it.
>   One thing more; there happened a scaffold below to fall, and
> we feared some hurt, but there was none, but she of all the great
> ladies only run down among the common rabble to see what hurt
> was done, and did take care of a child that received some little
> hurt, which methought was so noble. Anon there came one there
> booted and spurred that she talked long with. And by and by, she
> being in her hair [unwigged], she put on his hat, which was but
> an ordinary one, to keep the wind off. But methinks it became
> her mightily, as every thing else do. The show being over, I went
> away, not weary with looking on her.

Earlier that year he had had an even more evocative encounter with
her. 'In the Privy-garden saw the finest smocks and linen petticoats of
my Lady Castlemayne's, laced with rich lace at the bottom, that ever

I saw; and did me good to look upon them.' After this brush with the
lady's underwear, there followed a series of fairly close encounters
with the lady herself – usually at the theatre. Every time Pepys was
enchanted anew by the sight of her. The glorious upshot of it all
was that she came to him in his sleep one night in 1665. This life-
affirming dream occurred at a time when the waking world was full
of death and pestilence.

> ... something put my last night's dream into my head, which I
> think is the best that ever was dreamed – which was, that I had
> my Lady Castlemayne in my armes and was admitted to use all
> the dalliance I desired with her, and then dreamed that this could
> not be awake but that it was only a dream. But that since it was
> a dream and that I took so much real pleasure in it, what a happy
> thing it would be, if when we are in our graves (as Shakepeere
> resembles it), we could dream, and dream but such dreams as this
> – that then we should not need to be so fearful of death as we are
> this plague-time.

Pepys later bought three copies of a print taken from Lely's portrait of
the lady, and was most upset when, towards the end of the decade, she
seemed to be losing her good looks. Others who knew her as a person
rather than as a pin-up had a less rosy image of her.

> I love not to give characters of women, especially when there
> is nothing that is good to be said of them, as indeed I never
> heard any commend her but for her beauty, which was very
> extraordinary and has been now of long continuance. She was
> a woman of great beauty but most enormously vicious and
> ravenous; foolish but imperious, very uneasy to the king and
> always carrying on intrigues with other men, while yet she
> pretended she was jealous of him. His passion for her and her
> strange behaviour towards him did so disorder him that often
> he was not master of himself nor capable of minding business,
> which, in so critical a time, required great application. In short,

> she was a woman of pleasure, and stuck at nothing that would either server her appetites or her passions. She was vastly expensive, and by consequence very covetous. She was weak, and so was easily managed.

That was the verdict of Gilbert Burnet, Bishop of Salisbury, who was most concerned with her insidious political influence. For Lorenzo Magalotti, an Italian visitor to England, she was a beauteous monster, a scandalous has-been.

> This woman is in a position that cannot hide her very bad qualities. She was born a Protestant, and has prostitution bred into her by ancient inheritance in the maternal line. Before coming into the hands of the King she passed through those of many men, and among the others the Duke of Buckingham with all his relations were not the last to avail themselves of her. When the king came to desire her she at once abandoned herself to his pleasures with almost no resistance. Lord Gerard, who at that time held the privy purse and slept in the King's chamber, had the first information about this, for the king at first had her come to his bedroom, before he gave her apartments in the palace … One night he was in a terrible quandary when in bed with her, for a fire broke out near his room and they found themselves surrounded by the guards and all the court, who had run to extinguish it. Meanwhile the lady was in the king's bed, and he found it advisable to put her, naked, into the hands of Gerard, who thought of a place to stow her for safety, also profiting from the opportunity, according to some people.
>
> At the present time this lady is not very beautiful, although she shows the vestiges of marvellous beauty. She could not possibly carry herself in a worse way than she does. This is, in truth, a defect common to all the English ladies, who, as if they were moved by some internal power only from the waist up, trail their thighs and legs behind them in a ridiculous way. However, in her this is an advantage, for not only in her carriage, but in every

gesture of the arms and the hands, in every expression of her face, in every glance, in every movement of her mouth, in every word, one recognises shamelessness and whoredom. At times she gives way to terrible rages. Her jealousy ... poisoned her mind with such moral rancour that in these rages she often shut herself in her apartments, refusing to dine with the King.

Magalotti was writing in 1668, by which time Lady Castlemaine's sexual grip on Charles was loosening. Pepys had noticed this, but he did not underestimate her power over the king. In January 1669 he remarked that, 'my lady Castlemayne is now in a higher command over the king than ever; not as a mistress, for she scorns him, but as a tyrant to command him.' It was true that the king was entirely in her sway. For almost a decade she had lived a life of unfettered luxury at his expense. She had grown fabulously wealthy using her enormous sexual appetite as a means to satisfy the king. As an 'illustrious lady of pleasure' she had managed to persuade him to pay her immense gambling debts, and she had amassed vast quantities of jewels, which she wore with great ostentation. She had acquired land and property. One year she had even demanded that Charles give her all the Christmas presents he had received from other monarchs – and this he did without a murmur.

At last she decided that it was time to cash in her chips. A few days after Pepys made his remark about Castlemaine's tyrannical hold on the king, she had herself pensioned off. The illustrious lady was granted a life pension of £4,700 a year, and was later given the new title of Lady Cleveland as a kind of long-service medal. She was also presented with the beautiful Elizabethan Nonsuch Palace, near Cheam in Surrey, as a retirement gift. Rapacious to the last, she had the building stripped of anything of worth and sold it; she rented out the gardens and grounds as farmland; and she left the shell of the palace to fall down.

La Belle Stuart

At the height of his passion for the voracious Castlemaine, Charles also became infatuated with a very different kind of lady. Frances Stuart was a distant relative of the royal house. She was introduced to court by Charles's sister, the Duchess of Orléans, who let him know in advance that the new lady-in-waiting was 'the prettiest girl imaginable and most fitted to adorn a court'. The duchess's unspoken aim was to distance the king from the haughty Lady Castlemaine (it was a classic play in the regal bowling game) and Frances was the perfect choice for the task. She was stunningly beautiful, but in a way that was as far removed from Lady Castlemaine's vain and imperious comeliness as it was possible to be. She was petite and fresh-faced, bubbly and girly. She was only 15 years old when she came to England from the home in France where she had been raised. In a nod to her provenance and her good looks, she was immediately nicknamed 'la belle Stuart'. Every man at Whitehall Palace, up to and including the king, was captivated by her.

And not just at the palace. Pepys too was very taken with the new star of the court. He saw her one day when the king and queen and their entire retinue were out riding in the park. As he observed the colourful scene, the astute Pepys instinctively understood that new forces were at work in the seat of power, that the politics of beauty had wrought significant changes in Charles's world:

> By and by, the King and Queene, who looked in this dress, a white laced waistcoat and a crimson short petty-coate and her hair dressed *a la negligence*, mighty pretty; and the King rode hand in hand with her. Here was also my Lady Castlemayne rode among the rest of the ladies, but the King took methought no notice of her; nor when they light did anybody press (as she seemed to expect, and stayed for it) to take her down, but was taken down by her own gentleman. She looked mighty out of humour, and had a Yellow plume in her hat (which all took notice of) and yet is very handsome – but very melancholy; nor did anybody speak to her or she so much as smile or speak to anybody. I followed them up into White-hall and into the Queenes presence, where all the ladies walked, talking and fiddling with their hats and feathers, and changing and trying one another's, but on another's heads, and laughing. But it was the

finest sight to me, considering their great beautys and dress, that ever I did see in all my life. But above all, Mrs Steward [Miss Stuart] in this dresse, with her hat cocked and a red plume, with her sweet eye, little Roman nose, and excellent *taille* [waist], is now the greatest beauty I ever saw I think in my life; and if ever woman can, doth exceed my Lady Castlemayne; at least, in this dresse. Nor do I wonder if the King changes, which I verily believe is the reason of his coldness to my Lady Castlemayne.

Frances was a fresh and novel presence, and that was her advantage over Lady Castlemaine. But she had a much more powerful asset even than that: her innocence. The fact was that Frances, for all her giggling and flirting, did not succumb to Charles's advances or anyone else's. She made herself unavailable, and by so doing rendered herself infinitely more desirable. Charles could not get enough of her company. He spent hours with her, and even refused to go and see Lady Castlemaine unless Frances was going to be there too. Lady Castlemaine, wise old courtesan that she was, knew better than to oppose the king's infatuation. Instead she made friends with Frances and used her as a kind of bait. The king would come to Lady Castlemaine's apartments and find both women lying languidly in bed, a lubricious vision of angelic innocence on the one hand, and of knowing carnality on the other. Lady Castlemaine even managed to persuade Frances to take part in a mock marriage – complete with the traditional rite of putting to bed. The older woman played the groom and the younger the bride. To Frances it was doubtless just a piece of silliness; she was known to have 'a taste for infantile diversions'. But Pepys, when he got to hear of it, appreciated the full suggestiveness of the charade and was gleeful.

My Lady Castlemayne, a few days since, had Mrs. Stuart to an entertainment, and at night began a frolique that they two must be married, and married they were, with ring and all other ceremonies of church service, and ribbands and a sack posset in bed, and flinging the stocking; but in the close, it is said that my Lady Castlemaine, who was the bridegroom, rose, and the King

**came and took her place with pretty Mrs. Stuart. This is said
to be very true.**

The 'ribbands' that Pepys mentions are the ties that hold up a lady's
garter – a relic of the strange old custom of publicly undressing a bride
on her wedding night. The 'flinging of the stocking' is a reminder of the
same ceremonial disrobement. A bridesmaid would throw the groom's
stockings over their shoulder; if it hit the groom that meant that the
bridesmaid would soon be married herself. (The custom survives – in
a sanitized and back-to-front form – in the modern wedding ritual of
throwing the bride's bouquet at the end of the reception.)

Pepys's suspicions notwithstanding, Frances did not succumb to the
king that night or any other night. Like Anne Boleyn with Henry VIII,
she understood that everything depended on not giving the king what
he wanted. And like Henry VIII, Charles seriously considered divorcing
the foreign wife who had failed to give him a son, and marrying the
young lady-in-waiting. But this was not to be. In 1667, to Charles's
great fury, Frances eloped with the Duke of Richmond. She was for a
time *persona non grata*, but (as with Rochester) the king could not afford
to banish permanently the few people who meant something to him.

As Lady Richmond, Frances held a place in court and in the king's
affection for many years. She outlived the king, but his affection for
her outlived them both in two strange ways. Firstly, her face was used as
the model for Britannia in a medal struck to commemorate the victory
over the Dutch. That allegorical image of Britain was subsequently
reproduced on British copper coins, and is still in use today on the
50p piece. More intimately, Charles's feelings for Frances are preserved
in a poem he wrote for her at the peak of his obsession. Here it is:

I pass all my hours in a shady old grove,
But I live not the day when I see not my love;
I survey every walk now my Phyllis is gone,
And sigh when I think we were there all alone,
Oh, then 'tis I think there's no Hell
Like loving too well.

But each shade and each conscious bower when I find
Where I once have been happy and she has been kind;
When I see the print left of her shape on the green,
And imagine the pleasure may yet come again;
Oh, then 'tis I think that no joys are above
The pleasures of love.

While alone to myself I repeat all her charms,
She I love may be locked in another man's arms,
She may laugh at my cares, and so false she may be,
To say all the kind things she before said to me!
Oh then 'tis, oh then, that I think there's no Hell
Like loving too well.

But when I consider the truth of her heart,
Such an innocent passion, so kind without art,
I fear I have wronged her, and hope she may be
So full of true love to be jealous of me.
Oh then 'tis I think that no joys are above
The pleasures of love.

The verses are somewhat amateurish, and the rhymes are distinctly
pedestrian, but the words touching nevertheless because they are
genuinely tender. This alone is a remarkable coming from a man like
Charles II, whose soul, in the course of his reign, became so blighted
by vice, so bloated with excess.

The Rise of the Orange-Girl

It would be a mistake to think that the lascivious behaviour of the king
was replicated by his subjects. Many of them, after all, were committed
to the Puritan way of life, if not to the Puritan Republic, and were
horrified by the lecherous stories they heard about the royal circle.
Moralists worried that the entire nation was following the king into
a cesspit of sin.

Would it not be a shame to tell of the chambering and
wantonness, and privy lewdness which hath been committed in
London? wrote one dissenting preacher. Suppose that in all the ...
churches the sin of uncleanness should be reproved; and all, both
men and women, that have actually been guilty of it, should be
forced by an inward sting of conscience immediately to go out of
the place. What a stir there would be in some churches! What an
emptying of pews! What a clearing of some aisles! And how few
there would be remaining in some places!

Suppose a visible mark were put by God upon the foreheads of
all the adulterers in the city of London, as God put a mark upon
Cain ... Would not many who walk now very demurely, and with
much seeming innocency, walk with blushes in their cheeks?
Would not many keep house and hide their face, and not stir
abroad except in the night? Or if in the day, would they not
shuffle through the streets, and hate the fashion of little hats,
and the court mode of wearing them behind the head?

If there have not been public stews in London, as in other cities
in the world, yet have not some made their own houses little
better, some men bringing in their whores in little better than
public view; and of the other sex some by the open wear of naked
breasts, and their light attire and carriage, have enticed the eye
and courtship, and after, basely prostituted their bodies to the
lust of filthy ruffians?

O, the boiling, burning lusts that have been in London!

London was, perhaps, a permissive case apart. In the metropolis,
brothel-keepers did indeed tout for trade more brazenly and openly than
had been possible before the restoration. Women of all classes happily
embraced the fashion for revealing *decolleté* that so shocked this
sermonizing Puritan. The two newly licensed theatres did good box
office with bawdy plays about lustful libertines, doddery sugar-daddies
and their prettily deceiving wives. And booksellers discovered that
there was a lucrative market in written pornography. Pepys, after much
prevarication, bought a copy of a French work named *L'escholle des filles*,

'The School for Girls'. He judged it 'a lewd book, but what doth me no wrong to read for information sake.' He read it once, with great satisfaction, then burned it.

But the fact is: the loose conduct of the king and his courtiers did not profoundly alter the moral character of the nation as a whole. Births out of wedlock, to take one measure, were only fractionally higher in Charles's reign than they had been under Cromwell's punitive theocracy. The idea that the restoration plunged all levels of English society into an orgiastic free-for-all is a myth. Its origin lies partly in the story of a one remarkable and very public person, whose highly successful career was built on a foundation of solid sex appeal. That person was Nell Gwyn.

Eleanor Gwyn was the only commoner to establish herself as a fully fledged mistress of Charles II. And common she certainly was. She was raised in a back-street off Drury Lane, the younger daughter of a professional prostitute. While still a young teenager, Nell got a job selling China oranges in the King's Theatre. She doubtless also sold herself now and again to supplement her income. It was while she was hawking oranges night after night in the pit, that Nell came to the attention of Charles Hart, the leading actor of the theatre. He saw how this pretty girl joked and bantered with the men in the audience, how she used her attractiveness to get customers to come to her, and then used her clever tongue to fend them off when necessary. He thought he might be able to make an actress of her. Hart took Nell under his wing – and into his bed – and he taught her the rudiments of the actor's trade. She probably made her debut in 1665. Pepys saw her in a piece called *Mustapha* that April. He thought the play was dreadful, but was very contented with his night out for other reasons:

All the pleasure of the play was, the King and my Lady Castlemaine was there – and pretty witty Nell at the King's House, and the younger Marshall, sat next us; which pleased me mightily.

But Nell Gwyn's nascent career was interrupted by the plague soon after: all the theatres were closed until the autumn of 1666. Pepys saw her again at the same theatre almost two years later, and this time he got rather closer to her when he was introduced in person by two actress friends, Mrs Pierce and Mrs Knipp. Pepys found himself surrounded with attractive women, an eastern potentate for the night. The memory of it glowed warm for a long time after.

Here, in a box above, we spied Mrs. Pierce; and going out, they called us, and so we stayed for them and Knipp took us all in and brought to us Nelly, a most pretty woman, who acted the great part, Coelia, today very fine, and did it pretty well; I kissed her and so did my wife, and a mighty pretty soul she is. We also saw Mrs Ball, which is my little Roman-nose black girl [brunette] that is mighty pretty: she is usually called Betty. Knipp made us stay in a box and see the dancing preparatory to tomorrow for The Goblins, a play of Suckeling's not acted these 25 years, which was pretty; and so away thence, pleased with this sight also, and especially kissing of Nell.

It was around this time that Nell got the big break that took her out of the theatre and into the court. She agreed to become the full-time mistress of Charles Sedley, Lord Buckhurst, who was one of the charming and dissolute rakes who surrounded the king. According to the rumour Pepys heard, she took on the job for £100 a year. (When Pepys and others refer to her as a 'whore', it is this kind of situation that they have in mind: the term meant a kept woman, rather than a street prostitute.)

The professional agreement with Lord Buckhurst lasted no more than six months – one or both of them grew tired of it. The management of Nell's career was now taken on by the Duke of Buckingham. He saw her as a comely pawn that he could use to entrap the concupiscent king, and so gain an advantage over his enemy, Lady Castlemaine.

The Duke of Buckingham studied to take the King from her by new amours, wrote Bishop Burnet. And because he thought a gaiety of humour would take much with the King, he engaged

him to entertain two players, one after another, Davies and Gwyn. The first did not keep her hold long; but Gwyn, the indiscreetest and wildest creature that ever was in a court, continued in great favour. The Duke of Buckingham told me that when she was first brought to the King she asked for only £500 a year.

While Nell's asking price had quintupled in less than a year, she was still seen as a fantastic bargain compared with the astronomically expensive Lady Castlemaine. She became the king's main lover in 1668, and remained loyal to him for the rest of her life. He was, she always said, her Charles the Third – Charles Hart the actor and Charles Sedley, Lord Buckhurst, having preceded him in her affections.

At War with Squintabella

But Nell did not have the king's attention to herself. In 1670, Charles's eye fell on a new courtier, recently arrived from France. This was Louise Renée de Penancoët de Kéroualle, a lady-in-waiting of noble Breton birth who had long lived in the household of Charles's sister, the Duchess of Orléans. Like Charles's two main mistresses of the 1660s – the unstoppably promiscuous Lady Castlemaine and the virtuously chaste Frances Stuart – his two amours of the 1670s were also opposing types. The high-born, refined Frenchwoman loathed the coarse guttersnipe Nell Gwyn, who hated her just as much in return. Louise was haughty, fanatically snooty about her aristocratic past, cold-hearted and scheming, and given to schoolgirl tantrums and feigned illnesses whenever she did not get her own way. To Nell, Louise's inflated pretensions were almost too easy to puncture, particularly since the Frenchwoman was utterly lacking a quality Nell possessed in abundance: a sense of humour. Nell constantly mimicked her imperfect English, and routinely referred to her as 'Cartwheel' – a mocking distortion of her unpronounceable surname – or as 'Squintabella', a reference to a very slight facial tic of Louise's about which she was, no doubt, immensely self-conscious.

Nell's ad-libs spread like tabloid news. Once she was travelling in the king's coach when she was actually mistaken for the unpopular Louise by the street mob. When they began to hurl insults she stuck her head out of the window and declared, 'Pray be civil, good people, I am the *Protestant* whore.' Nell would also go to extraordinary lengths to play a cruel joke on her rival. On one occasion in 1674, Louise turned up at court dressed in mourning for the Chevalier de Rohan, a French nobleman to whom she was not related, and whom she did not even know personally. The following day, Nell also appeared at court, in the presence of the king and of Louise, dressed from head to toe in funereal black and weeping into a handkerchief. When she was asked (presumably by someone primed to play the role of straight man) who it was exactly that she was mourning she said:

'Have you not heard of my loss in the death of the Khan of Tartary.'

'And what relation, pray, was the Khan of Tartary to you?'

'Exactly the same that the Chevalier de Rohan was to Cartwheel,' came the punchline.

Nell's constant jokes at Louise's expense kept the king, the court and the country royally amused. A year into the ding-dong battle between them, Madame de Sévigné, a French marquise and a wry observer of life at court, found that her sympathies lay mostly with the vulgar, sluttish Englishwoman.

Kéroual [Louise] has every reason to be satisfied with the treatment she has received in England, wrote Madame de Sévigné to her daughter. **She has achieved her purpose, which was to be the king's mistress. He spends all his nights with her with the full knowledge of everyone at court. Her son has been acknowledged, and has received two dukedoms, and withal has amassed great wealth and has succeeded in being feared and respected, at any rate by some persons. But she had not counted on the advent of a young actress whose charms bewitched the king, and from whom she finds herself unable to detach him.**

In pride and resolution the actress is her match. If looks could kill, Kéroual would no longer be alive. The actress makes faces at

her, often manages to inveigle the king, and boasts of his favours. She is young, untamed, bold, agreeable and dissolute, and she plies her trade with a will. She has a son by the king, whom she insists should be recognised, and to justify herself she reasons thus: 'This duchess wishes to pass as a great lady, claims to be related to all the French quality, and when any one of them dies goes into deep mourning. Very well, then. If she is so high and mighty, why has she turned whore. She should die of shame. As for me, I ply my trade and pretend no other. The King keeps me for the time being, and has given me a son whom he should and will acknowledge, as he cares for me any day as much as Portsmouth'. The trull has the last word, and proves a great embarrassment to the duchess. You will agree as to the story being highly original.

Louise's son by the king was made Duke of Richmond, and she herself was rewarded with the title Duchess of Portsmouth. Nell, who wanted no aristocratic status for herself, was adamant that her son should be acknowledged as fully as the Frenchwoman's. She achieved her aim not by wheedling and crying fits, as her rival was wont to do, but by making use of her fine sense of drama. Charles came to visit her at her home on one occasion when her son was about six. As the king stood in the doorway, Nell called out to the boy, 'Come here, you little bastard, and say hello to your father.' When the king objected to this turn of phrase, Nell said that she did not know how to refer to him since 'Your majesty has given me no other name by which I may call him.' The boy – whose baptismal name was in fact Charles – was soon after made Earl of Burford.

Both women remained part of Charles's life to the very end. Nell was always faithful to him, and her reward was a life of ease in her house on Pall Mall. Louise was unfaithful when it suited her purpose, and returned to France after Charles died. Barbara, Lady Cleveland, lived opulently and disgracefully to the age of 69. She had many more lovers after Charles – among then Charles Hart, the actor who had first discovered Nell's talents as an actress and as a mistress.

As for the king himself, the long years of self-indulgence reduced him to a raddled, desiccated personality. His mistresses – with the exception of Nell – were grasping, greedy individuals, who drained him morally and left him as empty as the echoing interior of poor old derelict Nonsuch Palace. Bishop Burnet's epitaph for the king was almost as damning as his verdict on Lady Castlemaine.

He had great vices, but scarce any virtues to correct them. He had in him some vices that were less hurtful, which corrected his more hurtful ones. He was, during the active part of his life given up to sloth and lewdness to such a degree that he hated business, and could not bear any thing that gave him much trouble, or put him under any constraint. And though he desired to become absolute, and to overturn both our religion and our laws, yet he would neither run the risk, nor give himself the trouble, which so great a design required.

He had an appearance of gentleness in his outward deportment, but he seemed to have no tenderness in his nature, and in the end of his life he became cruel. He was apt to forgive all crimes, even blood itself. Yet he never forgave any thing that was done against himself.

He delivered himself up to a most enormous course of vice without any sort of restraint, even from the consideration of the nearest relations. The most studied extravagances that way seemed, to the very last, to be much delighted in, and pursued by him. He had the art of making all people grow fond of him, at first, by a softness in his whole way of conversation, as he was certainly the best bred man of the age. But when it appeared how little could be built on his promise, they were cured of the fondness that he was apt to raise in them.

When he saw young men of quality who had something more than ordinary in them, he drew them about him, and set himself to corrupt them both in religion and morality – in which he proved so unhappily successful, that he left England much changed at this death from what he had found it at his restoration.

His person and temper, his vices as well as his fortunes, resemble the character that we have given us of Tiberius so much that it were easy to draw the parallel between them. Tiberius's banishment, and his coming afterwards to reign, makes the comparison in that respect come pretty near. His hating of business and his love of pleasures; his raising of his favourites, and trusting them entirely; and his pulling them down and hating them excessively; his art of covering deep designs, particularly of revenge, with an appearance of softness, brings them so near a likeness that I did not wonder much to observe the resemblance of their face and person. At Rome I saw one of the last statues made for Tiberius, after he had lost his teeth ... It was so like King Charles that Prince Borghese and Signor Dominico to whom it belonged, did agree with me in thinking that it looked like a statue made for him.

Few things ever went near his heart.

The Carpenter's Wife

Like the king himself, Samuel Pepys was a sensual man in a licentious age. Happily married though he was for the most part, he was the kind of man who regularly and easily fell for barmaids, actresses, duchesses and anonymous temptresses that he passed on the street or saw at church. On at least one occasion he took a telescope to a house of prayer so that he could ogle the prettiest women in the congregation during the *longueurs* of the sermon. Sometimes, as on this occasion in 1667, he saw church simply as an opportunity for a little low-level sexual harrassment:

I walked towards Whitehall, but, being wearied, turned into St. Dunstan's Church, where I heard an able sermon of the minister of the place. And stood by a pretty, modest maid, whom I did labour to take by the hand and the body. But she would not, but got further and further from me. And at last, I could perceive her to take pins out of her pocket to prick me if I should touch her again – which seeing I did forbear, and was glad I did espy her design. And then I fell to gaze upon another pretty maid in a pew close to me, and she on me. And I did go about to take her by the hand, which she suffered a little and then withdrew. So the sermon ended, and the church broke up, and my amours ended also. And so took coach and home.

Like many of his peers, Pepys took advantage of the unbuttoned possibilities that London presented to a freewheeling man of middling status. He had several women that he went to for casual sex – all of them his social inferiors. Once he made the mistake of growing overfond of his own housemaid, a girl named Deb Willets. His wife caught him in flagrante delicto with her, an incident which caused prolonged grief to all concerned. That unhappy venture came right at the end of the diary period. It seems that the further the po-faced prudery of the Puritan government receded into the past, the more inclined Pepys was to follow where his libido led him.

The passages in the diary where Pepys recorded his 'dalliances', as he called them, are among the most frank in the entire work. He noted not only the erotic frisson he got from stealing a kiss in the back of a hackney carriage, but also the occasional self-loathing that he felt after more serious assignations (which are recounted in such graphic detail that no edition before the 1970s could commit them to print). Pepys could afford to be utterly frank in what he wrote about this aspect of his life, because he was after all only addressing himself. The diary, one senses, is both the voice of Pepys's conscience and a secret confessional.

Of all the secret dalliances recorded in the diary, Pepys long drawn-out affair with a certain Mrs Bagwell is the strangest. The first mention of her comes on 9 July 1663, soon after the end of the imagined assignations with Elizabeth's dance teacher. On that wet summer's day, Pepys's naval business had taken him – as it often did – to the shipyards downriver from London.

I by water to Deptford and there mustered the yard, purposely (God forgive me) to find out Bagwell, a carpenter whose wife is

> a pretty woman, that I might have some occasion of knowing him
> and forcing her to come to the office again; which I did so
> luckily, that going hence, he and his wife did of themselfs meet
> me in the way, to thank me for my old kindness; but I spoke
> little to her, but shall give occasion for her coming to me. Her
> husband went along with me to show me Sir W. Penn's lodging;
> which I knew before, but only to have a time of speaking to him
> and sounding him.

It is not clear what favour Pepys had done for the ship's carpenter.
Probably he had given the craftsman's career some small boost, because
much of what followed was made possible by Bagwell's hope for
professional advancement. Equally obscure is the question of what
Pepys meant by 'sounding' the man. It could be that Pepys the manager
was assessing his subordinate on a purely professional level, or it could
be that Pepys wanted to weigh up how serious an obstacle the man
would be to what he had in mind. Because having seen her again,
Pepys was certain that he wanted to seduce Mrs Bagwell if he could.

A week later he was back in Deptford, and this time he got a little
closer to the couple.

> Thence coming home, I was saluted by Bagwell and his wife
> (the woman I have a kindness for) and they would have me into
> their little house; which I was willing enough to, and did salute
> his wife. They had got wine for me and I perceive live prettily;
> and I believe the woman a virtuous modest woman. Her
> husband walked through to Redriffe [Rotherhithe] with me,
> telling me things that I asked of in the yard; and so by water
> home, it being likely to rain again tonight, which God forbid.
> To supper and to bed.

Pepys must have been hoping deep down that Mrs Bagwell was not
quite as virtuous as she seemed. At this stage he had no way of finding
out one way or the other. But an opportunity presented itself a month
later on one of his regular visits to the dockyards.

> I stayed walking up and down, discoursing with the officers
> of the yard of several things, and so walked back again, and
> on my way young Bagwell and his wife waylayd me to desire
> my favour about getting him a better ship, which I shall pretend
> to be willing to do for them, but my mind is to know his wife
> a little better.

It was six months before Pepys acted on this thought, and then it was
at Mrs Bagwell's instigation. She came to see him early one morning
in February 1664.

> Before I went to the office there came Bagwell's wife to me
> to speak for her husband. I liked the woman very well and
> stroked her under the chin, but could not find in my heart
> to offer anything uncivil to her, she being I believe a very
> modest woman.

It is curious that the ambitious Mr Bagwell sent his wife to make his
case. They must have discussed among themselves how best to persuade
Pepys, and decided that she would make the better advocate. Mr
Bagwell surely knew, in other words, that his wife's attractiveness was
an asset he could use in his quest to get a transfer. Perhaps the carpenter
and his wife were more complicit in the affair than Pepys ever realized.

But come the spring of 1664, Pepys had yet to do anything to improve
Bagwell's station. So Mrs Bagwell called again.

> And so to the office, where a great while alone in my office,
> nobody near, with Bagwell's wife of Deptford; but the woman
> seems so modest that I durst not offer any courtship to her,
> though I had it in my mind when I brought her in to me. But
> am resolved to do her husband a courtesy, for I think he is a
> man that deserves very well.

That word 'modest' again. Pepys, timorous Lothario that he is, could not
yet pluck up the courage to make a pass. He does not say whether he told

Mrs Bagwell that he planned to do Mr Bagwell a professional 'courtesy' – if not, then she will have gone home as frustrated as he did. But at least he is no longer 'pretending to be willing'. Pepys and Mrs Bagwell were edging their way towards an unspoken bargain. At their next meeting, in October, the terms of the contract became a little clearer.

> **Meeting Bagwell's wife at the office before I went home, I took her into the office and there kissed her only. She rebuked me for doing it; saying, that did I do so much to many bodies else, it would be a stain to me. But I do not see but she takes it well enough; though in the main, I believe, she is very honest. So after some kind discourse, we parted, and I home to dinner.**

Pepys seems to have understood that Mrs Bagwell's protestations are a formality, and that their deal was close to being struck. In the meantime, he was neglecting the formalities of his own happy marriage, the anniversary of which fell less than a week after his first tentative embrace with Mrs Bagwell.

> **This day by the blessing of God, my wife and I have been married nine years, wrote Pepys on 10 October. But my head being full of business, I did not think of it, to keep it in any extraordinary manner. But bless God for our long lives and loves and health together, which the same God long continue, I wish from my very heart.**

On the 20th of the month, Mrs Bagwell was back in Pepys's private office. Alone together, the parties spelled out what they expected from the arrangement. 'I caressed her, and find her every day more and more coming, with good words and promise of getting her husband a place, which I will do,' wrote Pepys. But at their next assignation a fortnight later, the affair almost came to an end before it had properly begun.

> **At noon to the Change [the Exchange, in the City]; and thence by appointment was met with Bagwells wife, and she fallowed me**

> into Moorefields and there into a drinking-house – and all alone
> eat and drank together. I did there caress her; but though I did
> make some offer, did not receive any compliance from her in
> what was bad, but very modestly she denied me; which I was glad
> to see and shall value her the better for it – and I hope never
> tempt her to evil any more.

That pious resolution did not last long, and in any case Pepys had still
done nothing to help Mr Bagwell get a place on a better ship. He met
Mrs Bagwell in the office on 8 November, and arranged to see her away
from work the following week. He knew this was going to be an
important tryst, the one that would place him under an obligation
to fulfil his oft-repeated promise to the Bagwells.

> That I might not be too fine for the business I intend this day, did
> leave off my fine new cloth suit lined with plush and put on my
> poor black suit; and after office done (where much business but
> little done), I to the Change; and thence Bagwell's wife with
> much ado fallowed me through Moor-fields to a blind alehouse,
> and there I did caress her and eat and drank, and many hard
> looks and sithes [sighs] the poor wretch did give me, and I think
> verily was troubled at what I did; but at last, after many
> protestings, by degrees I did arrive at what I would, with great
> pleasure.

Distressing though this consummation seems to have been for Mrs
Bagwell, it gave her a position of power in her relationship with Pepys.
From this point he began to develop a doggish obsession with her.
'among others Bagwell's wife coming to speak with me put new
thoughts of folly into me which I am troubled at,' he wrote in the
first week of December. He now started to look for excuses to go to the
shipyards and seek her out, and was pathetically disappointed when he
could not contrive to bump into her. 'Up, and by water to Deptford,
thinking to have met *la femme de* Bagwell, but failed,' he noted a few
days later.

The three words of French in that entry for 16 December are not a fanciful flourish of the pen. Around now, Pepys began to record the details of his sexual adventures in a strange mix of foreign words – French, Latin, Spanish, Portuguese – often a chaotic amalgam of all four tongues. Why he resorted to this usage is hard to fathom. After all, no one knew he kept a diary, and it was always under lock and key. Since it was written in shorthand, his wife would not have been able to understand it even if she had happened upon it, and his macaronic terminology would in any case have been easy for her to understand, since French was her first language. It is not even as if he disguised the most incriminating words: the 'foreign' passages often consist for the most part of passionless lexical terms such as 'with', 'do' and 'I'.

It can only be that Pepys wrote in cod-French and mock-Portuguese for psychological reasons of his own. Perhaps the exotic words gave an extra thrill to the reminiscence or added a romantic glow to what was often a perfunctory and one-sided act. Conversely, perhaps this ruse allowed him to install a little mental moat between himself and his reprehensible behaviour. By imposing a linguistic filter on the facts of his sex life, he was able to maintain the same honest unedited attitude that he had to other events. As regards his deepening affair with Mrs Bagwell, two other oddities support the idea that the diarist needed to put some distance between Pepys the writer and Pepys the adulterer. One is that he never refers to Mrs Bagwell by her Christian name – she is always 'Bagwell's wife' (and no amount of scholarship has been able to establish her given name). The other strangeness is that Pepys tends to spell out the word 'Bagwell' in longhand when it refers to the husband (as was his usual practice with proper nouns); but when he is writing of his lover then 'Bagwell' is almost invariably rendered in opaque shorthand. So she is consigned very firmly to the shadowlands of his psyche, even when his longing for her dominates his conscious thoughts.

On the night of 18 December, Pepys struck his wife hard in the face during an argument about the servants. By morning she had a nasty bruise over her left eye. But Pepys went to work as usual, and in the afternoon arranged to meet with Mrs Bagwell. But first he had to go back home for a bite to eat.

I bid her go and stay at Mooregate for me; and after going up to my wife (whose eye is very bad, but she in good temper to me); and after dinner, I to the place and walked round the fields again and again; but not finding her, I to the Change and there found her waiting for me and took her away and to an alehouse, and there I made much of her; and then away thence and to another, and endeavoured to caress her; but *elle ne vouloit pas*, which did vex me but I think it was chiefly not having a good easy place to do it upon ...

I to supper with my wife, very pleasant. And then a little to my office and to bed – my mind, God forgive me, too much running upon what I can *faire avec la femme de Bagwell demain* – having promised to go to Deptford and *à aller à sa maison avec son mari* when I come hither.

The next day, Pepys carried out the plan he devised in the night.

Up and walked to Deptford, where after doing something at the yard, I walked, without being observed, with Bagwell home to his house and there was very kindly used, and the poor people did get a dinner for me in their fashion – of which I also eat very well. After dinner I found occasion of sending him abroad; and then alone *avec elle je tentoy à faire ce que je voudrais, et contre sa force je le faisoy, bien que pas a mon contentment.* By and by, he coming back, I took leave and walked home.

Morally, this was a low-point. Pepys was entirely untroubled by this cynical ruse – enjoying the hospitality of Mr Bagwell's house, then sending him on a pointless errand so that he could make love to his wife. But in the weeks that followed his conscience needled him a little. On 23 January, Pepys made one of his periodic vows to himself.

Thence to Jervas's, my mind, God forgive me, running too much after *sa fille*, but *elle* not being within I away by coach to the 'Change, and thence home to dinner. And finding Mrs. Bagwell waiting at the office after dinner, away *elle* and I to a cabaret where *elle* and I have *été* before, and there I had her company *toute l'après-diner* and had *mon plein plaisir* of *elle*. But strange to see how a woman, notwithstanding her greatest pretences of love *à son mari* and religion, may be *vaincue* ... So to my office a little and to Jervas's again, thinking *avoir rencontré* Jane, *mais elle n'etait pas dedans*. So I back again and to my office, where I did with great content *faire* a vow to mind my business, and *laisser aller les femmes* for a month, and am with all my heart glad to find myself able to come to so good a resolution, that thereby I may fallow my business, which and my honour thereby lies a-bleeding.

So Pepys admits that the affair is affecting his work and is a stain on his honour. It is interesting that Pepys's resolution to leave the women alone comes at the end of a day of erotic surfeit – the rendezvous with Mrs Bagwell being sandwiched in between failed attempts to flirt with his barber's pretty maidservant. More interesting still is that Pepys feels the need to tut-tut over his mistress's professed love for her husband. This can be read as a sub-conscious attempt to divert his mind from his own sense of guilt. On February 14, Mrs Bagwell committed a small faux pas:

I up about business; and opening the door, there was Bagwell's wife ... and she had the confidence to say she came with a hope to be time enough to be my Valentine, and so indeed she did, but my oath preserved me from losing any time with her.

The custom at the time was that people chose the first man or woman they saw that day as their Valentine. Generally it was an entirely innocent business – a young male neighbour had already come by early that morning to see Elizabeth and claim her as his Valentine – but the implication was too raw, and the gesture too close to home, for Pepys to be pleased. The oath he mentions is his guilty pledge to '*laisser aller les femmes*'.

In spite of Pepys's rudeness to her, or perhaps precisely because of it, Mrs Bagwell came back a few days later to insist again that he keep his promise to promote her husband. At long last, 18 months after the initial undertaking, he did so. 'I directed [Mrs Bagwell] to go home, and I would do her business, which was to write a letter to my Lord Sandwich for her husband's advance into a better ship ...' Now he felt that he was owed a favour from her. She evidently was not keen to grant it, but Pepys more or less forced himself upon her.

> And by and by did go down by water to Deptford, and then down further, and so landed at the lower end of the town, and it being dark did privately *entrer en la maison de la femme de Bagwell*, and there I had *sa compagnie*, though with a great deal of difficulty, *néanmoins enfin je avais ma volonté d'elle*.

The next day he had 'a mighty pain in my forefinger of my left hand, from a strain that it received last night in struggling *avec la femme que je* mentioned yesterday.'

In August, when the plague in London was at its height, Pepys twice visited Mrs Bagwell at her home – by now the usual venue for their trysts. On 12 August, Mrs Bagwell's father-in-law facilitated the meeting. 'Coming back to Deptford, old Bagwell walked a little way with me and would have me in to his daughter's. And there, he being gone *dehors, ego* had my *volunté de su hija*,' wrote Pepys coldly. A few days later it is Mrs Bagwell's mother-in-law who tactfully makes herself scarce when Pepys comes prowling round.

> To the King's Yard, walked up and down, and by and by out at the back gate and there saw the Bagwells' wifes, mother and daughter, and went to them; and went in to the daughter's house without the mother and *faciebam la cosa que ego tenebam* a mind to *con ella* – and drinking and talking.

These two incidents, within days of each other, suggest that the entire Bagwell family was complicit in the arrangement: they all knew that carpenter Bagwell's hopes of advancement depended on Pepys's libido. The still-raging plague was a double opportunity for Pepys to carry on the affair. It gave him good reason to conduct much of his navy business in Deptford rather than at the office in the City; and at the same time it meant he did not have to give account to his wife, who was safely stowed away in Woolwich. But the plague reached as far as Deptford too.

Down by water to Deptford and there to my Valentine's, wrote Pepys in October. **Round about and next door on every side is the plague, but I did not value it but there did what I would con ella. And so away to Mr Evelings. And here he showed me his gardens, which are for variety of evergreens, and hedge of holly, the finest things I ever saw in my life. Thence in his coach to Greenwich, and there to my office, all the way having fine discourse of trees and the nature of vegetables.**

Mr Evelings is Pepys's distinguished friend, John Evelyn. He had a house in Deptford, Sayes Court, with a vast acreage of land attached. Here he had created a wonderful, experimental garden while exploring ideas about botany and horticulture – hence the 'discourse of trees'. So it was that on that day, Pepys gratified his basest instincts and his high-minded intellectual curiosity in the space of one afternoon.

But the affair with Mrs Bagwell was beginning to pall. In November we find Pepys behaving like a stalker, walking in the field till dark before going 'à la maison of my valentine, and there je faisais whatever je voudrais avec her'. It is then almost a year before she is mentioned again. A few days after the Great Fire, (with Elizabeth once more out of sight in Woolwich) he paid her a visit. But his lust, like London, had turned to ashes.

There nudo in lecto con ella did do all that I desired; but though I did intend para aver demorado con ella toda la night, yet when I had done ce que je voudrais, I did hate both ella and la cosa; and taking occasion from the uncertainty of su marido's return esta noche, did me levar; and so away home late.

A different man might have ended it there. But Pepys was still seeing her in February 1667. On the first of the month he spent the afternoon in her bed, 'con much *voluptas*', and was still in the house when her husband came home. He promised Bagwell another promotion – which one might think was the very least he owed him – before going off to meet one of his shopgirl mistresses, a woman curiously named Doll Lane, in Westminster.

The following month Pepys was almost seen in the Bagwells' house by one of his own servants. It was a close call, and it gave Pepys a fright. He seems not have met with Mrs Bagwell again in the course of that year. The final mention of her is in June 1668. In the description of their last encounter, the Spanish/Portuguese pidgin sounds less than usually ridiculous. In a strange way, the passage is tender, almost lyrical.

> And so by water, it being now about 9 a-clock, down to Deptford, where I have not been many a day. And there, it being dark, I did by agreement *andar a la* house de Bagwell. And there, after a little playing and *besando*, we did go up in the dark *a su cama*, and there *fasero la grand casa* upon the bed, and that being *hecho*, did go away to my boat again, and against the tide home.

It is possible that Pepys continued to see Mrs Bagwell after the diary years – we cannot know for sure. We do know, however, that Mr Bagwell's career as a naval carpenter flourished for years to come. In 1677 he was put in charge of the construction of the *Northumberland*, a ship then being built in the dockyards at Bristol. Whether he thought that fair recompense for what he had bartered away, and how far this apparently able craftsman would have gone without his wife's advocacy, we cannot know.

It is also hard to know what to make of Pepys's conduct in this tawdry business. Even as one feels distaste for Pepys actions, one cannot but admire his unvarnished honesty in setting them down. He could, after all, have omitted the affair altogether, or at least painted his own venal motives in a much more flattering light. He does not do so because, he is as scientifically curious about his own psychology as he is about the world at large. He is fascinated by himself, and never consciously betrays that fascination by averting his gaze from the murky tides and currents of his own mind. The result in this instance is a kind of Dorian Gray portrait, an ugly picture of the philandering, unkind aspects of Sam Pepys. It is an image that he contrived to keep hidden away, in the dark attic spaces of the journal, while the God-fearing, upstanding Samuel Pepys went about his respectable and important business on the streets of London.

Mister Pepys *Abroad*

The streets of London were Pepys's natural habitat. Most days he spent a good deal of time 'abroad' – that is, out and about in the busy city. Some of the liveliest passages in the diary are crowd scenes in which we see Pepys in the audience at the theatre; in the congregation at church; watching cats in bell jars at a Royal Society lecture; among the mob at an execution; with friends in a coffee house or an inn; slumming it with the proletariat in Vauxhall Gardens; promenading with the king and his court in Hyde Park. In all these pursuits Pepys remains a consummate observer. He is continually hypnotized by great, gaudy pageant of life in general – and of London life in particular.

The change of regime in 1660 transformed the range of pastimes available to the public. All laws passed during the Commonwealth were annulled, so the prohibition on profane entertainments vanished in an instant. Christmas was reinstated (and the Anglican Church was re-established); new bears were acquired for the bearpit at Clerkenwell; maypoles were erected in outlying villages; and annual fairs were revived with their gingerbread stalls, menageries of tigers and snakes, and enactments of the adventures of Scaramouche, the Italian clown. And most significantly of all, the ban on the theatre was lifted. After a gap of 18 years, it once again became possible to go and see a play in London.

The King's Men and the Duke's Company

King Charles was fond of the theatre, and one of his first acts on being restored to the throne was to grant licences to two theatrical companies, one to be led by the actor Thomas Killigrew, the other by the playwright William Davenant. The companies were known respectively as the King's and the Duke's, and no one else was allowed to stage plays. Killigrew and Davenant were a duopoly in a new and lucrative business: their only rivals were each other.

Killigrew at first had the upper hand. He somehow managed to persuade the king that his company was the legal descendant of the King's Men – the troupe that had performed many of Shakespeare's plays at the Globe, and to which Shakespeare himself may have belonged. This connection, reasoned Killigrew, meant that he should have exclusive access to all the riches of Jacobean and Elizabethan theatre. The king gave him this right, and so Davenant was left with the problem of providing his troupe with a constant stream of new material. Davenant could not even stage his own works, since these were written before the restoration and so deemed to be part of Killigrew's repertory. As a result, Davenant's Duke's Company was the driving force behind the new form of drama that we now term 'Restoration comedy' – the light, bawdy, witty, satirical stories of greed and lust that now seem to sum up the reign of Charles II.

Pepys had not seen a stage play since he was a small boy, and he lost no time in going to see the revived entertainment. On 18 August 1660 he records that, 'Captain Ferrers, my Lord's Cornett, comes to us, who after dinner took me and Creed to the Cockepitt play, the first that I have had time to see since my coming from the sea.' The Cockpit was the name of a makeshift theatre on Drury Lane, not the name of the play, which was *The Loyal Subject*. It was an old work, written in 1618, but its felicitous title made it a good piece with which to mark the royally sponsored rebirth of English theatre. Whether it was a good play is another matter, but Pepys seems to have enjoyed his night out.

One Kinaston, a boy, acted the Dukes sister but made the loveliest lady that ever I saw in my life – only her voice was not very good. After the play done, we three went to drink, and by Captain Ferrers means, Mr Kinaston and another that acted Archas the Generall came to us and drank with us.

From this small beginning grew Pepys's obsession with the theatre. In the middle years of the decade he sometimes went to see a play four or five times a week, and happily watched the same work over and over again. By that time, the theatrical experience had become more fulfilling for both audience and players. Once they had become profitable, the two companies moved from their original impromptu venues into purpose-built theatres. This created all kinds of possibilities for the use of stagecraft: moving scenery helped foster atmosphere, trapdoors and pulleys meant characters could vanish or fly through the air. Some of the profits of the business were invested in improved costumes. Most radically of all, by Charles's own decree, women were allowed to play the female parts. The Elizabethan practice of having young men play the women's roles, the last gasp of which Pepys saw at the Cockpit, very quickly died out.

Pepys highly approved of the new profession of 'actress'. He first saw a woman on stage in February 1661. Later that month he went to see *The Scornful Lady*, a play in which he had previously seen the title role performed by a man. It was 'now done by a woman, which makes the play appear much better than ever it did to me.' By October, Pepys was getting into the spirit of Restoration drama.

I to the Theatre, and there saw Argalus and Parthenia; where a woman acted Parthenia and came afterward on the Stage in man's clothes; and had the best legs that ever I saw; and I was very well pleased with it.

Admiring the actresses became an essential part of an evening at the theatre for Pepys. In fact, sometimes it was the only thing that made the outing worthwhile:

My wife and I and Sir W. Penn to the King's playhouse, where the house extraordinary full; and there was the King and Duke of York to see the new play, *Queen Elizabeths Troubles, and the History of Eighty-Eight*. I confess I have sucked in so much of the sad story of Queen Elizabeth from my cradle, that I was ready to weep for her sometimes. But the play is the most ridiculous that sure ever came upon stage, and endeed is merely a show; only, shows the true garbe of the queens in those days, just as we see Queen Mary and Queen Elizabeth painted – the the play is merely a puppet-play acted by living puppets. Neither the design nor language better; and one stands by and tells us the meaning of things. Only, I was pleased to see Knipp dance among the milkmaids, and to hear her sing a song to Queen Elizabeth – and to see her come out in her night-gowne, with no locks on, but her bare face and hair tied up in a knot behind; which is the comeliest dress that ever I saw her in to her advantage.

The actress Elizabeth Knipp became a particular friend of Pepys. He had one of his fumbling, fondling affairs with her, and was always enthralled by her backstage gossip. It was through her that he managed to get to meet Nell Gwyn for a second time – without his wife, and in the actress's dressing room.

So to the King's House; and there going in, met with Knipp and she took us up into the Tireing-rooms and to the women's Shift, where Nell was dressing herself and was all unready; and is very pretty, prettier then I thought; and so walked all up and down the House above, and then below into the Scene-room, and there sat down and she gave us fruit; and here I read the Qu's [cues] to Knepp while she answered me, through all her part of *Flora's Figarys*, which was acted today. But Lord, to see how they were both painted would make a man mad ... and what base company of men comes among them, and how lewdly they talk – and how poor the men are in clothes, and yet what a show they make on the stage by candle-light, is very observable. But to see how Nell cursed for having so few people in the pit was pretty, the other House carrying away all the people at the new play, and is said nowadays to have generally most company, as being better players. By and by into the pit and there saw the play; which is pretty good, but my belly was full of what I had seen in the House.

The experience of going backstage was always tinged with disappointment for Pepys. With his gimlet eye he could not help but notice the tattiness and tawdriness of it all.

> **After dinner we walked to the King's play-house, all in dirt, they being altering of the Stage to make it wider – but God knows when they will begin to act again. But my business here was to see the inside of the Stage and all the tiring roomes and Machines; and endeed it was a sight worth seeing. But to see their clothes and the various sorts, and what a mixture of things there was, here a wooden leg, there a ruff, here a hobby-house, there a Crowne, would make a man split himself to see with laughing – and perticularly Lacys wardrobe, and Shotrell's. But then again, to think how fine they show on the stage by candle-light, and how poor things are to look now too near-hand, is not pleasant at all.**

The fact is, Pepys did not want to know about the mechanics of the theatre (which makes him a frustrating source for historians of the stage). What he loved about the theatre was the magic, the illusion. He wanted to be carried away by story-telling, the high-flown and uplifting language, the dancing and the music. All of which, one might think, would make him an admirer of Shakespeare's more fanciful plays – but not so. Shakespeare's *Tempest*, which surely contains the most sublime poetry ever written for the stage, drew only a lukewarm response. 'The play no great wit,' wrote Pepys, 'but yet good, above ordinary plays.' The explanation for this half-hearted seal of approval may be that Pepys saw an 'improved' version of the play: it had been rewritten by Davenant to suit the presumed tastes of his audience (and perhaps to get round the embargo on pre-Restoration works). But clumsy rewrites cannot explain Pepys's peculiar antipathy to *A Midsummer Night's Dream*, which he saw in the original version in 1662.

> **To the King's Theatre, where we saw *Midsummers nights dreame*, which I have never seen before, nor shall ever again,**

for it is the most insipid ridiculous play that I ever saw in my life.
I saw, I confess, some good dancing and some handsome women,
which was all my pleasure.

To Church Again

There was another very specific form of theatre that Pepys admired –
and that was the spectacle of divine worship. He enjoyed church music
as much as any other kind of music, and he appreciated a well-delivered
sermon in just the same aesthetic way as he took pleasure in a fine
soliloquy on stage. He would often go to church more than once on a
Sunday to hear the word of God spoken. The words 'to church again'
chime like a bell through the Sabbath-day entries in the diary. Pepys
was an indignant critic of substandard preaching because it was a waste
of his time and attention, and therefore a kind of personal insult.

Pepys did not expect to commune with God when he went to church
(that kind of excessive enthusiasm was for 'phanatiques' such as the
Quakers). But he certainly believed in God, and took it for granted that
Christianity was the one true faith. At the same time, he was not
religiously observant by the standards of the day – he rarely took
communion, for example – and he never allowed moral scruple to keep
him from an agreeable sin. The only sop he offered to his conscience
after some deceit or dalliance was the occasional retrospective 'God
forgive me' in his diary record. But even this was entirely formulaic: he
tacks on a 'God forgive me' when mentioning that he restrung his lute
on the day of rest.

For all that, Pepys was a churchman through and through. His home
church was St Olave's, Hart Street, which stood across the road from
his apartments on Seething Lane. He went there most Sundays, and was
as comfortable in his regular pew as he was in his own study. Church on
Sunday was part of a busy social round. Pepys expected to meet people
he knew, and to talk, as on this hectic Sunday in 1660:

Lord's day. In the morning before church-time, Mr. Hawly,
who hath for this day or two looked something sadly, which

methought did speak something in his breast concerning me, came to me, telling me that he was out 24 pounds, which he could not tell what was become of, and that he doth remember that he had such a sum in a bag the other day, and could not tell what he did with it; at which I was very sorry but could not help him. In the morning to Mr. Guning, where a stranger, an old man, preached a good honest sermon upon "What manner of love is this that we should be called the sons of God." After sermon I could not find my wife, who promised to be at the gate against my coming out, and waited there a great while; then went to my house and finding her gone, I returned and called at the Chequer, thinking to dine at the ordinary with Mr. Chetwind or Mr. Thomas; but they not being there, I went to my father and found her there, and there I dined. To their church in the afternoon, and in Mrs. Turners pew my wife took up a good black hood and kept it. A stranger preached a poor sermon, and so I read over the whole book of the story of Tobit. After sermon, home with Mrs. Turner; stayed with her a little while; then she went into the Court to a christening and we to my father's – where I writ some notes for my Brother John to give to the Mercers tomorrow, it being the day of their Apposition. After supper, home; and before going to bed, I stood writing of this day its passages ... This afternoon at church I saw Dick Cumberland at church newly come out of the country from his living. But did not speak to him.

On other Sundays, it was even possible to talk a little business, as on this day in 1661, when he found himself at St Nicholas's in Deptford along with his office colleague, Commissioner William Pett.

In the morning we all went to church and sat in the pew belonging to us. Where a cold sermon of a young [man] that never hath preached before. Here Commissioner Pett came with his wife and daughters – the eldest, being his wife's daughter, is a very comely black [dark-haired] woman. So to

**the globe to dinner. And then with Commissioner Pett to his
lodgings there (which he hath for the present while he is in
building the King's yacht, which will be a very pretty thing and
much beyond the Duchman's); and from thence with him and
his wife and daughter-in-law by Coach to Greenwich church –
where a good sermon, a fine church, and a great company of
handsome women.**

That last phrase pretty well sums up Pepys's ideal church service.

Pepys often attended churches other than St Olave's in the afternoon,
or even wandered from church to church throughout the morning,
sampling different sermons like a winetaster. Like all critics, he is more
interesting when he is displeased. Sometimes he expresses his lack of
appreciation in the wordless manner of churchgoers down the ages: 'To
church again, my wife and I, where we have a dull sermon of a stranger
which made me sleep'. Other times he is kept wide awake by a sense
of pique at a preacher's substandard technique, such as poor Greek or
faulty rhetoric. He usually sums up a sermon's shortcomings in a few
well-chosen words: 'up and to church, where a lazy sermon'; 'a pitifull
sermon of the young Scott'; 'a dull, drowzy sermon'; 'the most flat dead
sermon, both for matter and manner of delivery, that ever I heard; and
very long beyond his hour, which made it worse'. All these damning
judgments were made in the space of one month in 1663.

Pepys is rarely troubled by the moral message of a preacher; one
suspects that he rarely remembered much about what he heard by the
time he wrote it down (and he often misquotes the Bible text from
which the lesson is taken). In May 1666 he made this rare excursion
into doctrinal matters, but failed to state where he stood on the issue,
and was in any case very soon distracted by more wordly concerns:

**Fell by chance into St Margaret's, where I heard a young man
play the fool upon the doctrine of purgatory. At the church I
spied Betty Howlett, who indeed is mighty pretty, and struck
me mightily. I after church time standing in the churchyard,
she spied me; so I went to her ...**

Pepys was free-thinking about other religious practices. In 1661 he gatecrashed a Catholic Mass.

> I walked in the morning towards Westminster; and seeing many people at Yorke-house I went down and find them at Masse, it being the Spanish Embassadors; and so I got into one of the gallerys and there heard two masses – done, I think, in not so much state as I have seen them heretofore.

The chapels belonging to the embassies of Catholic states were the only places where Mass could legally be celebrated. Attendance by ordinary English citizens was forbidden, so Pepys was technically breaking the law by wandering in to the service. But he does not seem to care, and would have thought such a law foolish. He was not bigoted about other religions, and he was disapproving of people who were virulently or unthinkingly anti-Catholic. One Sunday evening Doctor Hollier, the surgeon who cut him for the stone, came to Pepys's house on a visit and spent the whole time 'proving as a most clear thing that "Rome is antichrist."' Pepys later lay awake in bed laughing at the idea.

Pepys's tolerance even extended to agreeing to be godfather to the son of a Catholic friend. Here is his description of the clandestine ceremony. The priest is in 'gentleman's dress' – that is, ordinary clothes rather than vestments – in order to keep his vocation hidden when out on the streets.

> It was pretty that being a Protestant, a man stood by and was my proxy to answer for me. A priest christened it, and the boys name is Samuel. The ceremonies many, and some foolish. The priest in a gentleman's dress, more then my own; but is a Capuchin, one of the Queen-mother's priests. He did give my proxy and the woman-proxy (my Lady Bills, absent, had a proxy also) good advice to bring up the child, and at the end, that he ought never to marry the child, or the godfather. But which is strange, they say that the mother of the child and the godfather may marry. This is strange. By and by the Lady Bills came in, a well-bred but crooked woman. The poor people of the house had good wine and

a good cake; and she a pretty woman in her lying-in dress. It cost me near 40s the whole christening: to midwife, 20s – nurse, 10s – maid, 2s 6d, and the coach, 5s – I was very well satisfied with what I have done.

Pepys was slightly less kindly disposed towards the Quakers, whose beliefs – as he and many others saw it – tended to be detrimental to good order in society. To him they were extremists, an impression confirmed when he happened upon this act of protest:

To Westminster Hall, the King being come to speak to the House today. One extraordinary thing was this day, a man, a Quaker, came naked through the Hall, only very civilly tied about the privities to avoid scandal, and with a chafing-dish of fire and brimstone burning upon his head did pass through the Hall crying 'Repent! Repent!'

The man in question was a certain Solomon Eccles, and he had a history of this kind of exhibitionism. Most Quakers were quieter souls, but they did have a knack of antagonizing people. This was due in part to their refusal to doff their hats to anyone, no matter what their rank. They also insisted on addressing everybody by the familiar 'thou' form of the personal pronoun, rather than the respectful 'you'. These peculiarities were an expression of the Quaker belief that every person, whatever their status, is of equal worth before God – but to their social superiors it looked like mere impertinence. The Quakers upset the Church authorities by refusing to accept that the Church had any authority. They eschewed all hierarchies, and said that there was no need for a priestly class, for 'steeple houses' or for any of the accepted paraphernalia of worship such as robes and crosses. In their view, every man and woman had direct access to God, and need only heed the 'inner light' that would lead towards spiritual perfection. They were as clean-living as any Puritan, but they were entirely undogmatic about their beliefs. Their worship consisted – as it still does – in sitting in silence until someone was moved by the spirit to speak.

The Quakers were, in a word, gentle and completely harmless – and they were persecuted from every side. Their meek and highly visible demeanour made them easy prey for religious bigots and street thugs. On a judicial level, they fell foul of a law of 1662 requiring the swearing of an oath of allegiance to the king: this was something they refused to do. They also defied the so-called Conventicle Act of 1664, which forbade religious assemblies of more than five people outside the auspices of the Church of England. The Act was intended to strengthen the re-established Anglican rite, but at the same time it deliberately targeted Quakers. They were arrested dozens at a time for the crime of holding prayer meetings. Pepys saw a group carted off soon after the Conventicle Act came into force, and was moved to pity:

> **While we were talking came by several poor creatures, carried by Constables for being at conventicle. They go like lambs without any resistance. I would to God they would either conform, or be more wise, or not be ketched [caught].**

One Quaker in constant trouble with the authorities was a young man named William Penn. He was known to Pepys because he was the son of Pepys distinguished colleague and next-door neighbour, the naval commissioner Admiral Sir William Penn. Pepys first met the younger William Penn in 1661. He visited his father in Pepys's house shortly after being expelled from Oxford University for protesting against the reintroduction of surplices. He went to the continent soon after, which kept him out of trouble for a couple of years, but was back in England by 1664. Pepys seems to have thought him a rather bumptious youth:

> **Landing at Greenwich I saw Mr Pen walking my way; so we walked together and for discourse I put him into talk of France, which he took delight to tell me of his observations, some good impertinent, and all ill-told.**

Pepys seems to have been unaware of Penn's religious convictions, or thought that he had grown out of them in France, because he was annoyed when the younger man would not take on a wager when they had a light-hearted disagreement on some point of French vocabulary. But young William had not changed his unconventional outlook, and this was a constant source of worry to his highly conservative father. In fact, William's views grew increasingly radical, and he became a semi-professional protester, constantly being arrested for breaching the new anti-Quaker laws. In 1667 he spent some time in prison, where he wrote a polemical book called *Truth Exalted*. 'After supper to read a ridiculous nonsensical book set out by Will Pen for the Quakers,' wrote Pepys. 'But so full of nothing but nonsense that I was ashamed to read in it.' Penn was released from Newgate, but the following year was sent to the Tower for writing an ostensibly blasphemous pamphlet setting out the Unitarian position on the doctrine of the Trinity. This effort got him a better review from Pepys.

> **Pelling hath got me W. Pen's book against the Trinity; I got my wife to read it to me, and find it so well writ as I think it too good for him ever to have writ it – and it is a serious sort of book, and not fit for everybody to read.**

The elder William Penn died while his son was still in prison. By the time the younger William was released he was a very rich man, having inherited his father's great wealth and large estates in Ireland. He also inherited a promissory note from King Charles, who had borrowed heavily from Sir William. The king repaid the debt by signing over to William a huge tract of land in the American colonies. He gave the troublesome Quaker a slice of territory 170 miles wide and stretching 300 miles from the eastern seaboard to Lake Erie. It was one of the largest land grants to an individual in history, and it transformed the fortunes of the Quakers. William Penn's inheritance provided them with a place where they could go to live as they chose, without fear of persecution. William wanted to call the land 'Sylvania' – 'the woods' in Greek. But the king insisted on a name that honoured William's father, the late Admiral, and decreed that the new colony would be called not just 'The Woods' but 'Penn's Woods' – Pennsylvania. William Penn the

Younger never settled there, but his lands became a haven for Quakers from all over Europe. And not only for Quakers. Penn's 'frame of government' for the province enshrined the principle of universal tolerance, and this made Pennsylvania a magnet for many other persecuted religious groups: French Huguenots, Swiss Amish, German Lutherans and Mennonites – so long as they believed in God, they were made welcome.

The Resettlement of the Jews

Even stranger than the Quakers, to English eyes at least, was the tiny community of London Jews. Officially there had been no Jews in England since their expulsion by Edward I in 1290. In practice, some Jews continued to live in England throughout the medieval period – though they had to convert to Christianity, or at least appear to have done so. There is evidence that many court musicians and travelling minstrels of the Middle Ages were crypto-Jews, for example. But for the mass of English citizenry, Jews were just characters from the Bible, literary or legendary figures, as fabulous as angels or demons, and as far removed from real life as the Moabites or the Babylonians.

It was Elizabethan scholarship that led to a revived interest in the Jews, or – in the first instance at least – in the ancient language of the Jews. Since the Old Testament was written in Hebrew (reasoned Protestant thinkers) it followed that God, when he declared 'Let there be light' and brought the world into being, must have been speaking in that language. Hebrew was therefore the language of God, and also the first human tongue. When Adam gave names to all the animals, the words he chose must also have been Hebrew ones. So by studying the original language of the Old Testament, one was breaking down barriers between God and Man, which was one of the central aims of Protestantism. (This line of thinking eventually gave rise to that magnificent feat of scholarship and literature, the King James Version of the Bible.)

Serious English students of Hebrew language naturally consulted Jewish scholars in Holland and elsewhere on the Continent. The rabbis of Amsterdam, Hamburg and Vilna were, after all, the undisputed experts in the language. The scientist Robert Boyle, a man as committed to the Christian religion as he was to the study of chemistry, had travelled in Europe during the Civil War and made a point of meeting with an Amsterdam rabbi named Menasseh Ben Israel. Ten years later this same rabbi came to England to petition Cromwell for the readmission of the Jews to England. Many of the Jews in Amsterdam were Portuguese merchants and bankers who had fled to Holland to escape the clutches of the Inquisition. They saw England as a safer haven than continental Europe. Cromwell, for his part, was ruler of an all but bankrupt nation, and so was keen to win the backing of Jewish finance. He was also, as a Puritan, kindly disposed towards the children of Abraham. They were, after all, the people who had given rise to such heroes as Samson, King David and Solomon the Wise. After some deliberation he gave his personal assent to the resettlement of the Jews in England.

Not everybody was pleased with Cromwell's decision. A lawyer named William Prynne published a tract arguing against readmission, claiming that, since the Jews had been expelled by royal decree, they could not be allowed back without an act of parliament. He added that most right-thinking English people had been in favour of expulsion at the time and still were; and that Jews were a menace to England's religious, commercial and political interests. His tract was entitled, in the verbose manner of the time,

A short demurrer to the Jewes long discontinued barred remitter into England. Comprising an exact chronological relation of their first admission into, their ill deportment, misdemeanors, condition, sufferings, oppressions, slaughters, plunders, by popular insurrections, and regal exactions in; and their total, final banishment by judgment and edict of Parliament, out of England, never to return again: collected out of the best historians and records. With a brief collection of such English laws, Scriptures, reasons as seem strongly to plead, and conclude against their readmission into England, especially at this season, and against

the general calling of the Jewish nation. With an answer to the
chief allegations for their introduction.

Prynne's anti-Semitic diatribe was answered by a Semitophile named
Thomas Collier. His overwrought writing was almost as unhinged as
Prynne's:

> Oh! let us respect them! Let us wait for that glorious day when
> they will be made masters of nations! Oh! the time is nigh when
> men will think themselves happy if they can just but touch the
> skirt of a Jew! Our salvation comes from them! Jesus was one of
> them! We were begotten with their promises and privileges! The
> natural branches were cut off so that we might be grafted on! O!
> we should not be high-minded, but fear them! For the sake of
> God, let us not be unmerciful to them! No, it would be enough
> if we had all the riches they have!

Only small numbers of Jews came to London during the Interregnum.
There may have been no more than a dozen Jewish families in London
at the time of the restoration. Those pioneers established a synagogue
on Creechurch Lane, near Aldgate, and they were granted a cemetery
outside the City walls at Stepney. In 1660, the Jewish community was
concerned that, in the rush to overturn all the laws and practices of the
Protectorate, the new king might reverse Cromwell's welcome to them.
In the event it turned out to be a blessing that the resettlement was not
formalized in law (as Menasseh Ben Israel had wanted) because it
meant that there was no official Cromwellian policy to be reversed.
The Jews remained in London, their numbers began to grow, and the
money men among them made their services available to the new rulers
of England.

The synagogue on Creechurch Lane took root and flourished. In 1662
it was visited by a John Greenhalgh, an inquisitive schoolteacher who,
as a kind of hobby, made it his business to observe diverse acts of
worship. He had attended the divine services of Roman Catholics,
Anabaptists, Quakers and Fifth Monarchists, and he was keen to

broaden his experience by seeing how the Jews prayed to their God. His guide, a rabbi from Cracow, is a slightly mysterious figure, since in those early years almost all of London's Jews hailed from Portugal.

When any thing ever occurred in my reading any where concerning the manner of the Jews divine worship (though since the destruction of their City and Temple) I have always thought it worth the seeing of a Christian; at least for once where it could be obtained.

I considered and concluded with myself that there must in reason need be some number of Jews in this City, though only merchants, and that consequently they must have some place of meeting together for their divine worship. Whereupon, as occasion offered me to converse with any that were likely to inform me, I inquired hereof, but could not of a long time hear or learn whether or where any such thing was. But lately having a desire to spend some of my time here in learning the Hebrew tongue, and inquiring of some one that professed to teach it, I lighted upon a learned Jew with a mighty bush beard, a great Rabbi as I found him afterward to be, with whom after once or twice being together, I fell into conference and acquaintance; for he could speak Latin and some little broken English, having as he told me been two years in London. He said he was an Hebrew of the Hebrews of the Tribe of Levi, and his name (I had liked to have said his Christian name) Samuel Levi.

He told me his own mother is yet living, and dwelleth at this present in the City of Jerusalem, from whence he had received ten several Letters within these two years. For it is a custom amongst them, that those who are of able estate, though born and have lived in other countries, yet when they grow old they transport themselves thither to end their days, and lay their bones there in Holy place as he called it. He said he was brought up, and was a student eleven years, in the Jews College in Cracovia the chief City of Poland, where the Jews have an University, and that he had newly written over the Five Books

of Moses with his own hand in Hebrew, without points, in rolls
of parchment, for the use of a Synagogue: and that himself had
formerly been Priest to a Synagogue of his own nation in Poland.
A very modest man, and once with much ado I got him to accept
of an invitation to take part of a dinner with me: at which time
he told me that he had special relation as Scribe and Rabbi to a
private Synagogue of his nation in London, and that if I had a
desire to see their manner of worship, though they did scarce
admit of any, their Synagogue being strictly kept with three doors
one beyond another, yet he would give me such a ticket.

Greenhalgh was delighted by the opportunity to get past the triple
doors of the synagogue. 'I inwardly hugged the good hap,' he said,
meaning that he grabbed the chance. The following Saturday – the
Jewish Sabbath – he got up early and made his way to Creechurch
Lane, where he presented the *laissez-passer* given to him by the Polish
rabbi. Once past the three gates he conducted himself like an explorer-
anthropologist in the midst of some undiscovered tribe, making notes
of everything he saw without trying to explain or understand it.

I was at first a little abashed to venture alone amongst all them
Jews; but my innate curiosity to see things strange spurring me
on, made me confident even to impudence. I rubbed my forehead,
opened the innermost door, and taking off my hat (as instructed)
I went in and sate me down amongst them; but Lord what a
strange, uncouth, foreign, and to me barbarous sight was there.
I saw no living soul, but all covered, hooded, guized, veiled Jews,
and my own plain bare self amongst them. The sight would have
frightened a novice, and made him to have run out again.
   Every man had a large white vest, covering, or veil cast over the
high crown of his hat, which from thence hung down on all sides,
covering the whole hat, the shoulders, arms, sides, and back to
the girdle place, nothing to be seen but a little of the face; this,
my Rabbi told me, was their ancient garb, used in divine worship
in their Synagogues in Jerusalem and in all the Holy Land before

the destruction of their City: and though to me at first, it made altogether a strange and barbarous show, yet me thought it had in its kind, I know not how, a face and aspect of venerable antiquity. Their veils were all pure white, made of taffeta or silk, though some few were of a stuff coarser than silk; the veil at each of its four corners had a broad badge; some had red badges, some green, some blue, some wrought with gold or silver, which my Rabbi told me were to distinguish the tribes of which each was common.

Their Synagogue is like a Chapel, high built; for after the first door they go up stairs into it, and the floor is boarded; the seats are not as ours, but two long running seats on either side, as in a school: at the west end of it there is a seat as high as a pulpit, but made deskwise, wherein the two members of the Synagogue did sit veiled, as were all both priest and people. The chief Ruler was a very rich merchant, a big, black, fierce, and stern man to whom I perceive they stand in as reverential and awe as boys to a master; for when any left singing upon their books and talked, or that some were out of tune, he did call aloud with a barbarous thundering voice, and knocked upon the high desk with his fist, that all sounded again. Straight before them, at some distance but on a seat much lower, sate the Priest. Two yards before him, on midst of the floor, stood that whereon the Service and Law were read, being like to an high short table, with steps to it on one side as an altar, covered with a green carpet, and upon that another shorter one of blue silk; two brass candlesticks standing at either end of it; before that on the floor were three low seats whereon some boys sat their sons, richly veiled, as gentle comely youths as one should see; who had each his Service Book in hand, in Hebrew without points, and were are ready and nimble in it, and all their postures as the men.

There was brought in a pretty Boy at four years old, a child of some chief Jew, in rich coats, with black feathers in his hat, the priest himself arose and put a veil over the child's hat of pure white silk, fastening it under the hat band that he should not shake it off, and set him upon a seat among the boys; but he soon leaped off, and ran with his veil dangling up and down; once he came and looked at me, wondering perhaps that I had no veil; at length he got the inner door open and went to his mother; for they do not suffer the women to come into the same room or into the sight of the men: but on the one side of the Synagogue there is a low, long and narrow latticed window, through which the women sitting in the next room, do hear; as the boy opened it, I saw some of their wives in their rich silks bedaubed with broad gold lace, with muffs in one hand and books in the other.

Greenhalgh sat quietly and listened to the reading of the Psalms, which 'they sung much like as we do sing ballads'. He watched the ceremony in which the Torah scrolls are taken from the ark and carried shoulder-high around the synagogue. 'The people bowed towards it, and such as could reach took up the fringe of its costly covering in their hands and kissed it.' During the reading of the Law he was close enough to see that the words on the scroll – perhaps the ones painstakingly inscribed by his Polish acquaintance – were 'pure black, and all without points'. He noted that Jews, like Christians, conclude their prayers with a communal 'Amen'.

Then a comely youth standing in the midst of the Synagogue, and looking towards the Law, sung alone a long Anthem, and after this there was long Supplication, which was the most solemn part of all their service; which they all spake together standing (for they never kneel), with their faces East, often bowing down altogether; it being partly a complaint of the long desolation of their City and Temple, partly a prayer for the coming of Messiah and their Restoration (thank my Rabbi for the interpretation). 'Sion is become a ploughed field, and Jerusalem made an heap of stones, thy servants think upon her stones and it grieveth them to see her in the dust; our ancient and our beautiful House, where our fathers served thee, lieth waste; then gather us O Lord from amongst the Heathen; remember Abraham, Isaac, and

Jacob; remember thy promises made unto our fathers, in our
time, in our time, O Lord', &c.

I confess that looking earnestly upon them in this, and thoughts
coming into my mind of the wonders which God wrought for
their fathers in Egypt, and who heard the Voice of God speak to
them out of the midst of the fire on Sinai, and seed of Abraham
the friend of God, I was strangely, uncouthly, unaccustomedly
moved, and deeply affected; tears stood in my eyes the while, to
see those banished Sons of Israel standing in their ancient garb
but in a strange land, solemnly and carefully looking East toward
their own Country, confessing their sins and the sins of their
forefathers, humbling themselves and bowing down together (as
often they did in their Supplication) before the God of their
Fathers, who doubtless will hear them or their posterity better
than they desire, will open their eyes and let them see that the
true Messiah came long since, even he whom their fathers
pierced, and they shall mourn over him and be brought unto him,
and to their own land. After this, for a conclusion of all, the
Priest read certain select promises of their restoration, at which
they showed great rejoicing, by strutting up, so that some of their
veils flew about like morris dancers, only they wanted bells. This
forenoon service continued about three hours, from nine to
twelve, which being ended, they all put off their veils, and each
man wrapping his veil up, went and put it and his Hebrew
Service Book into his box, and locking it departed.

When I was in the Synagogue I counted about or above a
hundred right Jews, one proselite amongst them, they were all
gentlemen (merchants) I saw not one mechanic person of them;
most of them rich apparel, divers with jewels glittering (for they
are the richest jewellers of any). They are all generally black so
as they may be distinguished from Spaniards or native Greeks,
for the Jews hair hath a deeper tincture of a more perfect raven
black, they have a quick piercing eye, and look as if of strong
intellectuals; several of them are comely, gallant, proper
gentlemen.

Pepys visited the same synagogue roughly 18 months later, on 14 October 1663. That day happened to have been the feast of the Rejoicing of the Law, when a kind of low-key carnival mood prevailed. Pepys found the light-hearted atmosphere rather unseemly in a place of worship, and that made it easy for him to dismiss the Jews and their religion out of hand.

> **After dinner my wife and I, by Mr. Rawlinsons conduct, to the Jewish Synagogue – where the men and boys in their Vayles, and the women behind a lettice out of sight; and some things stand up, which I believe is their Law, in a press, to which all coming in do bow; and at the putting on their veils do say something, to which others that hear him do cry Amen, and the party doth kiss his veil. Their service all in a singing way, and in Hebrew. And anon their Laws, that they take out of the press, is carried by several men, four or five, several burthens in all, and they do relieve one another, or whether it is that everyone desires to have the carrying of it, I cannot tell. Thus they carried [it] round, round about the room while such a service is singing. And in the end they had a prayer for the King, which they pronounced his name in Portugall; but the prayer, like the rest, in Hebrew. But Lord, to see the disorder, laughing, sporting, and no attention, but confusion in all their service, more like Brutes then people knowing the true God, would make a man forswear ever seeing them more; and endeed, I never did see so much, or could have imagined there had been any religion in the whole world so absurdly performed as this.**

Rude and Nasty Pleasures

It was a love of the exotic and colourful that brought Pepys to the synagogue, and the same impulse drew him to watch working-class amusements. 'Three entertainments are put on in London for the lowest classes: sword-fighting, bull- and bear-baiting and cockfights,' wrote the Italian traveller Lorenzo Magalotti. 'I have never been to the first, which I imagine to be the most curious.' Pepys did see one in 1667, the year before Magalotti came to Britain.

> And then abroad by coach and stopped at the Bear-garden stairs, there to see a Prize fought; but the house so full, there was no getting in there; so forced to [go] through an alehouse into the pit where the bears are baited, and upon a stool did see them fight, which they did very furiously, a butcher and a waterman. The former had the better all along, till by and by the latter dropped his sword out of his hand, and the butcher, whether not seeing his sword dropped or I know not, but did give him a cut over the wrist, so as he was disabled to fight any longer. But Lord, to see how in a minute the whole stage was full of watermen to revenge the foul play, and the butchers to defend their fellow, though most blamed him; and there they all fell to it, to knocking down and cutting many of the each side. It was pleasant to see, but that I stood in the pit and feared that in the tumult I might get some hurt. At last the rabble broke up.

For once, Pepys fails to give us a clear idea of the nature of the event. But this description of a fight between two professionals named Millar and Buck, written some years after Pepys's account, vividly evokes what went on in the ring.

> Millar is a man of 6ft 8in, of a kind but bold aspect, well-fashioned, and ready of his limbs. [He came into the ring] preceded by two disabled drummers, to show, I suppose, that the prospect of maimed bodies did not in the least deter him. There ascended with the daring Millar a gentleman with a dogged air, as [if] unsatisfied that he was not a principal. This son of anger lowered at the whole assembly.

The two swordsmen stripped to the waist and shook hands. Each of them wore a ribbon on his sword arm, a throwback to 'the custom of wearing a mistress's favour on such occasions of old'. Then the duel began.

> Millar's heat laid him open to the rebuke of the calm Buck by a large cut to the forehead. Much effusion of blood covered his eyes in a moment, and the huzzas of the crowd undoubtedly quickened his anguish ... The next was a warm, eager onset, which ended in a decisive stroke on the left leg of Millar ... [The wound] was exposed to the view of all who could delight in it.

Gory as these encounters were, they were no less a piece of theatre than Pepys's excursions to see Nell Gwyn at Drury Lane. The fighters knew how to inflict wounds that would bleed spectacularly without causing serious damage. The same writer who watched the fight between Millar and Buck once heard two swordsmen discussing their fight beforehand in a tavern. 'Will you give cuts or receive?' asked one; 'Receive, provided that you cut no more and no deeper than we agree,' was the reply. Prize fights with swords continued well into the Hanoverian era, but in the best part of a hundred years only one combatant is known to have died as a result of taking part – and that death was due to blood-poisoning.

The rate of attrition in the equally popular sports of bear-baiting and cock-fighting was rather higher. Pepys thought a bear-fight a tame enough occasion to take his wife along to.

> After dinner with my wife and Mercer to the Beare-garden, where I have not been I think of many years, and saw some good sport of the bull's tossing of the dogs – one into the very boxes. But it is a very rude and nasty pleasure.

Magalotti, having missed out on the sword-fighting, made sure he got to see the battles of the animals. Here is his graphic summary.

> The bear is tied in the centre of this theatre on a cord long enough to let him move in a circle of perhaps seven or eight paces. Then they release some mastiff dogs, which go to attack it from the front; those who do otherwise, attacking its ears from the side, are considered no good.

Now the betting proceeds. The same is done with bulls, whose
horns and testicles are appropriately protected, the latter so that
they may not be damaged, the former so that the dogs will not be
gored when they are thrown into the air. It is indeed extremely
pleasant to see them fly high up and then fall to the ground with
a terrible crash, and more pleasant still to see their masters
running to them; these are butchers and similar kinds of people
with whom the bottom of the theatre is full. To save their dogs
from their fall they run stooping to receive them on their
shoulders in the place where they are going to fall, and it often
happens that the blow is so terrible that it knocks them heavily
to the ground, and if several are knocked down at once near the
same spot they make a very fine and ridiculous group. When the
infuriated bull charges them, their flight, their shrieks, and their
fear are wonderful to see.

The place for the cock-fight is a small theatre in which one sits
in a circle on step-seats covered with matting. The bottom of this
is a round table, of about six ells [22ft] in diameter and about two
ells [7ft] high. It too is covered with matting, all stained with the
blood of the cocks. On the day of the fight, which is indicated by
printed cards posted at the street corners and distributed
throughout the city, when many people begin to arrive, two cocks
come, carried in two sacks by two of those people who raise and
keep them. One of them goes to one side and the other to the
other side, and when they have taken out their birds, they hold
them in their hands until the first bets are made, which everyone
does according to no rules, one may say, other than their own
inclination, which makes them prefer one bird to another.

The cocks have their wings blunted, their crests cropped and
their backs plucked; they are not of a large size, but strong and
excessively courageous. Halfway down the leg they are armed with
a very sharp steel spur with which, jumping into the air and
thrashing about, attacked to each other by their beaks, they
wound each other. Parted, they watch for a little while and then
crouching, return to the attack, with their necks low and stretched

forward and the neck feathers standing up around their heads; thus, gradually advancing, they spring up in a flash and, driven by their wings, meet in mid-air and wound each other with their beaks, with a fury that at first gives some idea of a considerable battle. But it is true that as they tire little by little, the end becomes boring, coming down to one having to kill the other by pecking its head and eyes, which sometimes goes on for more than a good quarter of an hour and often for nearly half an hour. Often when one appears vanquished and near death, it recovers such wonderful vigour that it jumps on the stronger one and kills it. When this happens and the defeated cock is seen to regain its courage, then the largest bets take place, one to ten, twenty, a hundred. At times it happens that both remain on the field, and while they are dying, when one falls dead the other drags himself as well as he can on to the body of his enemy and with the little breath remaining to him flaps his wings and crows his victory, after which he himself also abandons himself to death.

Pepys saw a cock-fight in 1663, and like Magalotti was surprised by the apparently courageous behaviour of the birds. But being Pepys, he was just as interested in the conduct of the audience:

Being directed by sight of bills upon the walls, did go to Shooe lane to see a Cocke-fighting at a new pit there – a sport I was never at in my life. But Lord, to see the strange variety of people, from Parliament-man (by name Wildes, that was Deputy-governor of the Tower when Robinson was Lord Mayor) to the poorest prentices, bakers, brewers, butchers, draymen, and what not; and all this fellows one with another in swearing, cursing, and betting. I soon had enough of it; and yet I would not but have seen it once, it being strange to observe the nature of those poor creatures, how they will fight till they drop down dead upon the table and strike after they are ready to give up the ghost – not offering to run away when they are wearing or wounded past doing further. Whereas, where a Dunghill brood comes, he will, after a sharp stroke that pricks him, run off the stage, and then they wring off his neck without more ado. Whereas the other they preserve, though their eyes be both out, for breed only of a true cock of the game.

Sometimes, a cock that hath had ten to one against him will by chance give an unlucky blow will strike the other stark-dead in a moment, that he never stirs more. But the common rule is, that though a cock neither run nor dies, yet if any man will bet 10 pounds to a Crowne and nobody take the bett, the game is given over and not sooner. One thing more it is strange to see, how people of this poor rank, that look as if they had not bread to put in their mouths, shall bet 3 or 4l at one bet and lose it, and yet bet as much the next battell, as they call every make of two cocks – so that one of them will lose 10 or 20 pounds at a meeting.

Taverns and Coffee Houses

Cock-fights were one place where the different social classes might be seen to rub shoulders. The tavern was another. Magalotti has this to say about the public drinking habits of the English:

The places called taverns are for the most part very splendid and all superbly furnished, so that persons of high rank, women as well as men, have not the least hesitation in going to them. There are also a large number of innkeepers, who in France would be called *traiteurs*, that is to say people who provide lunches and dinners. Some are English and some French, and the first gentlemen of the court go to them in the morning with the same frequency as the first gentlemen in Florence go to the inn in the evening to escape constraint and enjoy liberty. The difference between the taverns and the inns is that people usually go to the first to drink and to the second to eat. Not that one does not sometimes eat at the former and drink at the latter, but this is unusual and takes them out of their elements. The truth is that both are very expensive.

There are an infinity of beer-shops where they sell many kinds of indigenous drinks, of which I have counted as many as thirty-two sorts. These places are not very expensive and so they are always full of the rabble downstairs, and upstairs of every sort and condition of persons from artisans to gentlemen. They differ from taverns in this way, that in those are drunk Spanish wine, which is here called sack, French wine, Malaga, Bordeaux, muscat, and other costly and foreign wines, whereas in these beer-shops they drink only ale, cock-ale, buttered ale, lamb-ale.

There are also common and much cheaper inns that serve for the lackeys and other poor and lower-class people. But there they eat roughly and do not drink wine. For twelve pence they will get three helpings, which all consist of beef, veal, mutton, or lamb, according to the season.

Pepys spent many happy hours in the taverns and alehouses of London. Taverns often occupied the upper part of a house, and some were equipped with 'ordinaries', restaurants where a meal could be had for two or three shillings. Wine was the main drink served; white Spanish sack (from *secco*, meaning 'dry') or red claret from France. It was decanted from the cask brought to the table in a jug or wide-lipped bottle. Most taverns consisted of a number of rooms of various sizes: Pepys seems never to have had any trouble finding a private corner for his 'dalliances'.

There were more than 1,500 taverns and alehouses in the City of London alone, and Pepys was familiar with a great many of them. Among his favourite haunts were the The Mitre on Cheapside, The Swan in New Palace Yard, The Pope's Head on Lombard Street, and the Halfway House in Rotherhithe. He was also a regular at The Dolphin in Tower Street, which was close to his office and so an obvious place to go and wind down with colleagues after work. On this day in 1661 the company played a game that appears to be akin to 'Truth or Dare'.

And I to the tavern, where Sir Wm. Pen and the Comptroller and several others were, men and women; and we had a very great and merry dinner. And after dinner the Comptroller begun some sports; among others, the Nameing of people round, and afterward demanding Questions of them that they are forced to answer their names to; which doth make very good sport.

Pepys quite often mixed a little business with his drinking pleasure, as on this visit to The Golden Hoop on Fish Street Hill.

Went to the Hoope taverne, and (by a former agreement) sent for Mr. Chaplin, who with Nicholas Osborne and one Daniel came to us and we drank off two or three quarts of wine, which was very good (the drawing of our wine causing a great quarrel in the house between the two drawers which should draw us the best, which caused a great deal of noise and falling out till the maister parted them, and came up to us and did give us a large account of the liberty that he gives his servants, all alike, to draw what wine they will to please his customers); and we did eat above 200 wallnutts. About 10 a-clock we broake up. And so home; in my way I called in with them at Mr. Chaplins, where Nich Osborne did give me a barrel of samphire ...

Beer was the universal thirst-quencher. Untreated well-water or conduit-water was (rightly) considered dangerous, and so everybody – even the most abstemious Puritan – drank beer every day. Children enjoyed a weak brew known as 'small beer'. But in the middle of the 17th century some novel non-alcoholic drinks began to make their presence felt. One of these was tea, which Dutch importers first brought to England from China in the late 1650s. Pepys first tried it at the office in 1660 – 'did send for a Cupp of Tee, a China drink of which I never had drank before' – but it seems not to have made much impression on him. It was, in any case, fabulously expensive at 50 shillings for a pound. He preferred a more affordable new drink – chocolate – which arrived in England from Spanish America a year or two before tea came from China. An advertisement dating from 1657 proclaims that:

In Bishopsgate Street in Queen's Head Alley, at a Frenchman's house, is an excellent West India drink called chocolate, to be sold, where you may have it ready at any time, and also unmade at reasonable rates.

Pepys occasionally took 'a morning draft in chocolate', and solid cakes of chocolate figure among the many comestible bribes that he received in the course of his naval duties.

Neither tea nor chocolate really caught on during the Restoration period. Chocolate remained a foreign delicacy, and tea began to be drunk widely in England only after the price had come down to levels that the middle-classes could afford, and that did not happen until the next century. But another innovative drink caught the public imagination in the 1660s and transformed the social habits of the middle-classes – coffee.

Coffee drinking came to London in 1652. The man who introduced it was a Mr Edwards, a merchant who traded with Turkey and had acquired the habit of taking coffee in the mornings. His house was on St Michael's Alley, near Cornhill, in the heart of the financial district. Word of Mr Edward's interesting tipple got around, and his house was soon besieged each day by people who worked nearby and wanted to taste this novel thing. It occurred to Edwards that he could charge for the privilege, and he cleverly delegated his Turkish servant, Pasqua Rose, to front the business. He published a flyer to advertise the new venture. It set for the benefits of 'the Coffee Drink First publiquely made and sold in England by Pasqua Rose', among which were:

It will prevent drowsiness, and make one fit for business, if one have occasion to watch; and therefore you are not to drink it after supper, unless you intend to be watchful, or it will hinder sleep for three or four hours.

The coffee house was such a hit that other entrepreneurs immediately got in on the business; within a few years there were more than 80 separate coffee houses in the area around Cornhill. The Puritan government approved of coffee houses because they did not serve alcohol, and therefore did not lead to debauchery. But for the bankers and dealers who worked at the Exchange the coffee houses were an information nexus, a place to trade news and make deals. So it was that coffee houses, from the very start, were associated with republican ideas on the one hand and wheeler-dealing on the other. Lloyds, the insurance market, began life as a coffee house near the Tower; the gentleman's club White's is also the descendant of a coffee house.

The character of an individual coffee house depended on its location. The ones around St Paul's were known to be centres of theological debate; the ones in Westminster were rife with political gossip.

In an ale-house you must gorge yourself with pot after pot, sit dully alone, or be drawn in to club for others' reckonings, wrote one supporter of the institution. But here, for a penny or two, you may spend two or three hours, have the shelter of a house, the warmth of a fire, the diversion of company; and conveniency, if you please, of taking a pipe of tobacco; and all this without any grumbling or repining. [A coffee house is] the sanctuary of health, the nursery of temperance, the delight of frugality, an academy of civility, and the free-school of ingenuity.

This may have been too rosy a picture. Ned Ward, writing in the 1690s, provides a more truthful sketch of the interior of a coffee house:

There was a rabble going hither and thither, reminding me of a swarm of rats in a ruinous cheese-store. Some came, others went; some were scribbling, others were talking; some were drinking [coffee], some smoking, and some arguing; the whole place stank of tobacco like the cabin of a barge. On the corner of a long table, close by the armchair, was lying a Bible. Beside it were earthenware pitchers, long clay pipes, a little fire on the hearth, and over it the high coffee pot. Beneath a small bookshelf, on which were bottles, cups, and an advertisement for a beautifier to improve the complexion, was hanging a parliamentary ordinance against drinking and the use of bad language. The walls were decorated with gilt frames, much as a smithy is decorated with horseshoes. In the frames were rarities; phials of a yellowish elixir, favourite pills and hair tonics, packets of snuff, tooth powder made from coffee grounds, caramels and cough lozenges.

In the 1660s, coffee houses were viewed with suspicion by monarchists who remembered how beloved they were of the old regime.

A coffee-house is a lay-conventicle, good-fellowship turned puritan, ill-husbandry in masquerade; whither people come, after toping all day, to purchase, at the expense of their last penny, the repute of sober companions: a rota-room, that, like Noah's ark, receives animals of every sort, from the precise diminutive band, to the hectoring cravat and cuffs in folio; a nursery for training up the smaller fry of virtuosi in confident tattling, or a cabal of kittling critics that have only learned to spit and mew; a mint of intelligence, that, to make each man his penny-worth, draws out into petty parcels what the merchant receives in bullion. He, that comes often, saves two-pence a week in Gazettes, and has his news and his coffee for the same charge, as at a three-penny ordinary they give in broth to your chop of mutton; it is an exchange where haberdashers of political smallwares meet, and mutually abuse each other, and the public, with bottomless stories, and headless notions; the rendezvous of idle pamphlets, and persons more idly employed to read them; a high court of justice, where every little fellow in a camlet cloke takes upon him to transpose affairs both in church and state, to shew reasons against acts of parliament, and condemn the decrees of general councils.

The king himself agreed, and in the 1670s made a foolish attempt to have the coffee houses closed down as 'seminaries of sedition'. But by then it was too late: as a branch of industry and as a social convention they were already too well rooted to be abolished by a stroke of the royal pen.

From the start the coffee houses were living newspapers: people went to them to read the latest pamphlets and to talk to the people in the know. Pepys, as a high official of the Navy, was a provider of news as well as a consumer. In December 1664 he had this snippet to share:

So to the Coffee-house, where great talk of the Comett seen in several places and among our men at sea – and by my Lord Sandwich, to whom I intend to write about it tonight.

The comet remained a topic of conversation for the rest of the month. Pepys heard that the king and queen had sat up to see it. He tried in vain to view it himself, having been told that it was a spectacular thing with a great tail of fire. Lord Sandwich saw it in Portsmouth and wrote to Pepys that 'it is the most extraordinary thing he ever saw.' When Pepys eventually did see it on Christmas Eve, he was disappointed.

This evening, I being informed, did look and saw the Comett, which is now, whether worn away or no I know not, but appears not with a tail; but only is larger and duller than any other star, and is come to rise betimes and to make a great arch, and is gone quite to a new place in the heavens than it was before – but I hope, in a clearer night something more will be seen.

There were plenty of theories as to what the comet meant. Some people remarked darkly that it was a omen: the year 1666 was not far off, and 666 was, after all, the number of the devil. The opinions of astrologers circulated on flysheets that could be bought for a penny inside a coffee house. They inclined to the view that the comet did indeed portend a calamity – not for 1666, but for the coming year of 1665. And they said so in terms intended to send a chill down the spine.

Threatening the world with famine, plague and war. To Princes, death! To Kingdoms, many crosses. To all estates, inevitable losses. To Herdsmen, rot. To ploughmen, hapless seasons. To sailors, storms. To Cities, civil treasons.

The *Great* Plague

The penny astrologers did not know it, but their dismal prophecies were already beginning to come true. In the parish of St Giles-in-the-Field, one of the poorest and filthiest of the London suburbs, three cases of plague were reported just before Christmas 1664. On its own, this was nothing remarkable. Plague was endemic in England – just one of any number of fatal diseases that thrived on dirt and poverty. There were a few plague deaths every year. Twelve were recorded in the 'Bills of Mortality' for the City of London in 1663, and four in 1664 – not including those three in St Giles in the last weeks of December.

But there was anecdotal evidence that this incipient outbreak was something out of the ordinary. Nathaniel Hodges, a doctor who worked on Watling Street, had heard through the professional network that two members of the same family had died of plague in Westminster. Before the year's close he was to treat a plague victim himself – the first of many hundreds of cases he would see over the coming months.

In the middle of the Christmas holidays I was called to a young man in a fever, who after two days' course of alexiterial [anti-poison] medicines had two risings about the bigness of a nutmeg broke out, one on each thigh; upon examination of which I soon discovered the malignity, both from the black hue and the circle around them, and pronounced it to be the plague; in which opinions I was afterwards confirmed by subsequent symptoms, although by God's blessing the patient recovered.

This case I insert both to show that this season did not wholly destroy the distemper, although it greatly restrained it. But upon the frost breaking the contagion got ground, and gradually got out of its confinements, like a flame that for some time seems smothered, and suddenly breaks out with aggravated fury.

Certainly an unusually cold winter seems to have stopped the plague in its tracks. But in April, as soon as the warm weather came, the symptoms that Hodges described came budding forth like spring flowers. Everybody lived in fear of the appearance of 'pestilential tokens' on their skin, or on the skin of someone close to them. And almost as alarming as these physical marks of plague were the internal symptoms. These were documented at the time by a medical man named William Kemp. He wrote that the plague …

… sometimes begins with a cold shivering like an ague, sometimes continues with a mild warmth like hectic fever or a diary [one-day illness], and increaseth with violent heat like burning fever. It corrupteth the blood and all the humours, it afflicteth the head with pain, the brain with giddiness, the nerves with convulsions, the eyes with dimness, making them look as if they had wept and depriving them of their lively splendour. It makes the countenance look ghastly, troubling the ears with noise and deafness. It infecteth the breath with stinking, the voice with hoarseness, the throat with soreness, the mouth with drought, and the tongue with thirst; the stomach with worms and want of appetite, with hickop, nauseousness, retching and vomiting; the bowels with looseness and the bloody flux; the sides with stitches; the back with pains, the lungs with flegme, the skin with fainty and stinking sweats, spots, blains, blotches and carbuncles; the pulse with weakness, the heart with sounding and faintness. It makes feeble like the palsy, it causes sleepiness like the lethargy, watchfulness and madness like a phrensie, and sudden death like the apoplexy. And these symptoms happen not alike to all.

Clearly the symptoms were so diverse that almost any medical condition – from an arthritic twinge to a headcold – might be the first sign of imminent and agonizing death. It is hardly surprising, in the circumstances, that a kind of mass hypochondria swept London as spring turned to summer. The solicitious Doctor Hodges, who cared for victims throughout the year, noted this strange example of auto-suggestion in one of his patients.

> A girl ... came to my house full of sadness and consternation, already even to sink down. Upon examination she told me that she had broke out of house where she was shut up with a nurse, all the rest of her family being dead, to shew me the certain forerunner of death upon her, saying she had the tokens upon her leg. But I soon found a mistake that might have been fatal to her for it was only a wart, which neither she nor the nurse had ever taken notice of before. She was soon undeceived, and by my encouragement shook off all her fear, returning home cheerful.
> But I really believe that had not her mind soon been made easy ... she would have died merely by the force of her imagination.

The government in London reacted to the epidemic in a manner every bit as panicky as that young girl's. Wherever a case of plague was officially diagnosed the first step was (as with Hodges' patient) to shut the victims in their house along with every member of the household. A watchman armed with a halberd was set on the door to stop them trying to escape. This enforced quarantine was to remain in place all the time plague was in the house, and for 40 days after. Imprisoned inside their own homes, victims' only contact with the outside world was through the guard. He might be persuaded to go and buy bread if they had any money in the house. But many watchmen took advantage of the situation by demanding extortionate payment for running errands, and so piled misery upon misery for households that had been 'visited', as the euphemism of the time had it.

Pepys saw some infected houses on 7 June 1665, when he was out and about on business. At this point plague houses were still rare enough to be worth remarking upon. These ones were a long way from Pepys's home: no cases of plague had as yet been reported where he lived, at the eastern end of the City. But this was his first light brush with the 'pest'. and it sent a nervous shiver down his spine.

> This day, much against my will, I did in Drury-lane see two or three houses marked with a red cross upon the doors and 'Lord have mercy upon us' writ there – which was a sad sight to me, being the first of that kind that to my remembrance I ever saw, so that I was forced to buy some roll-tobacco to smell and chaw – which took away my apprehension.

Pepys in his anxiety spared no thought for the poor infected wretches inside the houses. The inescapable fact of the matter was that shutting up was most usually a death sentence for everyone within. In the confined, dirty, airless hovels, entire families succumbed one by one. A contemporary writer sketched this scene of the terrors of those who had been shut up with a dying relative:

> No drop of water ... but what comes at the leisure of a drunken or careless halberd bearer at the the door ... Not a friend to come night them in their many, many heart and house cares and complexities. They are compelled, though well, to lie by, to watch upon the death-bed of their dear relation, to see the corpse dragged away before their eyes. Affrighted children stand howling at their side. Thus they are fitted by fainting affliction to receive the impressions of a thousand fearful thoughts ... as the family ... sink one after another in the den of this dismal likeness of Hell, contrived by the advice of the English College of Doctors.

The only medical help available to those shut up was a nurse – usually an old woman with no knowledge or training whatsoever, and who often was at least as dangerous to a infected family's well-being as the plague itself.

This shutting up would breed a plague if there were none, wrote one enraged Londoner at the height of the epidemic. **Infection may have killed its thousands, but shutting up hath killed its ten thousands. Little is it considered how careless most nurses are in attending the visited, and how careless [uncaring] (being possessed with rooking avarice) they are to watch their opportunity and ransack their houses; the assured absence of friends making the sick desperate on the one hand, and them on the other unfaithful ... It is something beyond a plague ... to be in the hands of those dirty, ugly and unwholesome hags; even a Hell itself, on the one hand to hear nothing but screetches, cryes, groans, and on the other to see nothing but ugliness and deformity, black as night and dark as melancholy. Ah, to lie at the mercy of strange women is sad: to leave wife, children, plate, jewels to the ingenuity of poverty is worse. But who can express the misery of being exposed to their rapine that have nothing of the woman left but shape?**

There was more than a hint of misogyny in the complaints against nurses; they cannot all have been evil witches. But the plague gave rise to many a gruesome tale, and not just about 'unwholesome hags'.

I alledge the mischief and and sad consequence that may arise from the high fits of frenzy that usually attend this and all the other like distempers. A sad instance whereof we had this last week in Fleet lane, where the man of the house being sick, and having a great swelling, but not without hope of being almost ripe for breaking, did in a strong fit rise out of his bed, in spite of all that his wife (who attended him) could do to the contrary, got his knife and therewith most miserably cut his wife, and had killed her had she not wrapped up the sheet about her and therewith saved herself, till by crying out murther [murder] a neighbour who was himself shut up opened his own doors and forced into the house and came seasonably to her preservation. The man is since dead ...

The Flight from London

William Boghurst was a 34-year-old apothecary at the time the plague broke out. Though not qualified as a doctor, he had plenty of practical experience of treating illness, and had a good idea of what medicines were likely – or unlikely – to work against this deadly infection. He was, for example, scathing of Pepys's chosen preventative, tobacco. 'How many thousand tobacco-takers think you died this year?' he wrote afterwards. (Though so widespread was the belief in the efficacy of tobacco that at Eton College, one small boy was thrashed for failing to smoke his pipe.)

Boghurst made a long list of hopeless anti-plague measures. It was a hodge-podge of the medicinal and the municipal, and some of the 'antidotes' he cites are tragi-comic. He notes for example, that some people deliberately infected themselves with venereal disease – 'the French pox' – in the belief that the infection somehow blocked the progress of the plague. One or two of the measures catalogued might have been genuinely effective if they had been carried out consistently. Cleaning the streets would have helped; 'prohibiting goods and people from infected places' was instituted by the independent kingdom of Scotland, and it kept Scotland plague-free throughout the year.

But here are the measures that Boghurst described as 'foolish, superstitious, troublesome, weak and ridiculous'. Almost 400 years after the event, the meaning or usage of some of the things he mentions is obscure, but that somehow adds to the surreal effect of the litany:

Amulets, tobacco, taking strong waters, brandy etc., fumigating of houses, rubbing houses with herbs and sprinkling them, sweet powders, troches, odoriferous candles, civet boxes, nosegays, pomanders, rope's end tarred, spice caps, crosses, washing the temple and mouth with vinegar. Plasters to the groin, wrists, temples, armpits; lozenges, hair or silk or leathered clothes, stuffing the nose with rue, wormwood or what else; sleeping on flock beds or mattresses strewed with cold sweet herbs in summer and with hot sweet herbs in winter; frictions, bathing, purging, sweating, bleeding, vomiting, the French pox, issues [enemas], cordial quilts, avoiding all stinking things and places, making fires in the streets, smoking clothes with brimstone and storax etc; carrying venom about them, suppositories, Ruffi pills; washing of streets, shooting of guns, killing dogs and cats, choosing high ground or hills to live on, shutting up houses, burning infected linen or woollen, chewing tobacco, roots or herbs; warding towns, prohibiting goods and people coming from infected places, forbearing coming into a crowd, anointing the nostrils, eating six leaves of sorrel, fasting.

And no less ineffectual is the shunning and running away from dead-carts, shut-up houses, nurses, narrow alleys, dead bodies, dunghills, cobwebs, south winds. Also the sprinkling of chambers with vinegar, opening north and shutting south windows, keeping birds in cages or a goat in the house, flashing gunpowder, burning vinegar, or horns, or leather; setting milk up and down in the house, eating garlic and butter, drinking their own urine, continual mastication of roots, drugs, sweating once a week, carrying of relics or pictures about one, enchantment characters, pictures of stars, serpents, mystical numbers, taking of bezoar epithems over the heart, unctions.

Boghurst's shop was at the sign of the White Hart Inn, close to the seat of the epidemic in St Giles. From this vantage point he watched the spread of the plague from the slums to the better parts of town. By the start of the summer the disease was creeping out of the poor liberties and was encroaching on the City walls to the east and on Whitehall – the seat of government and the home of the king – to the south-west.

On 28 June Pepys had an official meeting with the Duke of York, but 'did not kiss his hand'. On King Street, close to the gates of Whitehall Palace, he saw several more houses bearing the red cross. As far as the court was concerned this was too close for comfort. The next day Pepys, back in Whitehall, found the 'Court full of waggons': King Charles, his family and entourage, were leaving town and heading for the rural safety of Hampton Court.

The king was by no means the first to decide to leave London. There had for some weeks been a steady outward flow of aristocrats – all of them heading for their country houses. So many merchants and traders had been leaving that commerce in the City was slowing to a standstill. 'Trading strangely ceaseth,' wrote one eyewitness. 'They shut up their shops, and such fear possesseth them as is wonderful [amazing] to see how they hurry into the country, as though the same God was not there that is in the city.' Most preferred not to tempt God by remaining in the midst of the sickness. And now that running from the plague had the royal sanction, the exodus became a stampede.

Thomas Vincent was rector of the church of St Mary Magdalen in Milk Street until 1662 when, like many Puritan ministers, he was removed from his post by the re-established Anglican hierarchy. He watched with pious disdain as the rich – 'the great orbs', as he called them – deserted their city and their poorer brethren. This, his eschatological take on the worsening situation, is full of vivid detail.

> Now a great consternation seizeth upon most persons, and fearful bodings of a desolate judgment. Now guilty sinners begin to look about them, and think with themselves into what corner of the land they might fly to hide them ... Now those that had, as it were, challenged the God of Heaven, and defied him by their horrid oaths and blasphemies when he begins to appear, they retreat, yea, fly away with terror and amazement. The great orbs begin first to move; the lords and gentry retire into their countries; their remote houses are prepared, goods removed, and London is quickly upon their backs [others went with them]. Few ruffling gallants walk the street; few spotted ladies [ladies wearing beauty spots] to be seen at windows. A great forsaking there was of the adjacent places where the plague did first rage.
>
> Now rich tradesmen provide themselves to depart. If they have not country houses, they seek lodgings abroad for themselves and families. And the poorer tradesmen, that they may imitate the rich in their fear, stretch themselves to take a country journey though they have scarce wherewithal to bring them back again.

Now the highways are thronged with passengers and goods, and London doth empty itself into the country. Great are the stirs and hurries in London by the removal of so many families. Fear puts many thousands on the wing, and those think themselves most safe that can fly furthest off from the city. In July the plague increaseth, and prevaileth exceedingly. The number of 470, which died in one week by the disease, ariseth to 725 the next week, to 1089 the next, to 1843 to next, to 2010 the next. Now the plague compasseth the walls of the city like a flood, and poureth in upon it. Now most parishes are infected both without and within; yet there are not so many houses shut up by the plague as by the owners forsaking them for fear of it. And though the inhabitants be so exceedingly decreased by the departure of so many thousands, the number of dying persons increaseth fearfully. Now the countries [country people] keep guards, lest infectious persons should from the city bring the disease unto them. Most of the rich are now gone, and the middle sort will not stay behind. But the poor are forced through poverty to stay, and abide the storm.

Fire-and-brimstone preachers such as Vincent were not the only ones disgusted by the mass flight of the well-to-do. George Thomson, another of those courageous physicians who stuck to the task of caring for the plague-sick throughout the crisis, had this to say about his fellow doctors who left their post.

If stragglers, deserters or runaways in an army ... ought to suffer loss of life and estate, I see no reason why these men, whose function obliges them to stand out to the last, should deserve less punishment if they deliver such a vast and populous city to the fury of so implacable a foe. For my part, though I could enjoy my ease, pleasure and profit in the country ... yet I would rather choose to lose my life than violate in this time of extreme the band of charity towards my neighbour, and de-decorate that illustrious profession I am called to.

The high-minded apothecary William Boghurst took the same view regarding his slightly less illustrious line of work. He was especially scathing of doctors that left town so that they could continue to treat those who had the money to pay for their services.

> I think all may fly that are free and not obliged to stay either by their office, relations or necessities. But those apothecaries which have their work and dependence from the physicians are not, I think, obliged to stay behind when their masters lead the way; for who shall direct them. But those apothecaries which stand upon their own legs, and live by their own practice, are bound by their undertakings to stay and help ... Every man that undertakes to be of a profession or takes upon himself any office must take all parts of it, the good and the evil, the pleasure and the pain, the profit and the inconvenience altogether, and not pick and choose. For ministers must preach, captains must fight, physicians attend upon the sick. But two or three of the youngest [doctors] are appointed in plague time to look to 30 or 40 thousand sick people; you should have five or six hundred hanging after them if they be well lined with white metal: 'tis the rich whose persons are guarded with angels.

An 'angel', it should be noted, was a coin worth ten shillings – the usual fee for a doctor. This little pun of Boghurst's is perhaps the only good joke to come out of the plague.

Pepys, too, had money on his mind as he considered the pros and cons of getting out of London. 1665 was turning into an especially remunerative year for him, and he was loath to abandon his lucrative job. So, characteristically, he found a middle way. In June he arranged to send his wife and servants to the quiet village of Woolwich, well out of town; he would stay and do his work despite the dangers. He packed off his household on 5 July. It was a busy working day, split between paperwork in his office and high-powered naval business in Whitehall. The plague was apparently not discussed, but in the afternoon he spotted that a house in Pall Mall, 'where heretofore in Cromwell's time we young men used to keep our weekly clubs', was now shut up. After work he took a boat downriver to Woolwich to see how Elizabeth was settling in.

> I found my wife come and her two maids, and very prettily accommodated they will be. And I left them going to supper, grieved in my heart to part with my wife, being worse by much without her, though some trouble there is in having the care of a family at home in this plague time.

After dark he hired a boat and had himself rowed slowly back to the sickly city against the outgoing tide. 'Late home and to bed,' reads the last line of the day's diary entry, 'very alonely'.

Death Rides Triumphant

The plague that raged in the suburbs now breached the City walls. In the week that Pepys sent his wife away, the number of plague deaths inside the City of London rose from four to 23. From then on the total doubled week on week until, in the first week of August 208 people died of plague within the City. Over the same period the number of fatalities in the out-parishes went from 166 in one week to almost 200 a day. And in Westminster the death count went from 105 in the first week of July to 450 in the first week of August. The 'forehorses of death's chariot', to use Boghurst's lively turn of phrase, had also slipped across London Bridge and were running amok in Southwark and Surrey: in the built-up area on the south bank of the Thames, more than 2,000 died in the course of July.

Pepys kept a close eye on the weekly Bills of Mortality and was deeply troubled. He knew that even these frightening figures were an underestimate. Late in August he happened to bump into James Hadley, clerk of St Olave's, Pepys's parish church:

> Upon my asking how the plague goes, he told me it encreases much, and much in our parish: 'For,' says he, 'there died nine

this week, though I have returned but six' – which is a very ill practice, and makes me think it is so in other places, and therefore the plague much greater than people take it to be.

It was not just parish clerks who were playing down the figures. Many plague deaths were concealed by the 'searchers of the dead'. These officials, usually old women, had the right to enter any house where a person had died. Their job was to determine the cause of death, but (like the feared nurses) they had no training. The searchers received a fee of fourpence for every death that they diagnosed and reported, but were happy to supplement their income by taking bribes. Families of plague victims were more than willing to pay for the cause of death to be listed as anything other than plague, and so avoid the horrors and hazards of shutting up. John Graunt, a member of the Royal Society and one of the first scientists to make a study of demographics, looked closely at the Bills as they were published and saw the discrepancy:

There lyeth an error in the accounts or distinctions of the casualties, he wrote. That is, more died of the plague than were accounted for under the name ... The poor searchers, out of ignorance, respect, love of money or malice, returning, it's suspected, more or less as they are inclined.

Graunt calculated that the true count was 25 per cent higher than the Bills suggested, because so many plague deaths were hidden under some more or less transparent euphemism. The Bill for the week of 15–22 August, for example, listed 'frighted' as the cause of death of two individuals; three died of 'grief' and one of 'lethargy'. Two were said merely to have died 'suddenly'. 'Teeth' is given as the fatal illness of 111 people – all of them babies deemed to have died in the process of teething. To them must be added 22 more deaths listed baldly and unhelpfully as 'infants'. Most of these children would in reality have been plague victims. Many of the deaths from 'feaver' (348) and 'spotted feaver' (166) would have been people who died with the pestilential tokens upon them. The official plague total for this week was 4,237.

By this time, no one needed to read the Bills to know that the plague was taking a terrible toll. Hodges, still in the thick of it, was almost overwhelmed by the enormity of what was happening around him, of the sights he was seeing on his exhausting daily rounds of the plague houses.

In the months of August and September the contagion changed its slow and languid pace, and having as it were got master of all made a most terrible slaughter, so that three, four, five thousand died in a week, and once eight thousand. Who can express the calamities of such times? The whole British nation wept for the miseries of her metropolis. In some houses, carcasses lay waiting for burial, and in others persons in their last agonies; in one room might be heard dying groans, in another the raving of delirium, and not far off relations and friends bewailing both their loss and the dismal prospect of their own sudden departure.

Death was the sure midwife to all children, and infants passed immediately from the womb to the grave. Who would not burst with grief to see the stock for a future generation hanging upon the breasts of a dead mother? Or the marriage-bed changed the first night into a sepulchre, and the pair meet with death in their first embraces? Some of the infected ran about staggering like drunken men, and fell and expired in the streets; while others lie half-dead and comatose, but never to be waked but by the last trumpet; some lie vomiting as if they had drunk poison; and others fell dead in the market while they were buying necessaries for the support of life.

The occasional appearance of toxic madmen on the empty streets was, for those still free of the taint, one of the most terrifying aspects of life in the plague city. There were tales of people becoming infected after being accosted by some naked, raving lunatic. Even more appalling were stories like the one told to Pepys by a Mr Caesar, who said 'how bold people there were to go in sport to one another's burials. And in spite to well people would breathe in the faces (out of their windows) of well people going by.'

Thomas Vincent continued to patrol the deserted city on God's business, even at the height of the plague. Here is his description of a moribund London where 'the church-yards are so stuffed with dead corpses, that they are in many places swelled two or three feet higher than they were before; and new ground is broken up to bury the dead.' This part of his tale ends with two chilling stories – the first of a bereaved mother, and the second of a man's attempted suicide.

Now Death rides triumphantly on his pale horse through our streets; and breaks into every house almost, where any inhabitants are to be found. Now people fall as thick as leaves from the trees in autumn, when they are shaken by a mighty wind. Now there is a dismal solitude in London's streets. Every day looks with the face of a Sabbath day, observed with greater solemnity than it used to be in the city. Now shops are shut in, people rare and very few that walk about, insomuch that the grass begins to spring up in some places, and a deep silence almost in every place, especially within the walls; no rattling coaches, no prancing horses, no calling in customers, nor offering wares; no London Cries sounding in the ears: if any voice be heard, it is the groans of dying persons, breathing forth their last: and the funeral knells of them that are ready to be carried to their graves.

Now shutting up of visited-houses (there being so many) is at an end, and most of the well are mingled among the sick, which otherwise would have got no help. Now in some places where the people did generally stay, not one house in a hundred but is infected; and in many houses half the family is swept away; in some the whole, from the eldest to the youngest, few escape with the death of but one or two; never did so many husbands and wives die together; never did so many parents carry their children with them to the grave, and go together into the same house under earth, who had lived together in the same house upon it. Now the nights are too short to bury the dead; the long summer days are spent from morning unto the twilight in conveying the vast number of dead bodies unto the bed of their graves.

Now we could hardly go forth, but we should meet many
coffins, and see diseased persons with sores and limping in the
streets: amongst other sad spectacles, methought two were very
affecting; one of a woman coming alone, and weeping, by the door
where I lived (which was in the midst of infection) with a little
coffin under her arm, carrying it to the new church-yard: I did
judge that it was the mother of the child, and that all the family
besides was dead, and she was forced to coffin up, and bury with
her own hands, this her last dead child. Another, was of a man
at the corner of the Artillery wall, that, as I judge, through the
dizziness of his head with the disease, which seized upon him
there, had dashed his face against the wall, and when I came by,
he lay hanging with his bloody face over the rails, and bleeding
upon the ground; and as I came back, he was removed under a
tree in Moorfields, and lay upon his back; I went and spake to
him; he could make me no answer, but rattled in the throat, and,
as I was informed, within half an hour died in the place.

Vincent was secure in the belief that the plague was God's way of
rebuking London for its sins. He was morally certain that the city
was in the grip of divine retribution, and that London deserved its
punishment. But his tone softens somewhat when he comes to describe
how that plague touched his own household. It happened on a day that
he had spent ministering to the dying.

We were eight in family, three men, three youths, an old woman,
and a maid, all of which came of me, hearing of my stay in town,
some to accompany me, others to help me. It was the latter end
of September before any of us were touched; the young ones
were not idle, but improved their time in praying and hearing,
and were ready to receive instruction, and were strangely borne
up against the fears of the disease and death, every day so familiar
to the view.

But at last we were visited, and the plague came in dreadfully
upon us. The cup was put into our hand to drink, after a

neighbour family had tasted it, with whom we had much sweet
society in this time of sorrow. And first our maid was smitten.
It began with a shivering and trembling in her flesh, and quickly
seized on her spirits. It was a sad day, which I believe I shall
never forget; I had been abroad to see a friend in the city, whose
husband was newly dead of the plague, and she herself visited
with it; I came back to see another whose wife was dead of the
plague, and he himself under apprehensions that he should die
within a few hours; I came home, and the maid was on her
death-bed, and another crying out for help, being left alone
in a sweating fainting fit.

It was on the Monday when the maid was smitten; on Thursday
she died full of tokens. On Friday one of the youths had a
swelling in his groin; and on the Lord's day died with the marks
of the distemper upon him. On the same day another youth did
sicken, and on the Wednesday following he died. On the
Thursday his master fell sick of the disease, and within a day or
two was full of spots, but strangely beyond his own, and others
expectations, recovered. Thus did the plague follow us, and came
upon us one by one: as Job's messengers came one upon the heels
of another, so the messengers of death came so close one after
another, in such a dreadful manner, as if we must all follow one
another immediately into the pit. Yet the Lord in mercy put a
stop to it, and the rest were preserved.

Others preserved themselves without trusting entirely to God. King
Charles kept well away from his capital while it writhed in sickness.
He had gone to Hampton Court, but moved on from there when the
pestilence began to creep downriver from the city. He went first to
Salisbury, which seemed far enough away to be safe. But when a case
of plague was diagnosed there, he moved his entire entourage – queen,
mistresses, advisers and courtiers – to Oxford. Here, he and his court
whiled away the time in idle amusements. Visitors from London were
kept out, guards were placed on the bridges, and even the royal post
was diverted away from London to prevent any possibility of infection

reaching the royal person. These measures seemed to work – or maybe Oxford was just lucky – but at any rate plague never touched the city.

The court was accommodated in the many fine building of the colleges. Charles occupied Christchurch; the Duke of York and his children stayed in Oriel. The queen shared Merton with the king's mistress, Lady Castlemaine, who was due to give birth to the king's child (the future Duke of Northumberland) at the end of September. Lady Castlemaine, rather than the catastrophe that had overtaken London, was the main subject of discussion at court. The *cordon sanitaire* placed around the city meant that little news filtered through. And according to an astonished account written by a French eyewitness, bad tidings would only have spoiled the lovely light-hearted mood. Here is Denis de Repas's description of the court at Oxford, written in faulty but lively English. The first thing that struck him was the frivolous fashion among courtly ladies for wearing masculine clothes:

> For news from Court, I shall tell you that one cannot possibly know a woman from a man, unless one hath the eye of a lynx who can see through a wall, for by the face and garbe they are like men. They do not wear any hood, but only perwick hats [wigs] and coats. There's no other plague here but the infection of love; no other discourse but of ballets, danse and fine couse [clothes]. No other emulation but who shall look handsomere, and whose vermillion and Spanish white is best. None other fight but for 'I am yours'. In a word, there is nothing here but mirth, and there is talk that there shall be a proclamacon made that any melancoly man or woman coming into this towne shalled be turned out and put to the pillary; and there to be whep till he has learned the way to be mery à la mode.

If melancholy were a crime, then by now not a single Londoner would have been found innocent. Everyone had seen some friend succumb to the plague. The city seemed to be drowning in a rising tide of corpses. Stephen Bing was a petty canon at St Paul's Cathedral. From his house, in the shadow of the old cathedral, he wrote a fatalistic letter to

William Sancroft, the dean of the cathedral, who was safely installed at Tunbridge. The plague was striking in a way as terrifying and haphazard as the bombs that – 300 years later – would fall on the same streets.

> **God hath been pleased now to encompass us with his pestilential hand in three places in Carter Lane, in Sermon Lane, which is next to my house, in the lane at the end of Knightriders Street, in the lane at the end of Ave Maria Lane, in the lane where the Bishop of London's house was, and in an alley in Paternoster Row and on the backside in the Shambles ... Yet nevertheless, under the shadow of the Almighty shall be my refuge until this calamity be overpast.**

A doctor who lived around the corner from Bing also wrote to Dean Sancroft. 'We have no neighbours left,' he said tersely.

Pepys was also losing friends. Alexander Burnet, Pepys's physician, died in the last days of August, much to Pepys's sorrow. In June, Dr Burnett's house had been one of the first in the city to be visited. A servant of his caught the plague, at which the doctor took the rare altruistic step of confining himself to his house. The servant died of the plague, and no one else in Burnett's household was infected at the time. But later in the summer, the doctor was accused, bizarrely, of having murdered his servant. He had to go to the trouble of getting a certificate from the pest house attesting that plague was the cause of death. No sooner had Burnett cleared his name than he caught the disease himself. Pepys thought it strange that this should happen so long after the first death in his house, but it may be that he contracted the disease as a result of attending the first ever post-mortem of a plague victim. If so, he died honourably in the line of duty, which makes Pepys's brief epitaph – 'poor unfortunate man' – seem rather inadequate.

Bring out your Dead

Death had become an omnipresent fact of life in the City of London. Pepys was surprised at himself when he realized how little he was moved by the sight of corpses. They were as unremarkable a sight on the streets as a cat or dog might be in ordinary times. In these extraordinary times, cats and dogs had in fact become a rare sight. By order of the Lord Mayor, all the cats and dogs had been killed early in the summer. 'It was computed that 40,000 dogs, and five times as many cats, were massacred in consequence of this prescription,' said Doctor Hodges. The cull was a seen as a precautionary measure, but in fact it was counterproductive: now there were no natural predators to keep down the flea-ridden rats, which were the true source of the plague.

By August the graveyards of London were all literally overflowing with dead bodies, and the reek of putrefaction that emanated from them was utterly nauseating. Some people living near churches were forced to move house to get away from the all-pervading stench. When the churchyards could take no more, the authorities resorted to the expedient of mass graves on unconsecrated ground. The task of ferrying the dead to the pits was done by 'bearers'. Many of them were apprentices who had been made destitute when their masters had left London for a safer place. Pulling the dead carts was the only way a jobless apprentice could earn his keep. It was dangerous and disgusting work – but at least there was plenty of it.

> **Pits of great extent were dug in several parts,** wrote Hodges. **The dead were brought by cart-loads, collected by the ring of a bell, and the doleful cry of 'Bring out your dead!' They were put into the carts with no other covering than rugs or sheets tied round them by their friends, if they had any surviving; and were shot down in promiscuous heaps! Sometimes the drivers of those carts would drop in their employments, and the carts would be found without any conductor; in the parish of Stepney, it was said they lost within the year, 116 sextons, grave-diggers and their assistants!**

John Allin was unfortunate enough to live within sight of one of these plague pits. His letters to a friend in Rye read like dispatches from the frontline of a war:

I am troubled at the approach of the sickness nearer every week, and at a new burying place which they have made near us ... making great funerals for such as die of the distemper ... The sickness increaseth: 5,319 this weeks bill [the Bill of Mortality] in general, and 3,880 in the bill of the plague, of which disease Mr Symond Porter, Mr Miller's brother-in-law, died last week. I am afraid to write to Mr Miller of it lest he should be afraid of my letter. But pray let him know of his brother's death ... I am, though, mercy, yet well in the midst of death – and that too approaching nearer and nearer. Not many doors off, and the pit open daily within view of my chamber window. The Lord fit me and all of us for our last end!

September was the worst month of the plague and, in terms of the death toll, possibly the cruellest month in London's long history. More than 30,000 people died. There is an account that speaks of 'howling desolation' in London, and one eyewitness said that the bells of London seemed hoarse from tolling for the dead. Strange and grisly stories began to circulate. John Allin heard tell of a baby that spoke miraculously after it had died of the plague and prophesied 'great and sad persecution' in 1666. Hodges relates a second-hand but rather more likely anecdote concerning the murderous behaviour of some nurses.

These wretches from an inhuman greediness to plunder the dead, would not only strangle their patients and charge their deaths to the distemper in their throats; but would secretly convey the pestilential taint from the sores of the sick to those who were well.

Pepys was told this sentimental little parable one day after church. It is Moses in the bulrushes, transposed to the pest-ridden circumstances of London in 1665:

Among other stories, one very passionate methought – of a complaint brought against a man in the town for taking a child from London from an infected house. Alderman Hooker told us it was the child of a very able citizen in Gracious-street [Gracechurch Street], a saddler, who had buried all the rest of his children of the plague; and himself and his wife, now being shut up and in despair of escaping, did desire only to save the life of this little child. And so prevailed to have it received stark-naked into the arms of a friend, who brought it (having put it into new fresh clothes), to Grenwich; where, upon hearing the story, we did agree it should be permitted to be received and kept in the town.

The oddest story to emerge from the plague is the comic adventure of a piper who was so blind drunk he was almost buried alive in a plague pit. Like the tale of the speaking corpse of the infant, the yarn has a kind of Gothic allure. It certainly appealed to Daniel Defoe, who included it in his book, *Journal of the Plague Year*. Many commentators have dismissed it as a complete figment of Defoe's imagination. His *Journal* was, after all, not a diary like Pepys's. Defoe was only four or five years old in 1665, so his book, published in 1722, is a piece of historical journalism, compiled from first-hand accounts and interviews decades after the event. But there is enough evidence from other sources to corroborate Defoe's version. Here it is in his words:

It was under this John Hayward's care, and within his bounds, that the story of the piper, with which people have made themselves so merry, happened, and he assured me that it was true. It is said that it was a blind piper; but as John told me, the fellow was not blind, but an ignorant, weak, poor man, and usually walked his rounds about ten o'clock at night and went piping along from door to door, and the people usually took him in at public-houses where they knew him, and would give him drink and victuals, and sometimes farthings. And he in return would pipe and sing and talk simply, which diverted the people; and thus he lived. It was but a very bad time for this diversion while things were as I have told, yet the poor fellow went about as usual, but was almost starved. And when anybody asked how he did he would answer, the dead cart had not taken him yet, but that they had promised to call for him next week.

It happened one night that this poor fellow – whether somebody had given him too much drink or no (John Hayward said he had not drink in his house, but that they had given him a little more victuals than ordinary at a public-house in Coleman Street) – the poor fellow, having not usually had a bellyful for perhaps not a good while, was laid all along upon the top of a bulk or stall, and fast asleep, at a door in the street near London Wall, towards Cripplegate, and that upon the same bulk or stall the people of some house, in the alley of which the house was a corner, hearing a bell which they always rang before the cart came, had laid a body really dead of the plague just by him, thinking, too, that this poor fellow had been a dead body, as the other was, and laid there by some of the neighbours.

Accordingly, when John Hayward with his bell and the cart came along, finding two dead bodies lie upon the stall, they took them up with the instrument they used and threw them into the cart, and, all this while the piper slept soundly.

From hence they passed along and took in other dead bodies, till, as honest John Hayward told me, they almost buried him alive in the cart; yet all this while he slept soundly. At length the cart came to the place where the bodies were to be thrown into the ground, which, as I do remember, was at Mount Mill. And as the cart usually stopped some time before they were ready to shoot out the melancholy load they had in it, as soon as the cart stopped the fellow awaked and struggled a little to get his head out from among the dead bodies, when, raising himself up in the cart, he called out, 'Hey! where am I?' This frighted the fellow that attended about the work; but after some pause John Hayward, recovering himself, said, 'Lord, bless us! There's somebody in the cart not quite dead!' So another called to him and said, 'Who are you?' The fellow answered, 'I am the poor piper. Where am I?' 'Where are you?' says Hayward. 'Why, you are in the dead-cart, and we are going to bury you.' 'But I an't dead though, am I?' says the piper, which made them laugh a little though, as John said, they were heartily frighted at first; so they helped the poor fellow down, and he went about his business.

I know the story goes he set up his pipes in the cart and frighted the bearers and others so that they ran away; but John Hayward did not tell the story so, nor say anything of his piping at all; but that he was a poor piper, and that he was carried away as above, I am fully satisfied of the truth of.

The Martyrdom of Eyam

On 3 September, the first Sunday after the death of Dr Burnett, Pepys had a moment's plague-anxiety as he got himself dressed for church.

Up, and put on my colour'd silk suit, very fine, and my new periwigg, bought a good while since, but darst not wear it because the plague was in Westminster when I bought it. And it is a wonder what will be the fashion after the plague is done as to periwigs, for nobody will dare to buy any haire for fear of the infection – that it had been cut off the heads of people dead of the plague.

The plague did not, in the event, kill off the powdered wig as a fashion accessory – but Pepys nervousness about the dangers of inanimate objects was shared by many Londoners. Everyone believed that you could catch the plague from a tainted coin, and letters from London were routinely toasted over a fire before being read as a means of disinfecting them. A more real danger was posed by the clothing of the dead, which was generally sold off by nurses and door-watchers, and sometimes by the families of the recently deceased. One pamphleteer warned against the folly of 'buying the goods out of infected houses, and wearing the apparel of them that lately died,' saying that 'multitudes have been executed by the plague for this heresy'. The writer who had railed against the shutting up of houses spelled out in graphic form the risks of handling plague goods.

**There goeth a tankard that shall infect the fifth cupboard [as
many as five cupboards]; here a set of spoons that taint the
hundredth dish of broth; this man steals the bargain of a cloak
that kills ten men; another buyeth a suit that infects Bristol; and
a third gets a fine child's coat that shall cut off a first-born son. In
vain do you object the savere laws against the removal of infected
goods before the forty days are past, when the careful nurse does
not stay the forty hours, lest a rightful owner interpose, or
cunning lawyer seize on the house and the estate.**

The line about a suit of clothes infecting all Bristol looks like a
preposterous exaggeration. But a terrible incident occurred outside
London that is not far removed from this scenario. It was one of the
most tragic and heroic episodes in the history of the last round of plague
to blight England, and it happened not in the great port city of Bristol,
but in the tiny village of Eyam, high in the peaks of Derbyshire.

On or around the day that Pepys in London noted his worry over his
wig, a box was delivered to the house of Edward Cooper, a tailor who
lived near at the western end of the churchyard in the middle of Eyam.
The box was opened by Cooper's servant, George Vicars. It contained
some old clothes and cutting patterns sent from a tailors' shop in
London. The clothes were damp, so Vicars hung them around the fire
to air. He did not know – he could not have known – that the musty
clothes were infested with plague-carrying fleas. He would have had no
reason to suspect a package from London, because only the faintest and
vaguest rumours of the plague would have reached the isolated
communities of the Pennines. But the fact is, Vicars was probably
infected before the contents of the box were dry. He was sick within
two days, and he died before the week was out. His employer succumbed
to plague two weeks later, and then began, on a microcosmic scale in
Eyam, the same exponential rise in the death toll as was seen in the
capital. Twenty-six people died before the snows came in November,
and another 16 in the course of the winter. This already represented a
cull of about one in ten of the population. But far worse was to come.
The plague, which (as in London) seemed to die down during the

coldest months, came back with a vengeance in the spring of 1666. More died with every passing month. Some villagers fled to relatives elsewhere, and many more were making plans to get away.

It was about now, at some point in the spring, that the young rector of Eyam summoned the entire village to a meeting. His name was William Mompesson; he was a man in his late 20s, married with two children. He had taken charge of the parish only a few months before the sickness began, and so had had little time to win the respect of his parishioners. But he was an eloquent and passionate preacher, and his villagers listened to him. His message was stark and terrible. He told the people of Eyam that it was their Christian duty to remain in the village, because many of them surely carried the plague in them. To leave now that the infection had taken hold would only spread the disease far and wide. He told them that he would remain with them, and that he would write to the Duke of Devonshire at Chatsworth and ask him to keep the village supplied with food. The villagers unanimously agreed to the plan. Stakes were placed at the boundaries of the village, forming a circular enclave about half a mile across. No one was to go outside this circle, whether they were infected or not. This was the London practice of shutting up houses, writ large and arrived at independently of London's example. And as in London, it was a death sentence for many of the people on the inside.

And so, through the summer, the village watched itself die. Entire families were obliterated in a matter of days. In July, the village blacksmith, a man by the name of Richard Talbot, buried his wife, his three daughters and one of his two sons. Then Richard died, leaving his last child an orphan for a matter of days until he too succumbed. They were among the 59 dead in Eyam that month. One woman (her name is not known) attempted to abscond from Eyam at the height of summer. It was the only breach of the voluntary quarantine in the year-long course of the visitation. The woman slipped out the village and walked to Tideswell, a market town five miles away. She chose market day to make her escape, perhaps to maximize her chances of getting lost in the crowd. But the people of Tideswell knew very well what had befallen Eyam, and they posted watchmen on the road from that direction.

The woman was stopped and challenged. 'Whence comest thou?' asked the watch. 'From Orchard Bank,' answered the woman, giving the name of a row of cottages in Eyam. 'Where is that?' asked the watch. 'In the land of the living,' answered the woman. Oddly, this ambiguous answer was good enough for the amateur sentry, and he let the woman pass. But no sooner had she reached Tideswell than she was recognized. A cry went up: 'The plague, the plague! A woman from Eyam!' The market-day crowd immediately chased her out of town, pelting her with stones and clods of earth as they went.

In Eyam, the hard labour of digging graves for the dead fell to a strange fellow named Marshall Howe. He was, by all accounts, a giant of a man, and as bad-tempered as a troll. He had contracted the plague in the early days but recovered, and seems to have believed that he was therefore immune. His was necessary work, but it was not undertaken without ulterior motive, because Howe insisted on the right to claim the goods and chattels of any person who died without an heir. He often went to the house of a plague victim and began digging a grave in the nearest field before its intended occupant was quite dead. This method made the best use of his time, and reduced the effort involved in dragging the corpse (on the end of a rope to minimize bodily contact) from its bed to its burial. Howe took large amounts of furniture and linen from the houses of his heirless clients, and joked that he 'had pinners [pinafores] and napkins sufficient to kindle his pipe with while I live'. And live he did. Howe survived almost to the end of the century; and long after he was dead his name was used in Eyam to terrorize children into good behaviour: 'Do as you are told, or Marshall Howe will come for you ...' Howe's own family were not so long-lived. His wife Jean, who had begged him to stop doing his ghoulish work, fell victim to the plague in August – and so did his son. He buried them both, and enjoyed his hard-earned inheritance alone.

That same month, William Mompesson lost his wife. The story goes that they were walking in the fields when Catherine Mompesson declared: 'The air, how sweet it smells.' A strange perception of sweetness was one of the early signs of infection, as Mompesson knew very well. Catherine died, and was buried a day or two before Mrs

Howe. On 1 September, Mompesson wrote a letter to his children,
George and Elizabeth, who at their mother's insistence had long since
been sent away to friends in Yorkshire. He informed them of her death
in this rather formal letter:

Dear hearts,
   This brings you the doleful news of your dear mother's death –
the greatest loss which ever befell you! I am not only deprived
of a kind and loving comfort, but you also are bereaved of the
most indulgent mother that ever dear children had. But we
must comfort ourselves in God with this consideration, that
the loss is only ours, and that what is our sorrow is her gain.
The consideration of her joys, which I do assure myself are
unutterable, should refresh our drooping spirits.
   My dear hearts, your blessed mother lived a most holy life,
and made a most comfortable and happy end, and is now invested
with a crown of righteousness. Her discourse was ever grave and
meek, yet pleasant withal; a vaunting, immodest word was never
heard to come from her mouth. Again, I can set out in her two
other virtues i.e. charity and frugality. She never valued anything
she had, when the necessities of a poor neighbour required it; but
had a bountiful heart to all indigent and distressed persons. And,
again, she was never lavish, but commendably frugal ...
   I can assure you, my sweet babes, that her love to you was little
inferior than to me. She gave strong testimony of her love for you
when she lay on her death-bed. A few hours before she expired
I wished her to take some cordials which she told me plainly she
could not take. I entreated she would attempt for your dear
sakes. At the mention of your names, she with difficulty lifted
up her head and took them; which was to let me understand
that whilst she had any strength left she would embrace any
opportunity she had of testifying her affection to you ...
   My dear babes, the reading of this account will cause many a
salt tear to spring from your eyes; yet let this comfort you – your
mother is a saint in heaven. I could have told you of many more

of your dear mother's excellent virtues; but I hope that you will not in the least question my testimony, if in a few words I tell you that she was pious and upright in her demeanour and conversation.

Now to that blessed God, who bestowed upon her all those graces be ascribed all honour, glory and dominion, the just tribute of all created beings, for evermore. Amen!

William Mompesson

Mompesson had every reason to believe that he would soon contract the disease. He certainly had no expectation of coming out of Eyam alive. With this thought in mind he wrote this valedictory letter to his friend and patron, Sir George Savile:

Honoured and dear Sir,

This is the saddest news that ever my pen could write. The destroying Angel having taken up his quarters within my habitation, my dearest wife is gone to her eternal rest. Indeed had she loved herself as well as me, she had fled from the pit of destruction with the sweet babes, and might have prolonged her days; but she was resolved to die a martyr to my interests.

Sir, this paper is to bid you a hearty farewell for ever, and to bring you my humble thanks for all your noble favours; and I hope you will believe a dying man, I have as much love as honour for you, and I will bend my feeble knees to the God of Heaven, that you may be blessed with external and eternal happiness, and that the same blessing may fall upon Lady Sunderland and her relations.

Dear Sir, let your dying Chaplain recommend this truth to you and your family, that no happiness or solid comfort can be found in this vale of tears, like living a pious life; and pray ever remember this rule, never do anything upon which you dare not first ask the blessing of God upon the success thereof.

Sir, I have made bold in my will with your name for executor, and I hope you will not take it ill. I have joined two others with you, who will take from you the trouble. Your favourable aspect, will I know, be a great comfort to my distressed orphans. I am not desirous that they should be great, but good; and my next request is that they be brought up in the fear and admonition of the Lord.

Sir, I thank God I am contented to shake hands with all the world; and have many comfortable assurances that God will accept me through His Son. I find the goodness of God greater than I ever thought or imagined.

Dear Sir, I beg the prayers of all about you that I may not be daunted at the powers of hell; and that I may have dying graces; with tears I beg that when you are praying for fatherless orphans, you will remember my two pretty babes.

Pardon the rude style of this paper, and be pleased to believe that I am, dear Sir, &c.

William Mompesson

To his complete surprise, Mompesson did not follow his wife directly to the grave. He remained in the village and carried out his pastoral duties until the plague suddenly came to an end in October, by which time just 33 souls remained alive in Eyam. Once it was clear that the horror was at an end, Mompesson wrote another letter, this time to the friend who was caring for his children in Yorkshire. Having a few months previously been ready for death, he was now somewhat wearily resigned to living:

Dear Sir,

I suppose this letter will seem to you no less than a miracle, that my habitation is *inter vivos*. I have got these lines transcribed by a friend, being loth to affright you with a letter from my hands.

The condition of this place has been so sad, that I persuade myself that *it did exceed all history and example*. Our town has become a Golgotha, the place of a skull: and had there not been a small remnant left, we had been as Sodom, and like to Gomorrah. My ears never heard such doleful lamentations, my nose never smelled such horrid smells, and my eyes never beheld such ghastly spectacles. There have been 76 families visited within my parish, out of which 259 persons died. Now (blessed be God) all our fears are over, for none have died of the plague since the eleventh of October, and the pest houses have been long empty.

I intend (God willing) to spend this week in seeing all woollen clothes fumed and purified. Here have been such burning of goods that the like, I think, was never known. For my part, I have scarcely apparel to shelter my body. During this dreadful visitation, I have not had the least symptom of disease, nor had I ever better health. My man had the distemper, and upon the appearance of a tumour I gave him some chemical antidotes, which operated, and after the rising broke, he was very well. My maid continued in health, which was a blessing; for had she quailed, I should have been ill set to have washed and gotten my provisions.

I have largely tasted of the goodness of the Creator, and the grim looks of death did never yet affright me. I always had a firm faith that my babes would do well, which made me willing to shake hands with the unkind, froward world; yet I shall esteem it a mercy if I am frustrated in the hopes I had of a translation to a better place, and God grant that with patience I may wait.

Be pleased, dear Sir, to accept the presentments of my kind respects, and impart them to your good wife and all my dear relations. I can assure you that a line from your hand will be welcome.

William Mompesson

In proportion to its population, Eyam's experience was by far the worst outbreak of plague in the provinces, and the dreadful rate of attrition was due entirely to the selfless actions of its inhabitants. But many other towns closer to London's orbit were stricken. 'At Yarmouth, Colchester, Ipswich, the sickness is very much, and now pretty much at Norwich. Southampton reported to be almost depopulated', wrote John Allin to his friend in Rye. All the towns mentioned by Allin suffered dreadfully throughout 1666. In Ipswich, so many people fled the plague that the rates could not be collected. Colchester, like Southampton, was reduced to a ghost town. The commercial life of Norwich came to a complete standstill in the summer of 1666, and the survivors were reduced to such penury that a collection was taken in all London churches that August. Derby, the closest city to Eyam, was badly hit, but the north of England was hardly touched. Nottingham was struck in 1667, and so holds the sad distinction of being the last place in Britain to be visited by plague.

In London, it was all over by the late autumn of 1665. At the end of October Pepys noted that 'the town fills up again'. One returning Londoner went to a church in Acton and 'found the churchyard like a plow'd field with graves'. The grass grew on the burial grounds soon enough, but the stench of rotting flesh hung around many a church for a full year after the plague.

By the end of the year, Pepys's own personal universe at least was more or less back to normal.

Thus ends this year, to my great joy, in this manner,' he wrote on the eve of 1666. **'I have raised my estate from 1300 pounds to 4400 pounds … It is true that we have gone through great melancholy because of the great plague, and I put great charges by it, by keeping my family long at Woolwich … But now the plague is abated almost to nothing.**

My whole family hath been well all this while, and all my friends I know of, saving my Aunt Bell, who is dead, and some children of my Cosen Sarah's, of the plague. But many of such as I know very well, dead. Yet to our great joy, the town fills apace, and shops begin to be open again. Pray God continue the plague's decrease.

Pepys did not link his considerable wealth to his good luck in avoiding the plague, but there was a connection. He could afford to take precautions such as sending his family away. And though he remained in London throughout, he lived in a place and a manner far removed from the squalid, fetid slums where the plague first took hold and hit hardest. One historian has pointed out that among London's 100,000 dead there was not a single aristocrat or member of parliament, not one judge or magistrate, no high-ranking member of the clergy, hardly a wealthy merchant. The London elite, to which Pepys aspired, came throught the ravages of 1665 virtually unscathed. The courageous doctor Nathaniel Hodges noted this at the time, and laconically characterized the epidemic as 'the poores plague'. The same socio-economic dimension was apparent to Roger L'Estrange, publisher of a court newspaper called *The Intelligencer*, but he drew a different lesson from the fact that the plague was at its most virulent in the 'sluttish parts' of town:

> **In this raging pestilence it hath pleased God to spare those public ministers, magistrates and officers upon whose lives the peace and order of the government so much depend, insomuch that I do not find this visitation to have taken away any person of prime authority and command.**

The fawning L'Estrange would have been horrified to know that the next catastrophe to befall London would cost the rich, property-owning classes very dear indeed.

London's Burning

To the day he died, the baker Thomas Farynor never accepted that he was responsible for the catastrophe that destroyed the greatest city in the world. He insisted that on the night of Saturday 1 September 1666, he had drawn his baking ovens as he did every night. They were not alight when he went to bed at ten, 'leaving his providence with his slippers'. He was doubly certain that his ovens were dead, because around midnight he needed a candle, and went downstairs to see if there were any embers in the oven he could use to light it: there were none. Though it was undeniable that the fire began on his premises on Pudding Lane, the baker always insisted that it could not have been caused by his negligence. It could only have been arson.

Farynor was woken by his apprentice at about two in the morning. The house was already thick with smoke. The baker roused his wife, his son and daughter, and the maidservant. They 'felt themselves almost choked with smoke, and rising, did find the fire coming up the stairs'. Farynor noted that the fire was nowhere near his ovens, and that the stack of kindling that lay next to them was not alight – further proof, to his mind, that the fire was started deliberately, by an outsider. Since the stairs were aflame, escaping by the front door was out of the question, so the four Farynors and the two servants made their way to the top of the house where there was a garret window that gave out on to the roof of the house next door. One by one they climbed out and shimmied along the gutter to their neighbours' roof window. But the maidservant lost her nerve and refused to clamber along the roof. She stayed behind and was burned to death – the first victim of the Great Fire of London.

By now the fire had an audience. Lodgers at The Star Inn, a coaching house immediately behind the baker's on Fish Street Hill, crowded into the galleried courtyard to watch the show. At about three o'clock in the morning, the roof of the baker's shop fell, sending a fountain of sparks into the sky. The burning fragments rained down on the heads of the onlookers, sending them running for cover. Some sparks fell on the bales of hay intended for feeding the horses. Instead the hay fed the fire: The Star was ablaze within minutes.

It was about now that the glow of the fire was spotted by Pepys's servant-girl Jane, who was working into the night to get things ready for the next day's lunch: Samuel and Elizabeth had guests coming. To her the fire looked serious enough to warrant troubling the master. He disagreed:

> I rose and slipped on my nightgown, and went to her window, and thought it to be on the backside of Mark Lane at the farthest. But being unused to such fires as followed, I thought it far enough off. And so went to bed again and to sleep. About seven rose again to dress myself, and there looked out at the window, and saw the fire not so much as it was and further off.

In the meantime Thomas Bludworth, the Lord Mayor, had been called to the scene. He arrived bleary-eyed at about four in the morning, and was evidently none too pleased to have been dragged out of bed at this unseemly hour. No more than three or four houses were afire at this point, and there seemed to be no special cause for alarm. So Bludworth made the remark that damned him in the eyes of his contemporaries and of posterity: 'A woman could piss it out,' he said, and then went back to his house, which was far away at the other end of the City.

The First Morning

It is not surprising that both Pepys and Bludworth underestimated the little local fire on Pudding Lane. Fires were commonplace in London, and they rarely spread over more than a street or two at most. But circumstances were conspiring to maximize the destructive potential of this blaze. First, there was the time of night when it started – 'on a Sunday morning, a time when most persons, especially the poorer sort, were but newly in bed and in their first dead sleep,' wrote a London preacher named Edward Waterhouse.

> **And thence might the fire get a more than ordinary rooting, from the leisure of its burning before it was met with check or suppression. Yea, when it was discovered, the usual custom being to lie in bed on Sunday might make men more indulge their ease and remit their early stirring and wonted vigour.**

In other words, most citizens were, like Pepys, happy at first to watch, or better yet to sleep, in the expectation that the fire would burn itself out. This meant there was time for the fire to take hold, and for another factor to come into play: the weather. On the night that the fire started there was a strong east wind. It had been rattling the shop signs on their hinges and whistling through the chimney stacks since Saturday evening, and in the hour or two before dawn, the high wind drove the flames down Fish Street Hill and Pudding Lane at a rate that astonished eyewitnesses. The swift spread of the flames was abetted by the fact that London had been hot and rainless all summer. The timber-framed houses that made up most of the City's buildings were as dry as twigs.

Then there was the inaccessibility of the exact spot in which the fire broke out. Pudding Lane, says Waterhouse, was a ...

> **... pitiful little lane, crowden in behind Eastcheap on the west, St Botolph's Lane on the east and Thames Street on the south of it ... [The fire] ... met with no opposition from engines or other artifices because it was impossible in such a strait [narrow place] and in such a rage of fire that they should be serviceable. For if all the engineers of mischief would have compacted the irremediable burning of London, they could not have laid the scene of their fatal contrivance more desperately, to a probable success than there where it was, where narrow streets, old**

buildings all of timber, all contiguous to each other, all stuffed with aliment for the fire, all in the very heart of the trade and wealth of the city. These all concentring in this place put a great share of the mischief upon the choice of the place.

Topography also played a part in the third circumstance that allowed the fire to grow so rapidly. Fish Street Hill led straight down to London Bridge, and to Thames Street, which ran alongside the north bank of the river. The street was lined with warehouses, all of which were packed with highly inflammable goods. It was 'the lodge of all combustibles,' said Waterhouse.

Oil, hemp, flax, pitch, tar, cordage, hops, wine, brandies and other materials favourable to fire, all heavy goods being warehoused there near the water side and all the wharfs for coal, timber, wood &c. being in a line consumed by it.

So the first lick of fire to reach Thames Street was like a taper put to a fuse. As soon as one warehouse went up, the next one was bound to catch alight, and so on down the street almost as far as the Tower of London.

By first light on Sunday, the flames were out of control. The church of St Magnus the Martyr, at the bottom of Fish Street Hill, was burning merrily. The fire had also crept on to London Bridge, which was lined with shops and houses like an ordinary street. The flames had reached as far as an accidental gap in the houses – a legacy of a fire that had occurred in 1632. The fire on the bridge effectively cut off the only southerly escape route for Londoners, and made it impossible for help to reach the city from the far side of the river. A few flying sparks reached Southwark and set alight a stableyard, but the fire was quickly extinguished – nipped in the bud, as perhaps should have been the case on Pudding Lane.

At some time around eight o'clock in the morning, Pepys began to take notice of the situation half a mile away to the west. It was Jane the maid who, once again, alerted the consummate reporter Pepys to the fact that this really was an event worthy of his attention.

By and by, Jane comes and tells me that she hears that above 300 houses have been burned down tonight by the fire we saw, and that it is now burning down all Fishstreet by London Bridge. So I made myself ready and walked to the Tower, and there got up upon one of the high places, Sir J Robinsons little son going up with me. And there I did see the houses at that end of the bridge all on fire, and an infinite great fire on this and the other side the end of the bridge ... So down, with my heart full of trouble, to the Lieutenant of the Tower, who tells me that it begun this morning in the King's baker's house in Pudding-lane, and that it hath burned St. Magnes Church and most part of Fishstreete already. So I down to the water-side, and there got a boat and through bridge, and there saw a lamentable fire. Poor Michell's house, as far as the Old Swan, already burned that way, and the fire running further, that in a very little time it got as far as the Still Yard, while I was there.

In the passage that follows, Pepys's description of the fire is impressionistic and immediate, like pages torn from a journalist's notebook. But alongside the lively scenes of panic and the memorable image of the dying pigeons, there is a growing sense that this is a personal disaster for Pepys, for he was watching the immolation of the streets he grew up in, and the destruction of the homes of people he knew and loved.

Everybody endeavouring to remove their goods, and flinging into the river or bringing them into lighters that lay off. Poor people staying in their houses as long as till the very fire touched them, and then running into boats, or clambering from one pair of stairs by the water-side to another. And among other things, the poor pigeons, I perceive, were loth to leave their houses, but hovered about the windows and balconies till they were, some of them burned, their wings, and fell down.

Having stayed, and in an hour's time seen the fire rage every way, and nobody, to my sight, endeavouring to quench it, but to remove their goods, and leave all to the fire, and having seen it get as far as the Still Yard, and the wind mighty high and driving it into the City; and every thing, after so long a drought, proving combustible, even the very stones of churches, and among other things the poor steeple by which pretty Mrs Horsley lives, and whereof my old school-fellow Elborough is parson, taken fire in the very top, and there burned till it fell down: I to Whitehall, and there up to the King's closet in the Chapel.

So it was that Pepys, having been rather slow to appreciate the gravity of the situation, was the first to bring news of the fire to the king. While he waited to be summoned into the royal presence, he told anyone who would listen what he had seen, and gathered quite a crowd around himself – very much the messenger from the front line and, for a short while, the centre of attention. Charles and his brother heard Pepys's report and 'seemed much troubled'. News quickly spread around Westminster. William Taswell, a schoolboy at the time, was in church when the news reached him.

On Sunday, between 10 and 11 forenoon, as I was standing upon the steps which lead up to the pulpit in Westminster Abbey, I perceived some people below me running to and fro in a seeming disquietude and consternation. Immediately almost a report reached my ears that London was in a conflagration. Without any ceremony I took my leave of the preacher and, having ascended Parliament Steps near the Thames, I soon perceived four boats crowded with objects of distress. These had escaped from the fire scarce under any other covering except that of a blanket. The wind blowing strong eastward, the flames at last reached Westminster. I myself saw great flakes carried up in to the air at least three furlongs. These at last, picking up and uniting themselves to various dry substances, set on fire houses very remote from each other.

Taswell was writing years after the event, and has exaggerated the extent of the fire. The flames never reached Westminster, or even came close. But he surely would have seen the smoke and flames from his vantage point close to the river. He saw something else even more sinister that morning: the first stirrings of the London rabble looking for someone to blame.

The ignorant and deluded mob, who upon the occasion were hurried away with a kind of frenzy, vented forth their rage against the Roman Catholics and Frenchmen, imagining these incendiaries (as they thought) had thrown red hot balls into the houses. A blacksmith in my presence, meeting an innocent Frenchman walking along the street, felled him instantly to the ground with an iron bar. I could not help seeing the innocent blood of this exotic flowing in a plentiful stream down to his ankles. In another place I saw the incensed populace divesting a French painter of all the goods he had in his shop and, after having helped him off with many other things, levelling his house to the ground under the pretence that they thought himself was desirous of setting his own house on fire that the conflagration might become more general. My brother told me he saw a Frenchman almost dismembered in Moorfields because he carried balls of fire in a chest with him, when in truth they were only tennis balls.

The rumours about French firestarters grew in size and ferocity even faster than the fire itself. By midday on that first day, it was being said that entire regiments of foreign enemies were on the march.

In this interval of time, when the fury of the common people burst forth with an irresistible torrent upon these unhappy objects of distress, a report ... prevailed that four thousand French and Papists were in arms, intending to carry with them death and destruction and increase the conflagration. Upon which every person both in City and suburbs, having procured some sort of weapon or other, instantly collected themselves together to oppose this chimeral army.

The Fire Spreads Wider

Some devout Londoners went to church that Sunday morning – fire or no fire.

> Never was there the like Sabbath in London. Some churches were in flames that day, and the Lord seems to come down, and to preach himself in them, as he did in Mount Sinai when the Mount burned with fire. Such warm preaching those churches never had. Such lightning dreadful sermons never were before delivered in London.

So wrote Thomas Vincent, the Puritan preacher who had documented the plague the previous year. He was certain that this was another Biblical punishment – not Egypt this time, but the cities of the plain.

> Goods are removed from the lower parts of the city, and the body of the people begin to retire ... rather as Lot drew out from his house in Sodom before it was consumed by fire from heaven. Yet some hopes were retained on the Lord's day that the fire would be extinguished, especially by them that lived in the remote parts. They could scarcely imagine that the fire a mile off should be able to reach their houses ... Some are upon their knees, interceding for poor London in the days of its calamity, but ... London's sins were too great, and God's anger against the city was too hot so easily and presently to be quenched and allayed ... And if, by the intercession of some a mitigation be obtained, so that the Lord doth not stir up all his wrath utterly to destroy the place as he did Sodom and Gomorrah, yet none can prevail to call back that wrath and reverse that decree which is gone forth against the city. The time of London's fall is come ... and therefore all attempts to hinder it are in vain.

Pepys, for one, was doing his best to hinder it. By mid-morning he was on his way back to the burning city. The king had ordered him to find

the Lord Mayor and tell him to tear down the houses in the path of the
fire. Pepys set off in a coach, but soon came up against the contrary flow
of people escaping the fire with all they could carry. He got out of the
coach and proceeded on foot. It was the middle of the afternoon by
the time that Pepys found the mayor. The formerly nonchalant Mayor
Bludworth was close to panic:

**I walked along Watling-street as well as I could, wrote Pepys.
Every creature coming away loaden with goods to save, and here
and there sick people carried away in beds. Extraordinary goods
carried in carts and on backs. At last met my Lord Mayor in
Canning Streete, like a man spent, with a hankercher about his
neck. To the King's message he cried, like a fainting woman,
'Lord! what can I do? I am spent! People will not obey me. I have
been pulling down houses, but the fire overtakes us faster than we
can do it.' That he needed no more soldiers; and that for himself,
he must go and refresh himself, having been up all night.**

With this self-aggrandizing little fib – he had only been up for a couple
of hours in the night, after all – Thomas Bludworth fades from most
accounts of the burning of London. The next day the king's brother,
the Duke of York, was put in charge of all firefighting efforts in the
City of London.

Pepys now went home. His dinner guests had turned up despite the
fire. Pepys had it in mind to show off all the little treasures in his closet,
but that seemed inappropriate when the city was being consumed
outside. Instead, Pepys and one of his visitors, a Mr Moone, went
off for a walk after their meal to see how the fire was progressing.

**I and Moone away and walked through the City, the streets full
of nothing but people and horses and carts loaden with goods,
ready to run over one another, and removing goods from one
burned house to another – they now removing out of Canning-
street (which received goods in the morning) into Lumbard
Streete and further; and among others, I now saw my little**

> goldsmith Stokes receiving some friend's goods, whose house
> itself was burned the day after. We parted at Pauls, he home and
> I to Pauls-Wharf, where I had appointed a boat to attend me.

Pepys sailed back and forth, inspecting the growing extent of the flames.
He felt sure that the fire was unstoppable, but was more optimistic when
he went to discuss the situation with the king and the Duke of York,
who were watching events from their barge.

> Their order was only to pull down houses apace, and so below
> bridge at the water-side; but little was or could be done, the fire
> coming upon them so fast. Good hopes there was of stopping it
> at the Three Cranes above, and at Buttolphs-Wharf below bridge,
> if care be used; but the wind carries it into the City, so as we
> know not by the water-side what it doth there.

Therein lay the problem: no one had an overview of the extent of the
fire. There was no point in pulling down or blowing up houses at the
water's edge if the main thrust of the fire was now to the north, away
from the river altogether.

While Pepys was pondering the enormity of the problem, he effected
one of the sudden shifts of focus that make him so interesting a
chronicler of his times. He was suddenly intrigued by the fact that many
of the boats being used to salvage household treasures contained
keyboard instruments.

> River full of lighter[s] and boats taking in goods, and good goods
> swimming in the water; and only, I observed that hardly one
> lighter or boat in three that had the goods of a house in, but
> there was a pair of virginalls in it.

With this thought in mind, he went ashore and walked to Whitehall,
where he had arranged to meet up with his wife. They caught a boat
back home, and so were obliged to make a waterborne excursion
through the heart of the fire.

So near the fire as we could for smoke. And all over the Thames with one's face in the wind you were almost burned with a shower of firedrops – this is very true – so as houses were burned by these drops and flakes of fire, three or four, nay five or six houses, one from another. When we could endure no more upon the water, we to a little alehouse on the Bankside over against the Three Cranes, and there stayed till it was dark almost and saw the fire grow; and as it grow darker, appeared more and more, and in corners and upon steeples and between churches and houses, as far as we could see up the hill of the City, in the a most horrid malicious bloody flame, not like the fine flame of an ordinary fire ... We stayed till, it being darkish, we saw the fire as only one entire arch of fire from this to the other side the bridge, and in a bow up the hill, for an arch of above a mile long. It made me weep to see it. The churches, houses, and all on fire and flaming at once, and a horrid noise the flames made, and the cracking of houses at their ruine.

Samuel and Elizabeth arrived home to find all their neighbours 'discoursing, and lamenting the fire'. Then Tom Hayter, one of Pepys's clerks, came by. He had been burned out of his home on Fish Street Hill, and carried with him everything he had been able to rescue from his home.

Hayter needed a place to sleep, which Pepys readily gave him. But sleep was impossible, and soon both men were hard at work removing Pepys's possessions from the path of the fire.

I invited him to lie at my house, and did receive his goods, but deceived in his lying there, the noise coming every moment of the growth of the Fire, so as we were forced to begin to pack up our own goods, and prepare for their removal. And did by Moone-shine ... carry much of my goods into the garden, and Mr. Hater and I did remove my money and Iron-chests into my cellar – as thinking that the safest place. And got my bags of gold into my office ready to carry away, and my chief papers of accounts also

there, and my tallies into a box by themselfs. So great was our
fear, as Sir W. Batten had carts come out of the country to fetch
away his goods this night. We did put Mr. Hater, poor man, to
bed a little; but he got but very little rest, so much noise being in
my house, taking down of goods.

Thomas Vincent also watched the sun go down on the first full day
of the fire. To Vincent's Puritan eyes, the spectacle that presented
itself around midnight was the very picture of the fate that awaited
all sinners:

But the evening draws on, and now the fire is more visible and
dreadful. Instead of the black curtains of night, which used to be
spread over the city, now the curtains are yellow, the smoke that
arose from the burning parts, seemed like so much flame in the
night, which being blown upon the other parts by the wind, the
whole city at some distance seemed to be on fire.

Now hopes begin to sink, and a general consternation seizeth
upon the spirits of people: little sleep is taken in London this
night; the amazement which the eye and ear doth effect upon the
spirit, doth either dry up, or drive away the vapour which used
to bind up the senses: some are at work to quench the fire with
water, others endeavour to stop its course, by pulling down of
houses; but all to no purpose: if it be a little allayed, or beaten
down, or put to a stand in some places, it is but a very little
while; it quickly recruits, and recovers its force; it leaps and
mounts, and makes the more furious onset, drives backs its
opposers, snatcheth their weapons out of their hands, seizeth
upon their water-houses and engines, burns them, spoils them,
and makes them unfit for service.

On the Lord's day night the fire had run as far as Garlick-hithe,
in Thames-street; and had crept up into Cannon-street, and
levelled it with the ground, and still is making forward by the
water side, and upward to the brow of the hill, on which the city
was built.

A Universal Conflagration

On Monday, 3 September, John Evelyn went with his wife and son to see the fire. They took a coach to Bankside, across the river from St Paul's. It was a ringside seat.

We beheld that dismal spectacle, the whole city in dreadful flames near the waterside. All the houses from the Bridge, all Thames-street and upwards towards Cheapside, down to the Three Cranes, were now consumed, and so returned, exceeding astonished what would become of the rest.

Later Evelyn went back without his family to take a closer look. This time, as he wandered the streets north of the river, he was struck not so much by the spectacular horror of a city aflame, but by the many human tragedies that were playing out on the burning streets. Everyone seemed to be in a kind of trance:

The conflagration was so universal, and the people so astonished that ... they hardly stirred to quench it. So that there was nothing heard or seen but crying out and lamentation, running about like distracted creatures without at all attempting to save even their goods. Such a strange consternation there was upon them, so as it burned both in breadth and length, the churches, public halls, Exchange, hospitals, monuments and ornaments, leaping after a prodigious manner from house to house and street to street, at great distances one from the other ... The fire devoured after an incredible manner: houses, furniture and everything.

A full-scale evacuation was now under way. As London Bridge was impassable, people were trying to ferry themselves and their valuables across the river by boat, and then transfer them to a cart on the far side.

Here we saw the Thames covered with goods floating, all the barges and boats laden with what some had time and courage

> to save, as, on the other side, the carts &c. carrying out to the
> fields, which for many miles were strewed with movables of all
> sorts, and tents erecting to shelter both people and what goods
> they could get away.

Transport of any kind was of course at a premium, and it was a seller's
market. Vincent was disgusted by the way that carters and draymen
used the fire to make a quick profit.

> Carts and drays and coaches and horses, as many as could have
> entrance into the city, were loaden, and any money is given for
> help: £5, £10, £20, £30 for a cart to bear forth into the fields
> some choice things. Some of the countries [country people] had
> the conscience to accept of the highest price which the citizens
> did then offer in their extremity. I am mistaken if such money
> did not burn worse than the fire out of which it was raked.

Those who could not pay inflated prices for a cart saved only as much
as they could carry. 'Casks of wine and oil and other commodities are
tumbled along ...' continues Vincent,

> ... and the owners shove as much of their goods as they can
> towards the gates. Everyone now becomes a porter to himself,
> and scarcely a back, either of man or woman that hath strength,
> but had a burden on it in the street. It was very sad to see such
> throngs of poor citizens coming in and going forth from the
> unburnt parts, heavy loaden with some pieces of their goods, but
> more heavy loaden with weighty grief and sorrow of heart, so
> that it is wonderful they did not quite sink under these burdens.

Pepys had made arrangements for removing his own goods. It was a
prudent precaution: the fire was some way from the eastern end of the
city where he lived, and seemed to be heading west. But the wife of one
of his Navy Board colleagues had sent Pepys a cart before first light on
Monday. Pepys loaded it with 'all my money and plate and best things'

– including the notebooks containing the diary – and still in his nightgown rode with it to the house of a rich merchant friend in rural Bethnal Green. No one in London, Pepys included, had been able to get much sleep, so even at this early hour 'the streets and the highways are crowded with people, running and riding and getting carts of any rate to fetch away things.' It was a tortuous journey back from Bethnal Green, but worth it: 'I am eased at heart to have my treasure so well secured.' Pepys was at his desk on Seething Lane by the official start of the working week.

It was on that same Monday morning that James, Duke of York, began to take command of the firefighting effort. His authoritative presence was useful on its own. 'He did ride with his guard up and down the City to keep all quiet,' wrote Pepys, and the presence of armed soldiery must have made the looters and thieves think twice. But it was the Duke's organizational skills and military experience that made the real difference. Carts were banned from coming back into the city, so easing the great traffic jam that had formed at all the gates. Moves were made by the Privy Council to revoke the ancient city ordinance which said that any man who tore down a house was responsible for rebuilding it (the feckless Bludworth had felt bound by this by-law, and so was reluctant to start making firebreaks on the Sunday). Gawping spectators were put to work. The Westminster scholar William Taswell was one of those suddenly drafted to serve as a fireman:

> John Dobson, dean of Westminster, collected his scholars
> together in a company, marching with them on foot to put a
> stop to the conflagration. I was a kind of page to him. We were
> employed many hours in fetching water from the back side of
> St Dunstan's church in the East, where we happily extinguished
> the fire.

The Westminster boys might have won this little skirmish, but the fire was gaining ground in most places. It was rampant in the heart of the city, where soldiers were (at last) employed in pulling down houses with hooks and ropes. It was a losing battle, because sparks and burning brands were being carried on the wind over the top of the demolished houses and so new fires were constantly breaking out ahead of the main line of the blaze.

By Monday evening the fire had spread west along the riverfront as far as the old fortress of Baynard's Castle, which 'did yield like a paper building to the fire'. In the east it had reached Billingsgate at the river's edge, and was just short of St Dunstan's, where young William Taswell was on duty with his bucket. At Leadenhall, an alderman had turned up and distributed money to anyone who would help in the effort to fight the flames. His impromptu mercenaries managed to save nearby India House, the headquarters of the East India Company, along with most of the fabulous wealth in spices that the building in Leadenhall contained.

But there was terrible destruction further away from the river. The fire had pushed north, crossing Cannon Street, and scorching its way through the financial heart of the City. Lombard Street, Threadneedle Street, and the Royal Exchange were all gone. So were Cornhill, 'that large and spacious street' – and Gracechurch Street, where Mayor Bludworth had gone home to his warm bed two nights before.

Thomas Vincent witnessed the destruction of the Exchange. But it was the terrific noise of the fire, more than the sight of it, that took his breath away.

The flames quickly cross the way by the train of wood that lay in the streets untaken away, which had been pulled down from the houses. They mount up to the top of the highest houses; they descend down to the bottom of the lowest vaults and cellars; and march along on both sides of the way with such a roaring noise as never was heard in the city of London.

No stately building so great as to resist their fury. The Royal Exchange itself, the glory of the merchants, is now invaded with much violence. And when once the fire was entered, how quickly did it run round the galleries, filling them with flames; then descendeth the stairs, compasseth the walks, giving forth flaming volleys, and filled the courts with sheets of fire. By and by, down

fall all the kings upon their faces, and the greatest part of the
stone building after them, with such a noise as was dreadful
and astonishing.

Then, then the city did shake indeed, and the inhabitants did
tremble, and flew away in great amazement from their houses,
lest the flames should devour them. Rattle, rattle, rattle was the
noise which the fire struck upon the ear round about, as if there
had been a thousand iron chariots beating upon the stones. And
if you opened your eye to the opening of the streets where the
fire was come, you might see in some places whole streets at once
in flames that issued forth as if they had been so many great
forges from the opposite windows, which folding together were
united into one great flame. And then you might see the houses
tumble, tumble, tumble with a great crash, leaving the
foundations open to the view of the Heavens.

By Monday evening, flames were licking at the eastern end of
Cheapside, the main highway leading west through the centre of the
City to the great stone massif of St Paul's. Evelyn was almost overcome
by the extent of the desolation when he explored it all in the Monday
afternoon. It seemed to him that London was dead.

Oh, the miserable and calamitous spectacle, such as haply the world
has not seen since the foundation of it, nor be outdone till the
universal conflagration thereof. God grant mine eyes may never
behold the like, who now saw about ten thousand houses all in one
flame! The noise and the cracking and thunder of the impetuous
flames, the shrieking of women and children, the hurry of people, the
fall of towers, houses, and churches, was like a hideous storm; and
the air all about so hot and inflamed that at the last one was not able
to approach it, so that they were forced to stand still and let the
flames burn on, which they did, for near two miles in length and one
in breadth. The clouds also of smoke were dismal, and reached upon
computation near fifty miles in length. Thus I left it this afternoon
burning ... London was, but is no more.

Burning up the Bowels of London

On Monday night, the fire crept up Tower Street towards Seething
Lane, where Pepys and the naval commissioners lived and worked.
So Pepys spent the first part of Tuesday as he had Monday morning:
making sure that his personal property was secure. He carried some
bits and pieces down to the river and had them ferried away on a
lighter – if the Clerk of the Acts of the Navy Board couldn't lay his
hands on a boat in a crisis, then who could? After seeing his
possessions off to Woolwich, Pepys went home and helped Sir William
Penn dig a hole in the back garden at Seething Lane. Here they buried
some official papers that they had not been able to send away. That
job done, the two men sat in the garden, breathing the smoky air and
contemplating the imminent destruction of their homes. As they
talked over this sad prospect, Pepys had an idea. It occured to him that
the 'king's business' would be much hindered if the offices of the Navy
Board burned down, and so (without mentioning his ulterior motive)
he sent a message to the Duke of York asking that some houses be
pulled down on Tower Street to prevent the fire reaching the vital
building where he happened to live. The two naval men then had
a second self-serving thought: they should dig another hole in the
garden and inter their separate stocks of wine. This they did in the
hazy afternoon; Pepys famously deposited his 'parmazan cheese' in
the hole for safe keeping.

The Duke of York himself came by the office on Seething Lane
during the afternoon, but Pepys somehow missed him – perhaps he was
out the back burying his precious Parmesan. The Duke was surely too
busy to stay long. Like a general on the battlefield, he assigned different
portions of the front line to various lieutenants. The main thrust of
the firefighters' efforts was to prevent the fire from invading the seat
of government at Westminster. Here is an account, written by one
of his retainers, of how the future King James II led the charge.

> Being constant with the Duke, I presume to believe none have
> seen more of it than I have, he being so active and stirring in this

business, he being all the day long, from five in the morning till eleven or twelve at night, using all means possible to save the rest of the city and the suburbs. On Tuesday our only hope was to save Fleet Street, and so to Whitehall, by pulling down houses both sides of Bridewell Dock – so to make a good broad lane up from the river to Holborn Bridge. The Duke's station was from Fleet Bridge to the river; Lord Craven, next to the Duke most active in the business, was to come from Holborn Bridge to Fleet Bridge.

The Duke on Tuesday, about twelve o'clock, was environed with fire. The high wind blowed such flakes, and so far, that they fired Salisbury Court and several of the houses between that and Bridewell Dock, so the Duke was forced to fly for it, and had almost been stifled with the heat. The next hope there was to stop it at Somerset House, it raged so extreme in Fleet Street on both sides and got between us, and at six of the clock to the King's Bench Office at the Temple. Night coming on, the flames so increased by the wind rising, which appeared to us so terrible to see. At ten o'clock at night we left Somerset House, where they began to pull down some houses in hopes to save Whitehall.

Had the Duke not been present, and forced all people to submit to his orders, by this time I am confident there had not been a house standing near Whitehall. The city, for the first rank, they minded only for their own preservation; the middle sort so distracted and amazed that they did not know what they did; the poorer, they minded nothing but pilfering; so the city abandoned to the fire, and thousands believing in Mother Shipton's prophecy 'that London in sixty-six should be burnt to ashes.'

Mother Shipton's prophecy was an early urban myth: there was no such person, and there was no more to the oracular saying than that one sentence. Yet somehow everyone had heard of the mythical Shipton and her vision. And enough people saw the hand of fate in the conflagration to make the prediction self-fulfilling. Why fight the fire when the Mother Shipton had already said that London was doomed?

The Duke of York, at least, put more faith in water pumps than imaginary prophets.

At eleven of the clock on Tuesday night came several messengers to the Duke for help, and for the engines, and said that there was some hopes of stopping it; that the wind was got to the south, and by that means had took off the great rage of the fire ... and gave a check to it. We had not this mercy shown to us alone, but likewise hearts and hands from the people – the soldiers being almost all tired out with continual labour.

The Duke had been in mortal danger for a time, when the fire surrounded him at Salisbury Court, not far from the city boundary. (It is intriguing to think how differently the course of English history might have run if he had died that day – and England not found itself with a Catholic prince on the throne after the death of Charles II.) But for all his strenuous efforts, the Duke had been fighting a losing battle the entire day. And yet his retreat ahead of the fire in the west was not the gravest defeat of that terrible Tuesday. Far worse damage was done within the old City walls.

During Monday night the fire had been checked at the 'great conduit', where the east–west highway of Poultry becomes Cheapside. Here was a chance to make a really effective firebreak: Cheapside, the main shopping street of the city, was also one of the widest. Some judicious demolition here might have stopped the flames in their tracks. But time was short, because on Tuesday several independent blazes were making their way up the tributary streets leading up to Cheapside from the south.

On Tuesday was the fire burning up the very bowels of London, wrote Vincent. **Cheapside is all in a light fire in a few hours' time – many fires meeting there as in the centre. From Soper-Lane, Bow-lane, Bread-street, Friday-street and Old Change the fire comes up almost together and breaks furiously into the broad street, and most of that side of the way was together in flames, a dreadful spectacle.**

It was too late to save the ancient streets and buildings on the south side of Cheapside, and attempts to prevent the fire gaining a hold across the way came too late. The fire forded Cheapside and proceeded in separate columns up the streets on the north side. The entire medieval City, and with it a millennium and a half of history, was now doomed to go up in flames.

Partly by the fire which came down by Mercers' chapel, partly by the fall of the houses across the way, the other side is quickly kindled, and doth not stand long after it ... Now Cheapside fire marcheth along Ironmonger-lane, Old Jury, Lawrence-lane, Milk-street, Wood-street, Gutter-lane, Foster-lane. Now horrible flakes of fire mount up the sky, and the yellow smoke of London ascendeth up towards heaven like the smoke of a great furnace: a smoke so great as darkened the sun at noon-day. If at any time the sun peeped forth it looked red like blood.

Lawrence Lane led straight to the Guildhall, the jewel of the City. This 'fayre and goodly house' had been built during the reign of Henry V more than 200 years before. Its pavement and its glazing had been paid for in part with money bequeathed by Mayor Richard Whittington – the Dick Whittington of legend. Guildhall was the administrative headquarters of the City, London's townhall. Both in its Gothic structure and its civic function, it resembled the striking medieval *hôtels de ville* of Belgium and northern France. Its great hall was the place where the Lord Mayors and sheriffs were elected, and where Lady Jane Grey had stood trial for her life in 1533. It was the third largest such hall in the kingdom. All in all it was a beautiful building, and now it burned with a terrible beauty – 'without flames,' said Vincent, 'I suppose because the timber was such solid oak – in a bright shining coal, as if it had been a palace of gold, or a great building of burnished brass.' But the stone walls withheld when the oak timbers gave way and the roof fell in, and the whole was later repaired and restored. In architectural terms, Guildhall was one of the few noteworthy survivors of the Great Fire.

Old St Paul's

The most notable victim of the fire met its end this same night. St Paul's Cathedral rose above the medieval city like a great stone ark floating on a sea of rooftops. It was an immense presence – much larger than Wren's replacement was to be. Its spire was the tallest ever built while it lasted: it was struck by lightning in 1561 and fell down, never to be replaced. Consequently, the central bell tower was in Pepys time rather squat – it looked ominously like a stumpy little chimney.

The cathedral was the solid core at the centre of a maze-like network of lanes and alleyways where lived the many clerics who served the church. This ancient precinct had a definite boundary, which is marked even today by the streets that take their names from the Latin liturgy: Creed Lane, Paternoster Row, Ave Maria Lane – along with the more profane-sounding Old Change and Carter Lane. The area within the precinct was a seat of learning as well as of religion (the two things had only recently come to be seen as separate spheres of human activity). London's lively book trade flourished in many tiny shops around St Paul's Churchyard. Here and hereabouts were the stationers and bookbinders, the printers and purveyors of maps and ballads, the vendors of new works and antiquities whose tiny shops were haunted by Pepys and inveterate bibliophiles like him. All the different species of bookmen had as their guild church St Faith, which was located in the subterranean crypt of St Paul's. Just beyond the eastern end of the building, on Old Change was St Paul's School. It had founded by John Colet, dean of the cathedral, in 1509. The young scholars numbered 153, a number that, according to tradition, was the precise quantity of fish miraculously netted by the disciples after their first encounter with Jesus on the shores of Galilee.

The school contained an irreplaceable library. It went up in smoke along with the school building soon after midday. But the churchyard itself acted as a cordon: the fire did not touch St Paul's, but encircled it to north and south by burning along Paternoster Row and Carter Lane. These two fingers of fire joined up again at the western end of the cathedral and 'rushed like a torrent' down Ludgate Hill towards Fleet

Street. At this point, the cathedral was ringed with fire, but was unscathed. Like its successor, which remained gloriously intact through the devastating blitz of 1940, it seemed for a time to be guarded by some special providence.

But its luck ran out soon after dark. Wooden scaffolding on the tower caught alight, and led the flames upwards to some boards on the roof – stacked there carefully in anticipation of a major renovation, which had been approved the previous week. Vincent saw that the razing of the cathedral began on the roof, and was at a loss to explain how this had come to pass:

> The church, though all of stone outward, though naked of houses about it, and though so high above all the buildings in the city, yet within a while doth yield to the violent assaults of the conquering flames, and strangely takes fire at the top.

William Taswell saw the same strange phenomenon from three miles away.

> Just after sunset I went to the royal bridge in the New Palace at Westminster to take a fuller view of the fire. As I stood upon the bridge among many others, I could not but observe the gradual approaches of the fire towards that venerable fabric. About 8 o'clock it broke out on the top of St Paul's Church, already scorched up by the violent heat of the air and lightning too. And before long it blazed so conspicuous as to enable me to read very clearly an edition of Terence which I carried in my pocket.

The cathedral was now a kind of man-made volcano. Chunks of masonry exploded in the intense heat and 'flew like grenadoes'. The lead sheeting on the vast roof melted 'as if it had been snow before the sun'. It gushed down the walls of the church like lava and formed a molten lake on the floor of the nave, before 'running down the streets in a stream, and the very pavements glowing with fiery redness, so as no horse, nor man, was able to tread on them.' At the same time 'great

beams and massy stones with a great noise fall on the pavement and
break through into Faith Church underneath. And great flakes of stone
scale and peel off strangely from the side of the walls.'

The breach of the crypt, where St Faith's was located, was a financial
catastophe for the many booksellers whose premises were clustered
around the church.

> **Most of the booksellers in St Paul's Churchyard carried their
> books into the vaults under that Cathedral, where it was thought
> almost impossible for the fire to come,** wrote an observer named
> Richard Baxter. **But the church taking fire, the weighty stones
> falling down broke into the vaults and let in the fire, and there
> was no coming near to save the books.**

About £150,000 pounds' worth of stock were destroyed. The books
burned slowly but continuously over the course of the next week –
'a very great detriment to the interest of piety and learning', as well
as to the pockets of the bookmen.

John Evelyn was keen to assess the extent of the damage to St Paul's
as soon as possible. He surveyed the smouldering wreck on the Saturday
after the fire.

> **I was infinitely concerned to find that goodly church, St Paul's,
> now a sad ruin. And that beautiful portico now rent in pieces,
> flakes of vast stone split asunder and nothing remaining entire
> but the inscription in the architrave showing by whom it was
> built – and not one letter of it defaced.**
>
> **It was astonishing to see what immense stones the heat had in
> a manner calcined, so that all the ornaments, columns, friezes,
> capitals and projectures of massy Portland stone flew off, even
> to the very roof ... The lead over the altar at the east end was
> untouched, and among the divers monuments the body of one
> bishop remained entire. Thus lay in ashes that most venerable
> church, one of the most ancient pieces of early piety in the
> Christian world.**

The intrepid schoolboy William Taswell also wanted to see what had become of St Paul's. He got there before Evelyn and saw something more awful and poignant than the scorched portico.

On Thursday, soon after sunrise, I endeavoured to reach St Paul's. The ground so hot as almost to scorch my shoes, and the air so intensely warm that, unless I stopped sometimes to rest myself, I must have fainted under the extreme languour of my spirits. And giving myself a little time to breathe I made the best of my way to St Paul's.

And now let any person judge of the violent emotion I was in when I perveived the metal belonging to the bells melting, the ruinous condition of its walls, whole heaps of stone of a large circumference tumbling down with a great noise just upon my feet, ready to crush me to death. I prepared myself for returning back again, having first loaded my pockets with several pieces of bell metal.

I forgot to mention that near the east walls of St Paul's a human body presented itself to me, parched up as it were with the flames, whole as to skin, meagre as to flesh, yellow as to colour. This was an old decrepit woman who had fled here for safety, imagining the flames would not have reached her there. Her clothes were burnt, and every limb reduced to a coal.

Yet more gruesome to behold were the bodies of those long dead whose tombs had burst open as if the Day of Judgment had come. Within the choir was found the exposed remains of Robert de Braybroke, one-time Lord Chancellor of England, who had been at rest in the church for 262 years. It was found that his dessicated body had 'teeth in the head, red hair on the head, beard &c., skin and nails on the toes and fingers, without cirecloth, embalming spices, or any other condite'. Braybrooke had been Bishop of London when an earthquake shook the city in 1382. Now he became a posthumous witness to London's latest misfortune. His stiffened, wizened corpse was stood on its feet, then taken to the Chapter House, where it remained on show for a dozen years.

The grave of Dean Colet, founder of St Paul's School, was also laid open. His cadaver was subjected to an undignified and thoroughly nauseating experiment.

After the conflagration, his monument being broken, his coffin, which was lead, was full of a liquor which conserved the body. Mr Wyld and Ralph Greatorex tasted it, and 'twas of a kind of insipid taste, something of an ironish taste. The body felt, to the probe of a stick which they thrust into a chink, like brawn.

Ash Wednesday

On Wednesday, 6 September, scraps of charred paper fell on Eton and Windsor, 35 miles west of the City. The smoke of London had polluted the atmosphere for dozens of miles around. In Oxford, 55 miles to the north-west, an amateur meteorologist named Mr Locke stepped outside his house to make his daily observation of the weather. What he saw was the same blood sun that Vincent had remarked upon two days before. Locke was unaware of its sinister cause.

Dim reddish sunshine, wrote Locke innocently in his log. **This unusual colour of the air, which without a cloud appearing made the sunbeams of a strange red dim light, was very remarkable.**

Vincent was still tramping round the white-hot core of the blaze, thinking of how God spoke to Moses from within a burning bush, and listening for God's voice from the midst of the immolated city. On this fourth day, he detected a hint of divine mercy in the changing course of events.

On Wednesday morning, when people expected that the suburbs would be burnt, as well as the city, and with speed were preparing their flight as well as they could, with their luggage into the countries and the neighbouring villages, then the Lord hath pity on poor London. His bowels begin to relent, his heart is turned

within him, and he 'stays his rough wind in the day of the east wind'. His fury begins to be allayed. He hath a remnant of people in London, and there shall a remnant of houses escape. The wind is now hushed. The commission of the fire is withdrawing, and it burns so gently, even where it meets with no opposition, that it was not hard to be quenched – in many places with a few hands.

Now the citizens begin to gather a little heart and encouragement in their endeavours to quench the fire. A check it had at Leadenhall, by that great building; a stop it had in Bishopsgate-street, Fenchurch-street, Lime-street, Mark-lane, and towards the Tower. One means under God was the blowing-up of houses with gunpowder. Not it is stayed in Lothbury, Broad-street, Coleman-street. Towards the gates it burnt, but not with any great violence. At the Temple also it is stayed, and in Holborn, where it got no great footing. And when once the fire was got under, it was kept under.

In his eagerness to give God the credit, Vincent exaggerates the sudden diminution of the fire. It was still burning fiercely in many places. In the small hours of Wednesday morning it finally crept up on Pepys: 'About 2 in the morning my wife calls me up and tells of new cryes of "Fyre" – it being come up to Barkeing Church, which is [at] the bottom of our lane.'

Pepys had made a plan for this eventuality, and now he set it in motion. He went down to the dockyard and boarded a boat with his wife and his young friend Will Hewer. The three of them sailed downriver to Woolwich. With them they took one vital possession that he had kept in the house until now – his life savings in gold. These amounted to a very respectable £2,350. Elizabeth and Hewer were installed in Woolwich at the house of a work colleague named Mr Shelden, the same man who had played host to Mrs Pepys during the long months of the plague. Pepys locked his gold in the room where his family were to stay. He gave Elizabeth and Hewer strict instructions that they were never to leave the money unattended: one of them was to remain in the room with it all all times.

Having secured all that was most precious to him, Pepys took a boat alone back to London. He arrived at seven in the morning, fully expecting to find his home on fire, and was presently surprised to find that Seething Lane had been saved by the timely blowing-up of nearby houses. Barking Church was not afire – it had got away with a light singeing to the westward-facing tower and porch. Pepys climbed the church's steeple to take a look.

There was the saddest sight of desolation that I ever saw. Everywhere great fires. Oyle-cellars and brimstone and other things burning. I became afeared to stay there long, and therefore down again as fast as I could.

Pepys did not yet know it, but the church where he was standing, now known as All Hallows by the Tower, marked the high-tide of the Great Fire in the east of the city: it went no further in this direction. He went back home, had a bit of cold breakfast with Sir William Penn, and 'received good hopes that the fire at our end is stopped'. Then he and two colleagues walked into the City to see how far those hopes were justified.

Fanchurch-street, Gracious-street [Gracechurch Street] and Lumbard-street all in dust. The Exchange a sad sight, nothing standing there of all the statues or pillars but Sir Tho. Gresham's picture in the corner. Walked into Moore-fields (our feet ready to burn, walking through the town among the hot coles) and find that full of people, and poor wretches carrying their goods there, and everybody keeping his goods together by themselfs (and a great blessing it is to them that it is fair weather for them to keep abroad night and day). Drank there, and paid twopence for a plain penny loaf. Thence homeward, having passed through Cheapside and Newgate market – all burned. And took up (which I keep by me) a piece of glass of Mercers' chapel in the street, where much more was, and so melted and buckled with the heat of the fire, like parchment.

> I also did see a poor catt taken out of a hole in the chimney
> joyning to the wall of the exchange, with the hair all burned
> off the body and yet alive.

Pepys, with his thousands in gold safely stashed in Woolwich, still
baulks at paying double for a loaf of bread, and seems more concerned
for a frightened cat than for the thousands of homeless people stranded
on Moorfields, Tower Hill and in the open countryside beyond the city.
John Evelyn, walking the same streets a day or two later, found it in
himself to express a little compassion for the poor who had lost what
little they had.

> The people who now walked about the ruins appeared like men
> in some dismal desert, or rather in some great city laid waste by
> a cruel enemy. To which was added the stench that came from
> some poor creatures bodies, beds, and other combustible goods ...
> The vast iron chains of the City-streets, hinges, bars, and gates
> of prisons, were many of them melted and reduced to cinders
> by the vehement heat. Nor was I yet able to pass through any
> of the narrow streets, but kept to the widest. The ground and
> air, smoke and fiery vapour, continued so intense that my hair
> was almost singed, and my feet unsufferably surbated. The by-
> lanes and narrow streets were quite filled up with rubbish; nor
> could one have possibly known where he was, but by the ruins
> of some Church, or Hall, that had some remarkable tower, or
> pinnacle remaining.
>   I then went towards Islington and Highgate, where one might
> have seen 200,000 people of all ranks and degrees dispersed,
> and lying along by their heaps of what they could save from the
> fire, deploring their loss; and, though ready to perish for hunger
> and destitution, yet not asking one penny for relief, which to
> me appeared a stranger sight than any I had yet beheld. His
> Majesty and Council indeed took all imaginable care for their
> relief, by proclamation for the country to come in, and refresh
> them with provisions.

All this was at the eastern end of the city. In the west, the fire was still on the move. Workmen were frantically tearing down buildings on Chancery Lane to try and save Lincoln's Inn. Fleet Street was consumed in a matter of two or three hours. The hapless Mayor Bludworth, who had barely been seen since Sunday, was now supervising a demolition crew in Cripplegate, trying to stop the fire gaining ground to the north. Meanwhile, the flames had been brought to a standstill at Pie Corner near Smithfield and on Holborn Bridge. Efforts here were helped by the wind, which had dropped and veered to the south, in the manner that had so impressed Thomas Vincent.

But the flames were racing through the evil riverside slum known as 'Alsatia', south of Fleet Street. Its population of thieves, runaways, prostitutes and cutpurses were scattered to the four winds. Hard against Alsatia, cut off from it by a high wall, was the genteel lawyers' enclave of the Temple. It was now in imminent danger from the flames, and if it were to burn then there was a real possibility that the fire might spread beyond the Temple to Whitehall. The ladies and gentlemen of the Court were in a panic.

The tireless Duke of York was still in the vanguard of the battle, and made himself the man of the hour. He was called to the Temple late in the evening to find the Middle Temple Hall alight. When he arrived with a detachment of soldiers he found that the lawyers had locked the gates for fear of looters. The king's brother – himself a Bencher of the Inner Temple – could not get in to fight the fire. The 'templars' were eventually persuaded to open up, but by that time the Hall was merrily ablaze.

The Duke of York found no way of saving the Temple Chapel and the Hall by the Chapel but blowing up the Paper House in that court, wrote his attendant. Which experiment, if it had been used at first, might have saved a great many houses.

But even now, as their ancient chambers and tended gardens began to smoulder, there were some barristers who insisted that the firefighters observe the legal niceties.

> One of the templars, seeing gunpowder brought, came to the
> Duke of York and told him it was against the rules and charter
> of the Temple that any should blow that house with gunpowder,
> upon which Mr Germaine, the Duke's Master of Horse, took
> a cudgel and beat the young lawyer to purpose.

The writer adds 'the hope is that he will bring an action of battery
against Mr Germaine' – but it is hard to believe he really meant it.

The Aftermath

Having saved the Temple and Whitehall, the Duke of York went home
to his bed: he had had no sleep since Sunday. When he awoke on
Thursday morning, 6 September, the fire was effectively over. There
were still local bonfires – and embers were found to be smouldering in
basements as much as six months later – but the wholesale destruction
of London was at an end.

The smoking ruins were an awesome spectacle in themselves.

> The best and the fairest city in the world was turn'd into ashes
> and ruins in three days' space.
>   This was a sight that might have given any man a lively sense
> of the vanity of this world, and all the wealth and glory in it, and
> of the future conflagration of the the world. To see the flames
> mount up towards heaven and proceed so furiously without
> restraint; to see the streets fill'd with people astonish'd, that
> scarce has sense left them to lament their own calamity. To see
> the fields fill'd with heaps of goods. And sumptuous buildings,
> costly furniture, and household stuff, yea warehouses and
> furnished shops and libraries &c. all on a flame while none durst
> come near to receive any thing. To see the King and nobles ride
> about the streets, beholding all these desolations while none
> could attend the least relief. To see the air, as far as could be
> beheld, so fill'd with smoak that the sun shin'd through it with
> a colour like blood.

> But the dolefullest sight of all was afterwards, to see what a ruinous confused place the City was, by chimneys and steeples only standing in the midst of cellars and heaps of rubbish, so that it was hard to know what the streets had been – and dangerous of a long time to pass through the ruins, because of vaults and fire in them.

Eighty-nine of the City's 109 parish churches had been gutted. Many of them had stood since Norman or even Saxon times, as their lyrically French or robustly Germanic names proclaimed: St Mary-le-Bow, St Edmund King and Martyr, St Michael le Querne, St Peter Chepe, St Benet Sherehog (a shere hog is a ram castrated after its first shearing: this church stood in the heart of the old wool district).

Forty-four of the halls of the livery companies were gone. The halls were the pride of the medieval trades that built them, the very symbol of their professional standing as craftsmen. Some of those crafts were on the verge of obsolescence – broderers, girdlers, tallow chandlers, pewterers, bowyers, founders, salters, saddlers and scriveners – but were no less jealous of their rights as guildsmen for that. Other liveried professions are still with us in some form – the bakers, goldsmiths, vintners, brewers and masons. Eight livery companies came through the fire with their halls intact. They were the armourers, bricklayers, carpenters, cooks, glovers, ironmongers, leathersellers and upholsterers.

Among the other public buildings destroyed were the Exchange, the Custom House, three of the city gates, Newgate gaol (the inmates were evacuated to Southwark before the flames reached them), the Sessions house and four stone bridges over London's brooks and rivers. To this loss must be added the thousand of pounds' worth of goods destroyed in the wharves and warehouses. The earliest estimate of the financial cost of the fire was a little short of eight million pounds. Most devastating for the populace at large was the massive loss of the wooden houses, the homes that constituted most of the fabric of the city. More than 12,000 individual dwellings were razed, with the result that the urban landscape was strangely denuded. For the first time since the Romans it was possible to stand on Cheapside and see the River Thames.

The distress that all this entailed for the people of London is impossible to gauge. Even Pepys, usually so candid about every nuance of his feelings, has little to say about what it meant to him to be deprived of the locus of his every childhood memory, the backdrop to every triumph and setback. For a man who was a Londoner heart and soul, the fire must have occasioned a very odd kind of bereavement. But all we have from Pepys is a passing mention of the fact that his father's house is gone, and some complaints that he is troubled by nightmares about fire.

On Sunday, 9 September, a week after the fire broke out, rain fell like a blessing on London. It extinguished some of the smaller blazes that still burned, and it turned the mass of dry ashes into a quagmire of viscous mud. Pepys went to church in the evening. The preacher, in the course of a 'bad, poor sermon' remarked that the city had been reduced from 'a large folio to a decimo tertio' – that is, from and large and impressive piece of paper to a little scrap. Pepys thought it was a tasteless metaphor, but there was a kind of truth in it. Old London had been swept away. The tangled, organic hotchpotch of sunless alleyways and benighted garrets in defunct monasteries, the teetering Tudor houses like inverted ziggurats, the Norman stoneworks and the Saxon churches on Roman foundations – all this was no more. London was a blank sheet, and here was an unexpected chance to build a new city on the scorched medieval foundations – a metropolis that would be well-ordered, complex and designed to function as the capital of a great nation. Providentially, this chance came at the dawn of the New Science, at the very moment when the world at large was turning away from the dark and twisted alleyways of the medieval world-view, and beginning to explore the well-ordered cosmos, the designed-to-function natural world, the wonderfully complex human body.

So the modern scientific outlook happened to come into being at the same time as the modern city of London. Both were expressions of the new enlightened way of looking at the world, and both were forged by a handful of creative, inquisitive individuals. More remarkably still, the architects of the new world view and the builders of the new city were in some cases the very same men. The person who was appointed to be

City Surveyor was a specialist in geometry and the curator of experiments at the Royal Society, Robert Hooke. And the man whom Charles II chose to be King's Surveyor of Works – and so the prime mover in the resurrection of London – was a professor of astronomy named Christopher Wren.

The *New* Learning

The three separate projects for the rebuilding of London – Wren's, Hooke's and Evelyn's – were in many ways strikingly similar. Each one was drawn up before the embers were cool: all three men spent time separately tramping through the ruins, pacing out distances and plotting the topography of the blighted town. All three schemes envisaged reorganizing the messy, centuries-old cat's cradle of a streetplan that London had inherited, and replacing it with a city consisting of wide, straight thoroughfares and open piazzas. Above all, each vision of London bears the imprint of its author's scientific background, and is an explicit statement of his world view.

Robert Hooke presented his scheme to the city fathers on 21 September. It is very much a geometrician's ideal city. Hooke wanted to make a grid of identical squares, all perfectly aligned to the four points of the compass. If he had had his way, every trace of London's former history would have been obliterated. We do not know what Hooke had in mind for St Paul's and other immovable relics such as The Guildhall, because his plans have not survived. What is clear is that this was an American-style piece of town planning long before an American civic style existed. For that alone it was remarkable – but it was also entirely impracticable. The plan was quickly rejected, but Hooke was offered the job of City Surveyor, in which post he was to be deeply involved in the rebuilding.

As early as 13 September, John Evelyn, the thoughtful horticulturalist and royal adviser, took his plan to the king at Whitehall Palace. His diary entry for that day reads:

I presented his Majestie with a survey of the ruines, and a plot for a new Citty, with a discourse on it, whereupon, after dinner, his Majestie sent for me into the Queene's Bed-Chamber, her Majestie and the Duke onely present, where they examin'd each particular & discoursed upon them for near a full houre, seeming to be extreamly pleas'd with what I had so early thought on.

Evelyn's intention was to lay out the city like one of his gardens, so that a person moving through it would constantly encounter new and impressive vistas. And like a garden, the new London was to be a thing of beauty, a work of art. All the noxious but necessary trades – the tanners and the butchers, the soap-makers and the dyers – were to be banished beyond the city walls, tucked away like a compost heap in a corner of a back yard. Even the port of London was to be accommodated on the south bank of the river, so as not to impede the construction of a fine embankment lined with important public buildings (the Royal Exchange was to be moved to a large new square by the river) and the tall stately houses of rich private citizens. Old St Paul's was to be repaired and made a centrepiece of the entire scheme. It would stand like a quaint old sculpture in the midst of a large and modern oval piazza. The oval would be lined with harmoniously constructed residences for the bishop and church officers, regular bookshops to replace the jumble of stalls in the old churchyard, a public library and a new building for the scholars of St Paul's School. On a practical level, Evelyn recommended that the charred rubble of the old city be sorted with a view to reusing whole bricks and anything else that was recyclable, while the stuff that was no good for building should be deployed 'to fill up, or at least give a partial level, to some of the deepest valleys, holes, and more sudden declivities within the city, for the more ease of commerce, carriages, coaches and people in the streets, and not a little for the more handsome ranging of the buildings'.

Evelyn's 'London restored' was to be an altogether cleaner city:

Here is to be considered the channel running through Holborn [the Fleet River], which would be so enlarged as not only to be

preserved sweet (by scouring it through floodgates into the
Thames on all occasions) but commodious for the intercourse
of considerable vessels ...

A new and ample quay ... might run ... from the very Tower
to the Temple at least, and if it were possible extend itself even
as far as the very lowe water mark; the basin by this means kept
perpetually full, without slub [mud] ... What fractions and
confusions our ugly stairs, bridges and causeways make, and how
dirty and nasty it is at every ebb, we are sufficiently sensible of;
so as next to the hellish smoke of the town, there is nothing
doubtless which does more impair the health of its inhabitants.

This ecological vision of London was, like Robert Hooke's, very
contemporary its way. The green-fingered Evelyn had conceived a city
in which green ideas – in the modern sense of the word – were a
primary consideration. Evelyn's London is light and spacious and
unpolluted, and architecturally it is thoroughly European in character:

In the disposure of the streets, due consideration should be had,
what are the competent breadths for commerce and intercourse,
cheerfulness and state; and therefore not to pass through the city
all in one tenor without varieties, useful breakings, and
enlargements into piazzas at competent distances, which ought to
be built exactly uniform, strong, and with beautiful fronts. Nor
should these be all of them square, but some of them oblong,
circular and oval figures, for their better grace and capacity. I
would allow none of the principal streets less than an hundred
foot in breadth, nor any of the narrowest [less] than thirty, their
openings and heights proportionable ...

Between the piazzas, market places, and churches, might be the
halls for the ancient companies. These if fronted at least with
stone, adorned with statues and other ornaments, would infinitely
enrich the streets and render this city as famous for architecture
of the most refined gusto [noble style], and as worthy to be
considered of travellers as any city in Europe.

It is a testament to Evelyn's energy and to his intellect that he managed to produce such a complete vision of what London might be in the course of a week, and without any formal training in architecture. He was a true virtuoso in the 17th-century sense of the word: an amateur with a gentlemanly but wide-ranging and voracious interest in all areas of 'natural philosophy', as the pursuit of scientific knowledge was then known.

Wren's London

Christopher Wren, author of the third plan for the reconstruction of London, was a natural philosopher by training, but a professional scientist rather than a gifted dilettante. Evelyn had known Wren at Oxford in the 1640s and immediately recognized his genius, describing him at the age of 22 as 'that miracle of a youth'. By that time Wren was already Fellow of All Souls College, and well versed in mathematics, mechanics and anatomy as well as in his core subject, astronomy.

Wren built his first buildings while still a young man at Oxford. His uncle, an Anglican bishop, had been imprisoned in the Tower by Cromwell's regime. On his release after the restoration Bishop Matthew Wren commissioned his nephew to design a chapel to be built at Pembroke College, Cambridge, as an act of thanksgiving for his release. In these same years, Wren was asked by Gilbert Sheldon, Bishop of London, to design a theatre for Oxford University. These two magnificent buildings – Pembroke College Chapel and the Sheldonian Theatre – made Wren's reputation as an architect.

The construction of buildings was, for Wren, part of the wider intellectual quest. Architecture was seen as form of applied mathematics. A man of the age might even have said that architecture was mathematics rendered visible, in all its wondrous harmony, to the naked eye. This is why a lifelong natural philosopher such as Christopher Wren felt qualified to turn his hand to it, though there was not yet any such thing as a *professional* architect.

Wren's talent had by this time come to the attention of the king, who co-opted Wren and his old friend Evelyn to a Royal Commission

charged with investigating ways of repairing the delapidated fabric of
St Paul's Cathedral in London. The committee deliberated for a matter
of years. Wren made many suggestions, the most radical of which was
removing the too-heavy tower and replacing it with a lighter and more
elegant dome. Evelyn supported the idea:

> **We had a mind to build it with a noble cupola, a forme of church-
> building not as yet known in England, but of wonderful grace: for
> this purpose we offer'd to bring in a plan and estimate, which,
> after much contest, was at last assented to.**

Wren's plan for the restoration of the old St Paul's was accepted on
27 August 1666. Less than a fortnight later he had to come up with
completely new ideas, because the cathedral and most of the city
had been destroyed by fire.

Christopher Wren's outline of a new London was a masterpiece
of urban design. In the astronomer's plan, all the important locations
in the city related to a central, resurgent St Paul's – just as the planets
of the solar system revolve around the fixed point of the sun. Two
broad, dead-straight roads led east from the cathedral, like the arms
of a draughtsman's compass. The northerly road cut through the old
streetplan and connected St Paul's, the spiritual heart of the city, with
the Exchange – its financial heart and its *raison d'être*. This was to be
rebuilt at the centre of a big round plaza, and the halls of all the proud
guilds would have circled it like moons. The southerly arm of the
compass, running roughly along the line of Cannon Street, issued on to
another large new square close to the Tower. A third square, half way
down Fleet Street (near the point where the fire was stopped) provided
a focal point at the western end of the City. Eight roads issued from this
square like a geometric sunburst. From its centre an observer would
have had a clear view of a triumphal arch dedicated to Charles II,
'founder of the new city', at the bottom of Ludgate Hill – and beyond
it, the grand west façade of the new cathedral almost half a mile away.
Wren, like Evelyn, would have straightened and beautified the
embankment, but he would have provided deep docks at which laden

barges could unload easily and conveniently. To this end, he would have shifted London Bridge to the right and so that it was anchored at a spot on the north bank close to the bottom of the now razed Pudding Lane – where the purifying fire had started. Six new roads, ranged like the leaves of a fan, would have converged on a circus at the northern end of the bridge. London Bridge itself was to be cleared of its higgledy-piggledy clutter of buildings so that it could function properly as the start of the main highway to Surrey and the south of England.

Wren's ideas are so grandiose, and so logical and methodical, that even on a map the parts of the City that survived the blaze look somehow unkempt by comparison. Wren must have found himself regretting the fact that not quite all the City burned down. But in the end it made no difference, because none of these imaginative model cities ever got off the drawing board. It soon became clear that there were insurmountable legal problems involved in rescinding freeholds on individual plots of land, compensating the owners or handing out properties in the new urban layout. London may have been ruined, but the ruins belonged to individual Londoners who were determined to hang on to their little portions of scorched earth: often these were all they had left. Laws were passed to settle disputes between landlords and their burned-out tenants, and to ensure that henceforth all buildings would be constructed of brick or stone, according to officially approved designs. But most new buildings were raised on the exact sites of the ones that had been lost. The architectural style of the City was transformed, but the lined old face of London – the personality etched into its ancient streetplan – survived the fire intact.

The rejection of his masterplan was a disappointment for Wren. Instead of building an ideal city, he now devoted his energy and his genius to the reconstruction of individual buildings. But this alone was a task large enough to keep him fully occupied for more than 30 years. He rebuilt 53 of London's parish churches, and each one was a separate stone-made gem. Perhaps the brightest of them is St Bride's, which stands on Fleet Street close to the place where Pepys was born. The unusual tiered design of the spire and the matrimonial associations of the church's saint's name became an inspiration to the bakers and confectioners of London: every multi-layered wedding cake ever constructed owes a debt to Wren's design for this little church.

But the great jewel in the crown of Wren's *oeuvre* is of course St Paul's Cathedral. The construction of this masterpiece occupied him for most of his life – partly because progress was so slow. At first it was hoped that the old roofless church could be restored. Services were held in the ruins for months after the fire, and minor repairs were made, against the advice of Christopher Wren who could see with his architect's eye that the structure had been fatally compromised. He was proved right in 1668, when William Sancroft, the good dean who had remained with his flock through the plague months, wrote to Wren about an incident that had just occurred inside the stricken cathedral.

> What you whispered in my ear at your last coming hither is now come to pass, said the letter. Our work at the west end of St Paul's is fallen about our ears. Your quick eye discern'd the walls and pillars gone off from their perpendiculars, and I believe other defects, which are now expos'd to every common observer.
>
> About a week since, we being at work about the third pillar from the west end on the south side, which we had cased with new stone where it was most defective, almost up to the chapitre, a great weight falling from the high wall so disabled the vaulting of the side aisle by it that it threaten'd a sudden ruin, so visibly that the workmen presently remov'd, and the next night the whole pillar fell, and carry'd scaffolds and all to the very ground. The second pillar (which you know is bigger than the rest) stands now alone, with an enormous weight on top of it; which we cannot hope should stand long, and yet we dare not venture to take it down.
>
> What we are to do next is the present deliberation, in which you are so absolutely and indispensably necessary to us that we can do nothing, resolve on nothing without you.

Wren went to London and told the churchmen what they already knew, and what the avalanche of masonry demonstrated beyond any doubt.

The old cathedral had to be demolished altogether. This work, begun
in 1670, was quite a feat of engineering in itself. The account below
was written by Wren's son, who grew up with the building, became
an architect himself, and worked on St Paul's alongside his father.

**The pulling down of the walls, being about 80 feet high and 5
feet thick, was a great and troublesome work. The men stood
above, and worked them down with pickaxes, whilst labourers
below moved away the materials that fell, and dispersed them into
heaps. The want of room made this way slow and dangerous, and
some men lost their lives. The heaps grew steep and large, and
yet this was to be done before the masons could begin to lay the
foundations.**

**The City, having streets to pave anew, bought from the rubbish
most of the stone (called 'Kentish rag'), which gave some room
to dig and to lay the foundations – which was yet not easy to
perform with any exactness but by this method: the Surveyor
[Christopher Wren] placed scaffolds high enough to extend his
lines over the heaps that lay in the way. And then by
perpendiculars set out the places below, from the lines drawn
with care upon the level plan of the scaffold. Thus he proceeded,
gaining every day more room, till he came near to the middle
tower that bore the steeple. The remains of the tower being near
200 feet high, the labourers were afraid to work above.
Thereupon he concluded to facilitate this work by the use
of gunpowder.**

**He dug a hole of about 4 feet wide, down by the side of the
north-west pillar of the tower. When he had dug to the
foundation he then, with crows and tools made on purpose,
wrought a hole 2 feet square level into the centre of the pillar.
There he placed a little deal box containing eighteen pounds of
powder, and no more. A cane was fix'd to the box with a quick-
match (as gunners call it) within the cane, which reach'd from
the box to the ground above. And all along the ground was laid
a train of powder, with a match. After the mine was carefully**

clos'd up again with stone and mortar to the top of the ground, he then observ'd the effect of the blow.

This little quantity of powder not only lifted up the whole of the angle of the tower, with the two great arches that rested upon it, but also two adjoining arches of the aisles and all above them. And this it seem'd to do somewhat leisurely, cracking the walls to the top, lifting the whole weight about nine inches, which suddenly jumping down made a great heap of ruin in the place without scattering ... The fall of so great a weight from an height of 200 feet gave a concussion to the ground that the inhabitants round about took for an earthquake.

Encourag'd by this success, he thought to proceed this way, but being oblig'd to go out of town in the King's service, he left the management of another mine begun to the care of his next officer, who too wise in his own conceit, put in a greater quantity of powder, and neither went low enough, nor sufficiently fortified the mouth of the mine. And tho' it had the effect, yet one stone was shot out to the opposite side of the churchyard, through an open window, into a room of a private house where some women were sitting at work – without any harm done. This accident frighted the neighbours to that degree that he was importun'd to use no more powder, and was so directed also by his superiors, tho' with due caution it might have been executed without any hazard and sav'd much time and money.

He then turn'd his thoughts to another method. To gain time, prevent much expense, and the endangering of men's lives; and that was, to make an experiment of that ancient engine in war, the battering-ram. He took a strong mast of about 40 feet long, arming the bigger end with a great spike of iron fortified with bars along the mast, and ferrels [metal hoops]. This mast in two places was hung up to one ring with strong tackle, and so suspended level to a triangle prop such as they weigh great guns with. Thirty men, fifteen to a side, vibrated this machine to and again, and beat in one place against the wall the whole day. They believ'd it was to little purpose, not discerning any immediate

effect. He bid them not despair, but proceed another day. On the second day the wall was perceiv'd to tremble at the Top, and in a few hours it fell.

In the spirit of the age, the younger Wren was not content to see the wall come down; he had also to figure out the physics behind its collapse:

The reason to be given for it may be this: 'tis not by any present violence the Ram is able to overturn a wall of such Bulk and Compacture, but incessantly vibrating by equidistant Pulses, it makes a small intestine Motion through all the insensible partsof the Wall, and by Degrees loosens all the Bond of the Mortar, and moves every Stone from its Bed, and tho' not one hundredth part of an Inch and Every Blow, yet this Motion once begun hath its Effects more and more, till at length it is quite loose and falls. He made good use of this Machine in beating down all the lofty Ruins; and pleas'd himself that he had recover'd this noble Engine, of so great use to the Ancients in the besieging of Towns.

The portico so admired and lamented by Evelyn was the last part of the old cathedral to go. It was knocked down in 1686 – by which time work on the new St Paul's Cathedral was well under way. Throughout the last decades of the century, the project often ground almost to a halt for lack of money or because changes in the political wind carried Wren and his sponsors out of favour. But little by little Wren's great vision gained concrete form, and took its place at the zenith of London's new cityscape. The first service was held in the new edifice in 1697, by which date Charles II was long dead. But even at that time the cathedral was still headless and far from finished: the dome was not completed until 1708. The final stone was set in the lantern of the dome by Christopher Wren – not the architect, who was 78 years old by that time and too frail to climb up to the top of his creation, but by his son, who was born in 1675, the year that the cathedral was begun.

In that first year, a tiny incident occurred that Wren never forgot, and which sustained him through the long years of building. One day he was inspecting the newly cleared site of St Paul's, and had wanted to mark a particular spot. He asked a workman to bring him a stone for that purpose. The man went off, and came back carrying a fragment of tombstone. Carved on it was a single Latin word: *RESURGAM* – 'I shall rise again.'

The Prodigious Inventive Head

Wren was also sustained by his collaboration and friendship with Robert Hooke, who in his capacity as City Surveyor was, in effect, Wren's assistant. Hooke was responsible for many new buildings, including the Bethlehem Hospital and the Royal College of Physicians. He worked with Wren on the Royal Observatory at Greenwich and on the Monument to the Fire, which stands on Fish Street Hill.

Hooke said of Wren that, 'since the time of Archimedes, there scarce ever met in one man, in so great a perfection, such a mechanical hand; and so philosophical a mind.' It was probably the warmest remark he ever made, because as a rule he was crotchety, quick to take offence, and hard to get on with. One contemporary said of Hooke that he was 'the most ill-natured and self-conceited man in the world, hated and despised by most of the Royal Society, pretending to have had all the other inventions when once discovered by their authors to the world.' But this summation of his character – even if it were entirely fair – completely ignores his achievement as a scientist. His intellectual range was so panoramic and his insights are so many that he has been called the 'English Leonardo'. Hooke contributed to the design of the first efficient air pump, and so helped pave the way to the steam engine. He invented the universal joint that is still used in motor cars, and the iris diaphragm, which is an integral part of mechanical cameras. He also invented the balance wheel and the anchor escapement, which made it possible to make clocks without pendulums that would therefore function at sea. He formulated Hooke's Law, which concerns the elasticity of springs and other pliable materials; he was an adept of the microscope and the telescope – and was as interested in the minuteness of small things as he was in the immenseness of the cosmos. He was the first person to note the cellular structure of plants – indeed, he coined the word 'cell' as it relates to biology. He guessed that respiration is a form of combustion, and was awarded a doctorate for his services to medicine. He conducted experiments in skin grafting and blood transfusion. He was a magnificent draughtsman and a matchless technician who designed hundreds if not thousands of scientific experiments.

A kindly portrait of the man's character was penned by his friend, the biographer and antiquary John Aubrey:

> He is but of midling stature, something crooked, pale faced, and his face but little below, but his head is lardge; his eie full and popping, and not quick; a grey eie. He haz a delicate head of haire, browne, and of an excellent moist curle. He is and ever was very temperate, and moderate in dyet, etc. As he is of prodigious inventive head, so is a person of great vertue and goodnes.
>
> Now when I have sayd his inventive faculty is so great, you cannot imagine his memory to be excellent, for they are like two buckettes, as one goes up, the other goes downe. He is certainly the greatest mechanick this day in the world. His head lies much more to Geometry than to Arithmetique. He is a batchelour, and I beleeve, will never marie. *In fine,* (which crownes all) he is a person of great suavity and goodnesse.
>
> Twas Mr. Robert Hooke that invented the Pendulum-Watches, so much more useful than the other watches. He hath invented an engine for the speedie working of division etc., or for the speedie and immediate finding out the divisor. A new instrument he haz invented to make more accurate observertions in astronomy than ever was yet made, or could by made by any instruments hitherto invented, and this instrument performes more, and more exact, than all the chargeable apparatus of the noble Tycho Brache or the present Hevelius of Dantzick.

Pepys knew Hooke well, and saw the brilliant intellect that lay hidden beneath that curmudgeonly exterior. He said of Hooke that he 'is the most, and promises the least, of any man in the world that I ever saw.' Pepys bumped into Hooke on the street one day in August 1666, asked the professor what he was working on, and soon found himself out of his depth.

> ... discoursed with Mr Hooke a little about the nature of Sounds, and he did make me understand the nature of Musicall sounds made by Strings, mighty prettily; and told me that having come to a certain Number of Vibracions proper to make any tone, he is able to tell how many strokes a fly makes with her wings (those flies that hum in their flying) by the note that it answers to in Musique during their flying. That is, I suppose, a little too much raffined, but his discourse in general of sound was mighty fine.

'Too refined' for Pepys down-to-earth mind, perhaps. He was too much the dilettante to grasp fully what Hooke was trying to do, which was to deduce the frequency at which an insect's wing beats by matching its pitch to the note produced by a resonating string. But something about that unsatisfactory conversation rankled with Pepys, because almost two years later he challenged Hooke on the subject again. This time he came at it from an angle which he thought gave him an expert's advantage.

> I did desire of Mr Hooke and my Lord [Lord Brounkner, President of the Royal Society] an account of the reason of Concords and Discords in music – which they say is from the aequality of the vibrations; but I am not satisfied in it, but will at my leisure think of it more and see how far that doth go to explain it.

Hooke's experiments with insects' wings were a meeting of two of his lifelong interests: things that fly, and things that are too small to be seen with the naked eye. His great work was *Micrographia*, in which he documented the many things he had examined with his microscope.

It goes far beyond the flies' wings that so captivated his imagination.
The range of objects he looked at is astonishing: a flea, a hog's hairs,
a length of 'taffety ribbon', ice crystals, a piece of chalk, 'sparks of fire
struck from a flint and steel', the point of a needle, 'a pretty minute
shell found amongst sand', the edge of a razor, 'a printed dot or tittle'.
Hooke's own finely detailed sketches of these and many other objects
are the soul of the book. As is sometimes the case with top-flight
technical drawings (Wren's plans for St Paul's are another case in
point), they transcend their scientific purpose and become works of art
in their own right. Hooke's sketch of a magnified flea is rightly famous.
One can tell from the picture that he was touched by the beautiful
intricacy of what is generally a despised animal. That same joyful sense
of wonder in Creation is there in his affectionate written description
of the flea as seen through a microscope:

> The strength and beauty of this small creature, had it no other
> relation to man, would deserve description ... But as for the
> beauty of it, the microscope manifests it to be all over adorned
> with a curiously polished suit of sable armour, neatly jointed
> and beset with multitudes of sharp pins, shaped almost like
> porcupines' quills or bright conical steel bodkins. It has two
> biters, shaped very like the blades of a pair of round-topped
> scissors, and were opened and shut just after the same manner.
> With these instruments does this busy little creature bite and
> pierce the skin and suck the blood out of an animal, leaving the
> skin inflamed with a small round red spot.

Hooke clearly took great pleasure in his research. But he was also
ruthlessly rigorous. The preface to *Micrographia* contains a succinct
statement of his scientific creed:

> The truth is, the Science of Nature has been already too long
> made only a work of the Brain and the Fancy: It is now high
> time that it should return to the plainness and soundness of
> Observations on material and obvious things ... Philosophy

> [scientific knowledge] ... by wandring far away into invisible
> Notions, has almost quite destroy'd it self, and it can never be
> recovered, or continued, but by returning into the same sensible
> [tangible] paths, in which it did at first proceed.

In our time, it is taken for granted that new scientific ideas should
be rigorously tested by experiment, and that this is the only way to
establish the truth. But this was precisely the novelty of the approach
taken by men such as Hooke. Before the emergence of the 'new
science', knowledge of the natural world rested on the foundation
of received authority. If Aristotle said that everything was composed
of the four elements of fire earth, air and water, then it must be so; if
the Bible placed the earth at the centre of the universe, then that too
must be so. Men such as Hooke and Wren were involved in the work
of demolishing that medieval tower of knowledge and constructing a
better edifice to put in its place.

The Invisible College

At Oxford, Wren and Hooke had been part of a discussion group
dedicated to the pursuit of knowledge. Another member was Robert
Boyle, who was to become the leading scientist of the Restoration
period. He described this informal circle of earnest students as 'the
invisible college' because it was unconnected with the formal teaching
structure of the university.

> Our business, wrote John Willis, one member of the circle, was
> to discourse and consider of philosophical enquiries, and such
> as related thereunto, as physick [medicine], anatomy, geometry,
> astronomy, navigation, staticks, magneticks, chymicks,
> mechanicks, and natural experiments with the state of those
> studies as then calculated at home and abroad. We then
> discoursed of the circulation of the blood, the valves in the
> veins, the venae lacteæ, the lymphatic vessels, the Copernican
> hypothesis, the nature of comets and new stars, the satellites of

Jupiter, the oval shape of Saturn, the spots on the sun and its
turning on its own axis, the inequalities and selenography of
the moon, the several phases of Venus and Mercury, the
improvement of telescopes and grinding of glasses for that
purpose, the weight of air, the possibility or impossibility of
vacuities and nature's abhorrence thereof, the Torricellian
experiment in quicksilver, the descent of heavy bodies and the
degree of acceleration therein, with divers other things of like
nature, some of which were then but new discoveries, and others
not so generally known and embraced as now they are; with
other things appertaining to what hath been called the New
Philosophy, which from the times of Galileo at Florence, and
Sir Francis Bacon in England, hath been much cultivated in
Italy, France, Germany, and other parts abroad, as well as with
us in England.

The Elizabethan philosopher Francis Bacon, cited by Willis as the
group's inspiration, had been one of the first to define the scientific
method that Hooke and others were putting into practice. But the first
English scientist to achieve real success with the Baconian method was
William Harvey. He was court physician to King James I and Charles I,
and fought on the royalist side in the Civil War. As early as 1616 he
published his theory, based on gruesome but rigorous experiments on
animals, that blood circulated in a continuous and endless loop around
the body. This flew in the face of all accepted medical wisdom of the
time, and Harvey was ridiculed for it. But he had the strength of
personality to take the mockery of lesser men. To his immense
gratification he was proved right within his own lifetime. Harvey, like
Hooke, was known to Aubrey, who characterized him as follows:

He was not tall; but of the lowest stature, round faced olivaster
complexion; little eie, round, very black, full of spirit; his haire
was black as a raven, but quite white 20 yeares before he dyed.
He was alwayes very contemplative, and the first that I heare
of that was curious in anatomie in England. He had made

dissections of frogges, toades, and a number of other animals, and had curious observations on them, which papers, together with his goods, in his lodgings at Whitehall, were plundered at the beginning of the Rebellion, he being for the king, and with him at Oxon. But he often sayd, that of all the losses he sustained, no griefe was so crucifying to him as the losse of these papers, which for love or money he could never retrive or obtaine.

When Charles I by reason of the tumults left London, he attended him, and was at the fight of Edge-hill with him; and during the fight, the Prince and duke of Yorke were committed to his care: he told me that he withdrew with them under a hedge, and tooke out of his pockett a booke and read; but he had not read very long before a bullet of a great gun grazed on the ground neare him, which made him remove his station.

He did delight to be in the darke, and told me he could then best contemplate. He had a house heretofore at Combe, in Surrey, a good aire and prospect, where he had caves made in the earth, in which in summer time he delighted to meditate. He was pretty well versed in the Mathematiques, and had made himselfe master of Mr. Oughtred's *Clavis Math.* in his old age; and I have seen him perusing it, and working problems, not long before he dyed, and that book was always in his meditating apartment.

I have heard him say, that after his booke of the Circulation of the Blood came out, that he fell mightilly in his practize, and that 'twas beleeved by the vulgar that he was crack-brained. And all the physitians were against his opinion, many wrote against him. With much adoe at last, in about 20 or 30 yeares time, it was received in all the Universities in the world; and as Mr. Hobbes sayes in his book *De Corpore*, he is the only man, perhaps, that ever lived to see his owne doctrine established in his life time.

He was wont to say that man was but a great mischievous baboon. He would say, that we Europaeans knew not how to order or governe our women, and that the Turkes were the only people used them wisely.

He was far from bigotry.

The not-at-all bigoted Doctor Harvey died in 1657, three years before
the boy he had hustled from the battlefield at Edgehill became king of
England. Having had his physiological ideas vindicated in the eyes of
the world, Harvey would have been doubly delighted to see his political
views come out on top too. And he would have been pleased that young
Prince Charles turned out to be an enthusiastic patron of the sciences.
The youths who had joined together to form the 'invisible college' were
now all distinguished natural philosophers, men of note under the new
regime. In 1660, some of the original members – Wren, Hooke, Boyle
and Evelyn among them – had taken to meeting regularly once again.
The new venue was Gresham College, in the City of London. The
activities of this scholarly think tank were drawn to the attention of the
new king, who enthusiastically gave it his seal of approval and, in 1662,
a royal charter. The charter stated the aims of the newly named Royal
Society of London for Improving Natural Knowledge.

> **To improve the knowledge of all natural things, and all useful
> Arts, manufactures, Mechanick practises, Engines and Inventions
> by Experiments – (not meddling with Divinity, Metaphysics,
> Moralls, Politicks, Grammar, Rhetorick or Logick).**

> **To attempt the recovery of such allowable arts and inventions as
> are lost.**

> **To examine all the systems, theories, principles, hypotheses,
> elements, histories, and experiments of all things naturall,
> mathematicall, and mechanicall, invented, recorded, or practised
> by any considerable authors ancient or modern. In order to the
> compiling of a complete system of solid philosophy for explicating
> all phenomena produced by nature or art, and recording a rational
> account of the causes of things.**

This was a pretty sound definition of scientific endeavour in the modern
sense of the term. The charter goes on to give a statement of the
Baconian scientific method, and here too there is very little that a

21st-century scientist could disagree with. As in the statement of intent, the word 'philosophy' means knowledge of the natural world rather than abstract speculation – though significantly the word 'scientificall' crops up in a sense close to its present-day meaning.

> **This society will not own any hypothesis, system or doctrine of the principles of natural philosophy, proposed or mentioned by any philosopher ancient or modern, nor the explication of any phenomena whose recourse must be had to originall causes (as not being explicable by heat, cold, weight, figure and the like as effects produced thereby); nor dogmatically define nor fix axioms of scientificall things, but will question and canvass all opinions, adopting nor adhering to none, till by mature debate and clear arguments, chiefly such as are deduced from legitimate experiments, the truth of such experiments be demonstrated invincibly.**

The Society began to amass a library and a collection of specimens for study. Hooke was appointed curator of experiments, which meant that it was his responsibility to invent and build apparatus for the weekly lectures. Many of the ideas for suitable experiments came from Boyle, so Hooke was his assistant in the scientific endeavour, just as he was Wren's in the architectural one. The first two books published by the Society were Hooke's splendid *Micrographia* and Evelyn's treatise on trees and their uses – *Sylva*.

Pepys was a keen attender of the Gresham College lectures, though many of them, like Hooke's explanation of the nature of sound, went over his head. 'Very fine discourses and experiments,' wrote Pepys in 1665, 'but I do lack philosophy enough to understand them, and so cannot remember them.' Sometimes Pepys tries to explain to himself the significance of what he has seen (in this case some mechanical tracing devices and a camera obscura):

> **And hear a good lecture of Mr Hooke's about the trade of felt-making, very pretty. And anon alone with me about**

art of drawing pictures by Prince Rupert's rule and machine,
and another of Dr Wren's; but he says nothing doth like squares,
or, which is the best in the world, like a darke roome – which
pleased me mightily.

Other times he is content just to gawp in wonderment:

And so out to Gresham College and saw a cat killed with the
Duke of Florence's poison. And saw it proved that the oyle
of Tobacco, drawn by one of the Society, doth the same effect,
and is judged to be the same thing with the poison, both in colour
and smell and effect.

(Close to this Pepys has added, without comment, 'I saw also an
abortive child, preserved fresh in spirit of salt.')

Over the years, Pepys saw lectures and demonstrations on subjects
as diverse as the design of coaches, the making of bread, the effects of
poison on a hen and of a vacuum on a cat, on the refraction of light, on
gunpowder, lodestones, comets, music and molten glass. He saw the first
blood transfusion performed on a dog – a daring experiment that drew
directly on Harvey's pioneering work. The next time he saw Hooke he
enquired after the dog's health:

This noon I met with Mr Hooke, and he tells me the Dogg which
was filled with another dog's blood at the College the other day is
very well, and like to be so as ever. And doubts not its being
found of great use to men.

It was presumably part of Hooke's job, as the underrated drudge of
the Royal Society, to procure the dogs for these experiments – and
the society got through a great many dogs. Here is an account of an
experiment intended to explore the function of the lungs.

On Thursday last we repeated at our meeting that notable
experiment of opening a dog, and laying bare his lungs, and

blowing into him with bellows, keeping him thus alive as long as we pleased; which occasioned some discourse about the nature and use of respiration, some of the company declaring that this experiment made out what was not the use of respiration; others intimating that it seemed to teach that the principal end of respiration was the discharging of fumes of the blood, the animal keeping alive and lying still as long as the lungs were supplied and kept extended with fresh air, and falling soon into convulsions when we ceased to blow.

Pepys own dogged attendance must have made an impression on the professional scientists of the Royal Society, for in 1665 Pepys was proposed and accepted as a Fellow. His diary entry for that day is full of the pride of the newly elevated.

Thence with Mr Creed to Gresham College – where I had been by Mr Povy the last week proposed to be admitted as a member; and was this day admitted, by signing a book and being taken by the hand by the Praesident, my Lord Brunkard, and some words of admittance said to me. But it is a most acceptable thing to hear their discourses and see their experiments; which was this day upon the nature of fire, and how it goes out in a place where the ayre is not free, and sooner out when the ayre is exhausted; which they showed by an engine on purpose.

After this being done, they to the Crowne tavern behind the Change, and there my lord and most of the company to a club supper – Sir P Neale, Sir R Murrey, Dr Clerke, Dr Whistler, Dr Goddard, and others of most eminent worth. Above all, Mr Boyle today was at the meeting ... Excellent discourses till 10 at night, and then home.

The Sceptical Chymist

Robert Boyle, whose company Pepys was so glad to keep, was by this time the most outstanding scientist among the Royal Society men. His

eminence was due in part to his striking patrician looks and his wealthy
aristocratic background (he was the seventh son of the Earl of Cork).

**He is very tall (about six feet high), wrote Aubrey, and streight,
very temperate, and vertuouse, and frugall; a batcheler; keepes a
coach, sojournes with his sister, the lady Ranulagh. His greatest
delight is chymistrey. He haz at his sister's a noble laboratory, and
severall servants (prentices to him) to looke to it. He is charitable
to ingeniose men that are in want, and foreigne chymists have
had large proofe of his bountie, for he will not spare for cost to
gett any rare secret. At his owne costs and chardges he gott
translated and printed the New Testament in Arabique, to send
into the Mahometan countreys. He has not only a high renowne
in England, but abroad; and when foreigners come to hither, 'tis
one of their curiosities to make him a visit.**

But it was Boyle's stature as a scientist that made him stand out in that
crowd of intellectual titans. In his youth he had travelled to Italy and
spoken with 'the great star-gazer' Galileo before returning to England
and enrolling at Oxford University. At Oxford he used some of his
money to set up a laboratory and conduct experiments. It was here that
he met Robert Hooke. Together they built an air pump, which allowed
them to create vacuums and to pressurize air. This may not seem like
much of an achievement in itself, but the perfection of the air pump
was almost as important to the study of chemistry as the development of
the telescope was to astronomy. It opened up the possibility of studying
gases under various conditions: gases were a much more suitable subject
than solids and liquids because they are more uniform and less complex.
Boyle's work with the air pump led him to the hypothesis that gases are
made up of jumbled mass of fast-moving atoms, and therefore that all
matter is made of atoms: this is the first and most basic truth of
chemistry. Boyle's Law – that the volume of a gas at constant
temperature is proportional to the pressure – arose out of the work
with the air pump, and was the first physical law to be deduced from
the atomic theory of matter.

The air pump made possible a long series of experiments in the nature of combustion. The old view, inherited from the Greeks, was that the process of burning released a substance called phlogiston. Boyle was able to show that air was necessary for combustion to take place, and so pointed the way to the discovery of oxygen and to the chemical process of oxidization. The experiments themselves were highly ingenious. Here is an extract from Boyle's meticulous notes:

Of the Difficulty of Producing Flame without Aire.

Experiment I.

A Way of Kindling Brimstone *in vacuo Boyliano* Unsuccessfully Tried.

We took a small earthen melting Pot, of an almost Cylindrical figure, and well glaz'd (when it was first bak'd) by the heat; and into this we put a small cylinder of Iron of about an inch in thickness, and half as much more in Diameter, made red hot in the fire; and having hastily pump'd out the Air, to prevent the breaking of the Glass; when this vessel seem'd to be well emptied, we let down, by a turning key, a piece of Paper, wherein was put a convenient quantity of flower of Brimstone, under which the iron had been carefully plac'd; so that, being let down, that vehement heat did, as we expected, presently *destroy* the contiguous paper; whence the included Sulphur fell immediately upon the iron, whose upper part was a little concave, that it might contain the flowers when melted. But all the heat of the iron, though it made the Paper and Sulphur smoke, would not actually kindle either of them that we could perceive.

Experiment II.

An Ineffectual Attempt to Kindle Sulphur in Our Vacuum Another Way

Another way I thought of to examine the inflammability of Sulphur without Air; which, though it may prove somewhat hazardous to put it in practice, I resolved to try, and did so after the following manner:

Into a glass-buble of a convenient size, and furnish'd with a neck fit for our purpose, we put a little flower of Brimstone (as likely to be more pure and inflammable than common Sulphur;) and having exhausted the Glass [pumped out the air], and secured it against the return of the Air, we laid it upon burning coals, where it did not take fire, but rise all to the opposite part of the glass, in the form of a fine powder; and that part being turned downward and laid on coals, the Brimstone, without kindling, rose again in the form of an expanded substance, which (being removed from the fire) was, for the most part, transparent, not unlike a yellow varnish.

In 1661 Boyle published a book entitled *The Sceptical Chymist*. Part of it takes the form of an almost unreadably complex dialogue between a group of imaginary characters, each one expressing a different view about the nature of matter. Though it is written in this classically Greek genre, the purpose of the book is to refute the classical Greek notions. Boyle specifically argues against the received notion of the four elements, and draws a distinction between the practice of alchemy and the formative science of chemistry. Like Wren in London, he was clearing away the medieval inheritance and making room for a new edifice.

In his years as the leading light of the Royal Society, Boyle published dozens of papers which, taken together, earn him the right to the epithet 'the father of modern chemistry'. He guessed, for example, that the properties of substances must depend on the form of the atoms (or molecules) from which they are made. It also occurred to him that the shape of crystals must derive from the invisible architecture of their sub-atomic structures. These thoughts were the beginning of the road that led to the creation of the periodic table in the 19th century.

Oddly perhaps – at least to the modern way of thinking – Boyle was passionately interested in the alchemical mysteries that the Baconian scientist in him rejected. He always believed, for example, that it might be possible to transmute base metals into gold, and he never stopped trying to find ways to do it. For him the attempt was a symbolic mystery, almost a religious rite, connected to ideas about the transfiguration of Christ and the resurrection of the body at the Last Judgment. For Robert Boyle was a deeply religious man. He never spoke the name of God without pausing reverentially for a moment beforehand. He invested some of his money, as Aubrey said, in translations of the Bible into other languages – not just Arabic, but also the newly discovered languages of the 'Indians' in America, and the Gaelic of his Irish boyhood. He taught himself Hebrew, Greek, Chaldean, Syriac, Ethiopian and Arabic so that he could read theological texts in the original, and he wrote several works of moral theology himself. Among them are a *Free Discourse Against Customary Swearing* (he hated profanity), a work called *Seraphic Love*, which provided reasons for loving God, and a book that attempted to span the two great concerns of his life – science and religion – entitled *The Theological Use of Natural Philosophy*.

Boyle had great personal charm, and mixed happily with all kinds of people. He saw his gregariousness as a scientific asset, and inclined to the view that he could learn more about stone from talking to working masons than by reading a book. Pepys thought little of turning to the great Boyle for some personal advice. In the summer of 1668, when he was much troubled with his eyes, Pepys asked Boyle if he knew of a good oculist. 'He did give me the best advice he could,' wrote Pepys, 'but refers me to one Turberville of Salsbury, lately come to town, which I will go to.' Boyle had written on the subject of optics, and Daubigny Turberville was the best known eye doctor of the time. But presumably the great scientist was unaware that Turberville was not a practitioner in the strict Baconian tradition: the doctor's usual prescription for failing eyes was to have the patient shave his head and take tobacco.

Strange Seas of Thought

Pepys remained an active member of the Royal Society long after he ceased to keep the diary. His position of influence at the Navy Office, his ability as an administrator and his material wealth combined to make him an increasingly valuable asset in the decades that followed. He was held in such high regard that in 1684 Pepys, who could not even do his multiplication tables when he first became Clerk of the Acts, was elected president of this, the most prestigious scientific academy in the world. And once again, Pepys had an accidental encounter with greatness by being in the right place at the right time. For the greatest work of scientific thought ever written was published by the Society during his presidency. The work was *Principia*, and its author was Isaac Newton.

Newton was a very different kind of scientist from the convivial coterie that had founded the Society. He was younger than that first generation, and he did not share their collective ideals or their clubbable mentality. He was chary of sharing his ideas with other scientists (a trait that was to lead to a damaging and bitter feud with Hooke), and he took the attitude that his discoveries were his private property, to dispose of as he saw fit. All his life he worked alone, and for years at a time he lived almost as a hermit. He shut himself away in his rooms in Cambridge, far from London and from the distracting clamour of the wider scientific community. He often forgot to eat or sleep. Newton was the first modern scientist to exhibit this monk-like devotion to his craft. It was an attitude that was later romanticized – the poet Wordsworth imagined Newton, 'for ever voyaging through strange seas of thought alone'. Later still, the Newtonian archetype was parodied and caricatured in fictional characters such as Dr Frankenstein: the scientist as a troubled, unbalanced loner. But for Newton himself, this was just the obvious way to do science: intently, quietly and undisturbed.

Some scientists, like some poets, are at their best and most creative in the first flush of youth. This was the case with Newton. In 1665, when he was a 23-year-old student, the University of Cambridge temporarily closed as a precaution against the plague. Newton went home to his mother's farmhouse at Woolsthorpe, near Grantham. He took with him a prism, a glass toy that he had acquired at a country fair. He had become obsessed with the idea of investigating the properties of light, and he had it in mind to use the plaything for some experiments.

I procured me a Triangular glass-Prisme, to try therewith the celebrated phenomena of Colours. And in order thereto having darkened my chamber, and made a hole in my window-shuts to let in a convenient quantity of the sun's light, I placed my Prisme at his entrance, that it might thereby be refracted to the opposite wall. It was at first a very pleasing divertisement, to view the vivid and intense colours produced thereby; but after a while applying myself to consider them more circumspectly, I became surprised to see them in an oblong; which according to the received laws of refraction I expected to be circular.

It was well known that one could produce a rainbow with a prism. Part of Newton's achievement was to look at the phenomenon systematically. He conducted hundreds of experiments, and made careful notes and measurements of each one. He made observations that no one had thought to record before, for example, that refraction – like reflection – happens on the surface of the glass.

I have refracted it with prismes and reflected it with Bodies which in Day-light were of other colours; I have intercepted with the coloured film of Air interceding two compressed plates of glass; transmitted it through coloured mediums, and through Mediums irradiated with other sorts of Rays, and diversely terminated it; and yet could never produce any new colour out of it.

But the most surprising, a wonderful composition was that of Whiteness. There is no one sort of Rays which alone can exhibit this. 'Tis ever compounded, and to its composition are requisite all the aforesaid primary Colours, mixed in a due proportion. I have often with admiration beheld that all the colours of the Prisme being made to converge, and therefore to be again mixed, reproduced light intirely and perfectly white, and not at all sensibly differing from the direct light of the Sun. Hence therefore it comes to pass that Whiteness is the usual colour of light.

Newton had realized that, 'to the same degree of refrangibility ever belongs the same colour' – that is, that the colour of light depended on its wavelength, and that this was a property that could not be changed by further refraction. But it was the realization that colours could be recombined to make white light that thrilled Newton. He said that this insight was, 'in my judgment the oddest, if not the most considerable detection which hath hitherto been made in the operation of nature'. His suggestion that his discovery was trivial was a little piece of false modesty. Newton knew very well that astronomy consisted entirely in observing light from distant objects, and that scientific observation in general depended on light somehow emitting from solid objects and entering the human eye. An understanding of the nature of light went to the heart of science, and was an essential prerequisite to comprehending the universe in general.

For one young man to have gone so far, working in total isolation, is astounding enough. But Newton achieved far more than this during his enforced year-and-a-half of solitude on the family farm. Here is his own unselfconscious account of his work.

In the beginning of the year 1665 I found the Method of approximating series and the Rule for reducing any dignity of any Binomial into such a series. The same year in May I found the method of Tangents of Gregory and Slusius, and in November had the direct method of fluxions and the next year in January had the theory of colours and in May following I had entrance into the inverse method of fluxions. And the same year I began to think of gravity extending to the orb of the moon, and having found out how to estimate the force with which a globe revolving within a sphere presses the surface of the sphere, from Kepler's rule of the periodical times of the planets being in a sesquialteriate proportion of their distances from the centre of their orbs I deduced that the forces which keep the planets in their orbs must be reciprocally as the squares of their distances from the centres about which they revolve: and thereby compared the force requisite to keep the moon in her orb with the force of

gravity at the surface of the earth and found them to answer
pretty nearly. All this was in the two plague years of 1665
and 1666, for in those days I was in the prime of my age for
invention, and minded mathematics and philosophy more than
at any time since.

This was an explosion of creative genius unequalled in the annals of
science. Nothing like it had occurred before, and the only comparable
event since is Albert Einstein's 'annus mirabilis' of 1905, in which, at
the age of 26, he formulated the theories of relativity that eventually
overturned Newtonian physics. As for Newton's own miraculous year,
the discoveries he enumerates for that period are mind-boggling. To
take just one example, the 'fluxions' that Newton describes are what
we now term 'the calculus'. This powerful mathematical tool provides
a means of calculating the rates of change that occur in phenomena
such as acceleration and deceleration, and in the constantly altering
angle of a curve or an oval (ellipsis). Newton needed the calculus to
describe mathematically the paths of the planets as they turn around
the sun, and of the moon as it circles the earth, and the complex
interactions between these heavenly bodies. No method existed to do
this, so he invented it himself. He must have been aware that he had
founded a whole new field of mathematics, but this did not concern
him at the time. Once he had made the calculations he needed, he
put calculus aside and did not even think of publishing anything
about it.

But the crowning glory of Newton's inventive prime is contained in
the phrase 'gravity extending to the orb of the moon'. Everybody knows
the story (Newton sometimes even told it himself) of how he saw an
apple fall and realized that some force must be dragging it to the earth.
He now came to see that the same attraction that drew apples
downwards also bound the moon to the earth, and held the planets in
their orbits around the sun. Gravitational attraction, in other words,
was the defining characteristic of matter everywhere; it was what held
the universe together. Here, for its time, and long before the term was
invented, was a Unified Theory of Everything.

Framing the System of the World

But it was some years yet before Newton even came to the attention
of the Royal Society. In 1668 he made his first visit to London (at that
time, in the wake of the fire, one vast building site). He was then a
26-year-old professor, having just been granted the Lucasian Chair of
Mathematics at Cambridge by Isaac Barrow, who had relinquished it
in favour of his brilliant young protégé. Barrow introduced Newton by
letter to leading members of the Society. Newton ingratiated himself
by making a gift to the Society of a telescope he had constructed. In
1671 he became a fellow, and pulled off a splendid debut with a lecture
about his earlier optical researches.

But herein were the seeds of Newton's extraordinary long-running
quarrel with Robert Hooke. As curator of experiments, Hooke was
jealous of his reputation as the best maker of scientific instruments in the
country. When he saw Newton's telescope, Hooke claimed sniffily that
he made a smaller and more powerful telescope than that years ago. Soon
after, in the wake of the rapturous reception for Newton's ideas on light,
Hooke published a few trifling objections. This was a perfectly proper
thing to do, since the review was commissioned by the Society itself.
But Newton did not take kindly to criticism of any kind, and Hooke's
tone towards the younger scientist was somewhat condescending, which
cannot have helped. Hooke also felt that Newton's theory of light owed
an unacknowledged debt to ideas that had first been expressed in his
Micrographia, and he was not averse to pointing this out to anyone who
would listen. One of the people listening was Henry Oldenburg, secretary
of the Society. He disliked Hooke, and reported his remarks to Newton –
putting the most derogatory possible interpretation on them as he did so.
Newton began to smoulder with resentment.

Hooke apparently sensed that there was something unseemly in this
disagreement between colleagues, because in 1675 he wrote a
conciliatory letter to Newton. He begins by praising a letter of
Newton's which had been read out as a lecture at the Society, and
which seemed to contain some criticism of Hooke's own scientific
views. 'Sir,' wrote Hooke,

The Hearing of a letter of yours read last week in the meeting of the Royall Society made me suspect that you might have been some way or other misinformed concerning me. And this suspicion was the more prevalent with me, when I called to mind the experience I have formerly had of the like sinister practices. I have therefore taken the freedom which I hope I may be allowed in philosophicall matters to acquaint you of myself, first that I do noeways approve of contention or fending and proving in print, and shall be very unwillingly drawn to such kind of warr. Next that I have a mind very desirous of and very ready to imbrace any truth that shall be discovered, though it may much thwart and contradict any opinions or notions I have formerly imbraced as such. Thirdly that I doe justly value your excellent Disquisitions and am extremely well pleased to see those notions promoted and improved which I long since began, but had not time to compleat.

Having established that he is – despite what Newton may have heard – an honest scientist, that the gossiping Oldenburg was the cause of any discord between them, and that he has been in the business for longer than Newton, Hooke lays on the praise.

That I judge you have gone farther in that affair much than I did, and that as I judge you cannot meet with any subject more worthy your contemplation, so I believe the subject cannot meet with a fitter and more able person to inquire into it than yourself, who are every way accomplished to compleat, rectify and reform what were the sentiments of my younger studies, which I designed to have done somewhat at myself, if my other more troublesome employments would have permitted, though I am sufficiently sensible it would have been with abilities much inferior to yours. Your Designes and myne I suppose aim both at the same thing, which is the Discovery of truth and I suppose we can both endure to hear objections, so as they come not in a manner of open hostility, and have minds equally inclined to yield to the plainest deductions of reason from experiment.

Hooke then proposes that they keep any disagreements on a professional level by corresponding privately, as one scientist to another.

If therefore you will please to correspond about such matters by private letter I shall gladly imbrace it and when I shall have the happiness to peruse your excellent discourse (which I can as yet understand nothing more of by hearing it cursorily read) I shall if it be not ungrateful to you send you freely my objections, if I have any, or my concurrences, if I am convinced, which is more likely. This way of contending I believe to be the more philosophicall of the two, for though I confess the collision of two hard-to-yield contenders may produce light yet if they be put together by the ears of other's hands and incentives, it will produce rather ill concomitant heat which serves for no other use but [to] kindle cole. Sr I hope you will pardon this plainness of your very affectionate humble servant,
   Robert Hooke

Newton replied in similar friendly and deferential fashion, assuring Hooke that he would never knowingly fail to acknowledge an intellectual debt, and that he is always happy to be corrected on that score. But close to the end of his letter he made a telling (and now famous) remark.

Sir,
   At the reading of your letter I was exceedingly well pleased & satisfied with our generous freedom, & think you have done what becomes a true Philosophical spirit. There is nothing which I desire to avoyde in matters of Philosophy more then contention, nor any kind of contention more than one in print: & therefore I gladly embrace your proposal of a private correspondence. What's done before many witnesses is seldome without some further concern than that for truth: but what passes between friends in private usually deserves the name of consultation rather than contest, & so I hope it will prove between you and me.

Your animadversions will be therefore very welcome to me: for though I was formerly tired with this subject, & have not yet nor I believe ever shall recover so much love for it as to delight in spending time about it; yet to have at once in short the strongest or most pertinent Objections that may be made, I could really desire, & know no man better able to furnish me with them than your self. In this you will oblige me. And if there be any thing else in my papers in which you apprehend I have assumed too much, or not done you right, if you please to reserve your sentiments of it for a private letter, I hope you will find also that I am not so much in love with philsophical productions but that I can make them yield to equity & friendship. But in the meantime you defer too much to my ability for searching into this subject. What Descartes did was a good step. You have added much several ways, & especially in taking the colours of thin plates into philosophical consideration. If I have seen further it is by standing on the shoulders of Giants ...

That flattering dictum about giants cannot have pleased Hooke very much. For one thing, he would not have taken it as a given that Newton had 'seen further'; for another, he never gave the younger man permission to stand on his stooping, world-weary shoulders. The embers of personal dislike and professional jealousy continued to glow in both London and Cambridge. In 1679 the argument flared up again when Hooke noticed an error in one of Newton's calculations about the path taken by a falling object. Rather than address the matter in private, as they had agreed, Hooke gleefully presented Newton's mistake to a meeting of the Society along with his own, correct computation. Newton was furious at this betrayal – particularly since it concerned gravity, the subject in which he had already made his greatest conceptual leap – but had not as yet made his results known.

The publication of that world-changing idea was still five years away, and it was partly the rancour between Hooke and Newton that set the process in motion. Several members of the Royal Society had been considering the way that planets move around the sun. The 16th-century astronomer Johannes Kepler had shown that the pull of the sun on the planets decreased the greater the distance from it, and had proposed a mathematical basis for it. Edmund Halley, a young astronomer who had earned his spurs by mapping the stars of the southern hemisphere, was discussing this question one day at the Society with Christopher Wren and Robert Hooke. All three suspected that the mathematical key to the question was an 'inverse square relation' – but this proposition had never been proved. Hooke blithely declared that he was sure he could prove it, and Halley made a bet with him: if he could produce the mathematical proof inside two months, then Halley would buy him a book worth two pounds.

The deadline passed and Hooke produced nothing, but Halley was by now sufficiently intrigued to make a trip to Cambridge and ask Newton what he made of the inverse square hypothesis. Newton, who was wrapped up in opaque theological and alchemical questions, replied that he had proved it years ago. He looked for the proof among his papers, but couldn't find it. So he promised to send it on to Halley as soon as he dug it out. In the event he rewrote his proof on nine pages, entitled it *De Motu Corporum in Gyrum*– 'On the Motion of Bodies in Orbit' – and packed it off to Halley. The proof was concise, elegant and incontravertible, and Halley begged Newton to allow him to publish it. Newton refused, saying it needed more work. He went away and laboured on the question for a year and a half, at the end of which the nine-page paper had grown into three volumes to which Newton gave the name *Philosophiae Naturalis Principia Mathematica* – 'The Mathematical Principles of Natural Philosophy'.

The first volume contained Newton's three laws of motion, the cornerstone of the science of physics. They state that an object in motion will remain in motion unless acted upon by another force; that force equals mass times acceleration; and most famously of all, that for every action there is an equal but opposite reaction. The second volume dealt with motion through a resistive force such as water, and so is a foundation text of the discipline of fluid mechanics. The third volume is like the final movement of a Beethoven symphony, which draws together all the themes and strands of the earlier parts in a great and harmonious climax. This paragraph, from the preface to the third book, begins quietly, but builds crescendo-like to trumpet its final phrase like a fanfare:

> In the preceding Books I have laid down the principles of philosophy, principles not philosophical, but mathematical: such, to wit, as we may build our reasonings upon in philosophical inquiries. These principles are the laws and conditions of certain motions, and powers or forces, which chiefly have respect to philosophy; but, lest they should have appeared of themselves dry and barren, I have illustrated them here and there with some philosophical scholiums, giving an account of such things as are of more general nature, and which philosophy seems chiefly to be founded on; such as the density and the resistance of bodies, spaces void of all bodies, and the motion of light and sounds. It remains that, from the same principles, I now demonstrate the frame of the System of the World.

Halley received the manuscript from Newton on behalf of the Royal Society, but had to fund the publication of the first two volumes himself because the Society had spent its entire publications budget on a sumptuously illustrated history of fish. Nevertheless the book appeared under the official aegis of the Society. Beneath the title and the author's name are the words:

IMPRIMATUR
S Pepys, Reg Soc Praeses
Julii 5 1686

'May it be printed – Samuel Pepys, President of the Royal Society, 5 July 1686.'

After the publication of the *Principia*, Hooke reopened old wounds by insisting that he had thought of the inverse square solution first. Newton was incensed, and this time there was no rapprochement. Years later, when Wren was the obvious person to hold the post of President of the Royal Society, he refused to accept the honour because

Hooke was still living and working at Gresham College. Newton accepted the presidency with indecent haste as soon as Hooke died, and immediately began the process of moving the Society out of the building that was so closely associated with the enemy. More vindictively yet, he continued to speak ill of Hooke for years after he was dead and buried. This did permanent damage to Hooke's reputation, and diminished his fine legacy.

As for Newton, after the *Principia* he more or less retired from science, and took a government job running the Mint. Towards the end of his own life, he made another of those modest statements that he was apparently so fond of. It was a passing remark made to a young relative, and was not meant to become known to the world, so perhaps it should be taken as one old man's sincere assessment of his own life's work. It also functions as a kind of motto for scientists everywhere, and in every age. Isaac Newton said:

> I do not know what I may appear to the world; but to myself I seem to have been only like a boy, playing on the sea shore, and diverting myself in now and then finding a smoother pebble or a prettier shell than the ordinary, whilst the great ocean of truth lay all undiscovered before me.

The Right Hand
of the *Navy*

By the mid-1660s, Samuel Pepys had ceased to be a private person. He had become an establishment figure, a man of influence who was well known at court and in government circles. This was no mean achievement. He was still only 36 years old, after all, and had just passed the mid-point of his life.

Pepys's increasingly public profile came as a result of his unstinting work for the Navy Office. When he was appointed Clerk of the Acts he was a complete novice and the most junior of the principal officers. His immediate colleagues were Sir George Carteret, who had joined the service as a boy, risen to become a sea captain, and was now Treasurer of the Navy; Sir William Batten, Surveyor of the Navy, who had held that same post under Charles I and had served as a commander on active service during the civil war; Sir Robert Slingesby, Comptroller, a man who had grown up with the Navy and had been a sea captain as long ago as the 1630s; Commissioner William Penn, a former rear-admiral and veteran of many battles; and two other commissioners, William Pett, an expert in shipbuilding, and Lord Berkeley, a distinguished soldier.

Pepys was the only one of them who knew nothing whatsoever about the Navy at the time of his appointment. It would have been very easy for him, and hardly less lucrative, to settle into a junior role akin to an office manager. Instead Pepys took on the Herculean task of reforming and streamlining the entire administration of the Royal Navy, in the process teaching himself every aspect of the business. He began by learning his times tables (an accomplishment that had somehow not been required of him either at St Paul's School or at Cambridge University) and went on to become an expert in the procurement of essential supplies for the fitting-out of ships – timber, hemp (for ropes), sailcloth and tar, flags and spars. He studied the employment and payment of seamen, the provision of food for ships at sea, the methods and practices of the government dockyards at Deptford, the deployment of the eternally inadequate budget voted to the Navy by parliament. In the course of his work he encountered much corruption. Some of it he exposed and rooted out; some of it he indulged to his own enrichment. But he built up a clear overview of the visible and invisible machinery of the Navy, and acquired a level of insight that was unmatched by any of his more experienced colleagues. He became England's leading expert on naval affairs.

His command of his field was put dramatically to the test when war broke out between England and Holland in 1665. The immediate cause of the conflict was a dispute over trading rights in West Africa. But the war was also a skirmish in the larger battle for control of the seas. It was a clash between two nascent maritime empires. For Pepys, the Dutch war was first and foremost a huge logistical nightmare. All the old seadogs in his office abandoned their desk jobs at the first sign of war, and went of in search of a front-line command (which had the added benefit to them of taking them out of plague-ridden London). So Pepys was left to man the Navy Office pretty much alone. He wrote in the diary that William Coventry, secretary to the Duke of York, said to him that, 'the weight of despatch will lie most upon me.' So it turned out, and Pepys shouldered the weight masterfully. He was one of those men – like Lord Beaverbrook, Winston Churchill's minister of aircraft production in World War II – who in times of crisis can marshall a vast amount of disparate information and use it to conjure resources out of thin air. Pepys's war work often brought him into contact with George Monck, the hoary old general whose march south from Scotland Pepys had noted from afar on the first page of his diary. Monck was now Lord Albemarle, and commander-in-chief of all England's land and sea forces. Pepys did not much like him as a man, but was deeply flattered when Albemarle took him into his garden for a walk, 'where he expressed in great words his opinion of me: that I was the right hand of the Navy.' He had come a long way in five years.

The sea war against Holland went well at first. At the beginning of June the fleet, under the command of the Duke of York, inflicted a heavy defeat on the Dutch off Lowestoft. The Dutch flagship was sunk along with 17 other ships, and the remnant could only limp back to friendly shores. In July the English suffered a setback when Lord Sandwich attacked part of the Dutch fleet while it sheltered in Bergen, which was then part of the Danish empire. The Danish forts joined the Dutch ships in firing on the English attack force, which was heavily damaged and had to withdraw. Late in the summer Sandwich captured some heavy-laden Dutch East Indiamen and brought them to harbour – but that was small consolation for the disaster at Bergen.

The following summer the war was renewed. The high-point of the campaign was the Four Day Fight, a massive sea-battle in which the English warships were outnumbered 84 to 55. The fray lasted from 11–14 June, and is one of the longest single engagements in naval history. It was fought off the Flemish coast, and the sound of the guns could clearly be heard in London. Edward Barlow was an ordinary seaman on one of the English ships. This is his account of the fourth day of the Four Day Fight:

And by sunrising the Hollands ships bore up to us, and the fight began anew, very fiercely on both sides, Prince Rupert and his Vice-Admiral being engaged very hot, venturing into the midst of them and running into too much danger, whereby in a small time they were very much disabled, losing a great many men ... And the fight continuing very hard till four o'clock of the afternoon, and some of our ships having spent the most part of the powder and shot, and others being much disabled ... and few or none but were much disabled in one thing or another, and being engaged with so much odds, that some of our ships began to retreat towards our own coast and it being almost night and a mist arising, our General feared in the mist we might run on board of one another, as one frigate did, called The Essex; she running on board one of our Flemish-built ships, could not get clear again, though she made what haste she could to sink the Flemish ship, being little worth, for we reckon one English ship to be better than two Holland ships, but the Hollanders came so thick about her that she was forced to yield to them. So our General made the sign to retreat, the mist increasing and it beginning to be dark; but the Hollands fleet made no great haste to follow us, being willing to leave off, having their bellies full as well as we.

But if it had pleased God that we had our whole fleet together we had made an end in half the time, for we should have had them to have showed us their butter-box arses and run from us the first day, for they are nothing if they have no more ships than we have.

As Barlow grudgingly admits, the epic battle was lost. But at home it was seen as one of those heroic English defeats – like Dunkirk – that are almost better than a victory. Pepys knew otherwise: ten ships were sunk, two admirals were killed in action, and more than 4,000 sailors died or were taken prisoner. A deficit like that was going to be hard to make up.

The rest of that summer's fighting went better: the English fleet won a significant victory on St James's Day, and in August, Sir Robert Holmes managed to send fireships into the midst of the assembled Dutch East India merchant fleet as it lay at anchor in the estuary of the river Vlie. One hundred and fifty fully laden merchantmen went up in smoke with their precious cargo of spices. Holmes lost just 12 men in the action.

The perpetrators of 'Holmes's Bonfire', as it was called, were triumphant. But theirs was not the biggest bonfire of that autumn. Less than a month after their pyromanic attack, London burned to the ground. Holmes's heroes came back to a capital city that had been transformed into a desert of ashes. The Dutch crowed that the Great Fire was divine retribution for Holmes, but that did not prevent them exacting a revenge of their own. In June 1667 a Dutch fleet sailed up the Thames Estuary and into the Medway, the conveniently sheltered inlet on the Kent coast where England's shipyards were located. A chain had been laid across the mouth of the Medway to stop ships entering – but this was an entirely inadequate defence. The Dutch broke through it and landed some marines on the shore. They attacked several ships and watched as the English were forced to scuttle some of their own ships in an attempt to block the Dutch advance. Some of the Dutch ships were manned by English prisoners-of-war and deserters, who shouted from the deck that this navy, unlike England's, paid their wages.

The Dutch advanced to Chatham Docks, where they burned some of the finest ships in the English fleet. The population of nearby towns such as Rochester fled into the countryside, and there was panic in London. Rumours of a full-scale invasion were flying around the city. No invasion came, but something almost as dire did happen. The Dutch captured *The Royal Charles* – the pride of the fleet and the very ship on which, in happier times, the newly restored king had sailed back to England from exile in Holland. They towed it away with them under the noses of the enemy. The raid marked an end to the war with the Dutch, or at least of this phase of it: England sued for peace and settled for unfavourable terms under the Treaty of Breda of 1667.

Pepys was appalled by the raid on the Medway, which was a total humiliation for the Navy and, by extension, for his own Navy Office. He knew there would be political fallout, and he was desperate to avoid the blame, 'though, God knows, I have in my own person done my full duty'. His colleague William Pett became the first scapegoat because he was responsible for the well-being of the dockyards: he was sacked, and threatened with impeachment. The following spring, Pepys himself was summoned before the House of Commons to account for the actions of the Navy Office. In the weeks leading up to his appearance, he went through all the agonies of a man about to face trial for some terrible crime. He spent his days working feverishly on the case for the defence. He lay awake at night worrying, and he seriously considered resigning his job to avoid the ignominy of being dismissed. On 5 March 1668, he went by boat to Westminster, where he and his colleagues were arraigned to face the wrath of the House. He was, he wrote …

... full of thoughts and trouble touching the issue of this day; and to comfort myself did go to the Dogg and drink half a pint of mulled sack, and in the Hall did drink a dram of brandy at Mrs. Howletts, and with the warmth of this did find myself in better order as to courage, truly. So we all up to the Lobby; and between 11 and 12 a-clock were called in, with the Mace before us, into the House; where a mighty full House, and we stood at the Barr – *viz.*, Brouncker, Sir J. Mennes, Sir T. Harvey and myself – W. Penn being in the House as a Member. I perceive the whole House was full, and full of expectation of our defence what it would be, and with great praejudice. After the Speaker had told us the dissatisfaction of the House, and read the report of the Committee, I begin our defence most acceptably and smoothly, and continued at it without any hesitation or loss but with full scope and all my reason free about me, as if it had been at my own table, from that time till past 3 in the afternoon; and so ended without any interruption from the Speaker, but we withdrew. And there all my fellow-officers, and all the world that was within hearing, did congratulate me and cry up my speech as the best thing they ever heard, and my fellow-officers overjoyed in it ... and so out; and we were in hopes to have had a vote this day in our favour, and so the generality of the House was; but my speech being so long, many had gone out to dinner and come in again half drunk, and then there are two or three that are professed enemies to us and everybody else; among others, Sir T. Littleton, Sir Tho. Lee, Mr. Wiles (the coxcomb whom I saw heretofore at the cock-fighting) and a few others; I saw these did rise up and speak against the coming to a vote now, the House not being full, by reason of several being at dinner but most because the House was to attend the King this afternoon about the business of Religion (wherein they pray him to put in force all the laws against nonconformists and papists); and this prevented it, so that they put it off to tomorrow come sennit. However, it is plain we have got great ground; and everybody says I have got the most honour that any could have had opportunity of getting.

Pepys knew he had acquitted himself well, but it was not until the next day that he realized exactly how well. His performance in parliament had been recognized as a triumph by everybody in the government village. The hour of his disgrace had, by his own hand, been transformed into a personal and professional victory. For a single day, 6 March 1668, Samuel Pepys was the most admired and talked-about man in the kingdom. If his diary entry written that evening reads a little smugly, then one can hardly hold that against him: the unfolding scroll of plaudits was his reward for all the long years of early mornings, hard work and skilful management.

Up betimes, and with Sir D. Gawden to Sir W. Coventry's chamber, where the first word he said to me was, 'Good-morrow Mr. Pepys, that must be Speaker of the Parliament-house' – and did protest I had got honour for ever in Parliament. He said that his brother, that sat by him, admires me; and another gentleman said that I could not get less that 1000l a year if I would put on a gown and plead at the Chancery-bar. But what pleases me most, he tells me that the Sollicitor generall did protest that he thought I spoke the best of any man in England. After several talks with him alone touching his businesses, he carried me to White-hall and there parted; and I to the Duke of York's lodging and find him going to the parke, it being a very fine morning; and I after him, and as soon as he saw me, he told me with great satisfaction that I had converted a great many yesterday, and did with great praise of me go on with the discourse with me. And by and by overtaking the King, the King and Duke of York came to me both, and he said, 'Mr Pepys, I am very glad of your success yesterday;' and fell to talk of my well speaking; and many of the Lords there, my Lord Berkely did cry me up for what they had heard of it; and others, Parliament[-men] there about the King, did say that they never heard such a speech in their lives delivered in that manner. Progers of the Bedchamber swore to me afterward before Brouncker in the afternoon, that he did tell the King that he thought I might teach the Sollicitor generall.

Everybody that saw me almost came to me, as Joseph Williamson and others, with such eulogys as cannot be expressed. From thence I went to Westminster-hall, where I met Mr. G. Mountagu; who came to me and kissed me, and told me that he had often heretofore kissed my hands, but now he would kiss my lips, protesting that I was another Cicero, and said all the world said the same of me. Mr. Ashburnham, and every creature I met there of the Parliament or that knew anything of the Parliament's actings, did salute me with this honour – Mr. Godolphin, Mr. Sands, who swore he would go twenty mile at any time to hear the like again, and that he never saw so many sit four hours together to hear any man in his life as there did to hear me. Mr. Chichly, Sir Jo. Duncom, and everybody doth say that the Kingdom will ring of my ability, and that I have done myself right for my whole life; and so Captain Cocke, and other of my friends, say that no man had ever such an opportunity of making his abilities known. And, that I may cite all at once, Mr. Lieutenant of the Tower did tell me that Mr. Vaughan did protest to him, and that in his hearing it, said so to the Duke of Albemarle and afterward to W. Coventry, that he had sat 26 years in Parliament and never heard such a speech there before – for which the Lord God make me thankful, and that I may make use of it not to pride and vainglory, but that now I have this esteem, I may do nothing that may lessen it.

I spent the morning thus, walking in the Hall, being complimented by everybody with admiration.

The End of the Diary

The years of toil had brought rewards, but they had also taken a toll. On 20 June 1668, and not for the first time, Pepys found himself physically struggling to write up events for the diary. His short entry for that day ends with the words '… able to do nothing by candlelight, my eyes being now constantly so bad.' It was a few days later that, on the advice of Robert Boyle, he went to see the famous oculist Daubigny

Turbeville. The doctor prescribed some pills and drops, and for a time
Pepys was hopeful of an improvement. But strong light continued to
cause him pain; he now found it hard to read a book by any light.

The deterioration in Pepys's eyesight can be tracked through the
handwritten pages of the diary. In the notebook for 1668 and 1669
Pepys's practised shorthand gradually becomes larger and less regular.
The diary entries themselves are often shorter than in former years.
In May 1669 there are two occasions when he manages no more than
a line. 'Dined at home. The rest of the whole day at the office,' he
wrote blandly on the 22nd. And three days later an almost identical
entry: 'Dined at home, and the rest of the day, morning and afternoon,
at the office.' If his heart was no longer in it, then the reason was clear.
The daily chore of keeping the diary, writing for hours on end in the
flickering half-light of candle, was surely one of the causes of his eye
trouble. The diary had to stop.

For the sake of neatness, Pepys struggled on to the end of the month,
making his final entry on 31 May 1669. He describes a day that is a kind
of miniature of his busy life over the past ten years: he thinks about his
money, indulges in a little unfulfilling philandering with a shop girl,
does some navy business in the afternoon, drinks in a tavern all evening
– 'there merry, and so home late.' Then, leaving a gap that looks like a
sigh on the page, he writes this farewell:

**And thus ends all that I doubt I shall ever be able to do with my
own eyes in the keeping of my journall, I being not able to do it
any longer, having done now so long as to undo my eyes almost
every time that I take a pen in my hand; and therefore, whatever
comes of it, I must forbear; and therefore resolve from this time
forward to have it kept by my people in long-hand, and must
therefore be contented to set down no more then is fit for them
and all the world to know; or if there be anything (which cannot
be much, now my amours to Deb are past, and my eyes hindering
me in almost all other pleasures), I must endeavour to keep a
margin in my book open, to add here and there a note in shorthand with my own hand. And so I betake myself to that course**

which [is] almost as much as to see myself go into my grave – for which, and all the discomforts that will accompany my being blind, the good God prepare me.

He never pursued the idea of dictating the diary. So these are the last words in a work that runs to one and a quarter million words, and more than 3,000 pages. Samuel Pepys initialled that final entry as if setting a seal on it, then he closed the window on his private life forever.

Later that year Samuel and Elizabeth went on a short tour of the continent. It was a chance for Pepys to recuperate from the stresses of work, to rest his tired eyes, and to repair the damage caused to his marriage by his affair with the maid Deb Willets – the only one of his 'dalliances' ever to come unequivocally to his wife's attention. The trip took them to Holland (where Pepys could not keep himself from inspecting the shipyards), through Flanders and on to Paris, then back home via Brussels. John Evelyn, who knew the continent well, had provided Pepys with an immensely long list of travel tips and suggestions of things to see:

Abbeville. A pretty reasonable town – here they used to offer us Pistols and Guns to buy ... [In Paris] I would in the first place climb-up into St Jacques Steeple to take a synoptical Prospect of that monstrous City ... The principall Places where Persons of Quality dwell are in the Sub-urbs, especially that of St Germains ... In the City the first Place of note is the Louvre, or Court of that Great Monarch. The Galleries, Salle of Antiquities, Printing House, Monnoye, [Mint], Gardens of the Thuillieries, Furniture, Architecture and ten thousand Particulars will take you up a good time here. Besides that you ought to kiss the King and Queen's hand ...

And so on, for page after voluble page.

Pepys had promised to write to Evelyn on his return and give him an account of his travels. But the writing of the letter was delayed – and for an alarming reason. Elizabeth had become unwell on the journey back.

By the time they got to London, in mid-October, she was seriously ill. It was November before Pepys managed to dash off a note to his friend:

> Sir,
>   I begge you to believe that I would not have been ten daies returned into England without waiting on you had it not pleased God to afflict mee by the sickness of my wife, who, from the first day of her coming back into London, hath layne under a fever soe sever as at this houre to render her recoverey desperate. Which affliction hath very much unfitted mee for those acts of civillitie and respect which, amongst the first of my friends, I should have paid to yourselfe, as hee to whome singly I owe the much greater part of the satisfaction I have met with in my late voyage.

Pepys went on to say that he that a proper thank you would have to wait 'till I am better qualified', that is, until Elizabeth was over her illness. But the fever got worse and she died within the week. She was 29.

It is strange that Pepys, having spent ten years logging every gust of the emotional breeze, each barometric rise and fall in his moods and tempers, should have no word to say about the storm of grief that now engulfed him. He must have been tempted to go back to the last volume diary, which he had left with 54 blank pages, and write some kind of valedictory postscript about his wife. It would surely have been a comfort, like confiding in an old friend. But no. Instead of a funeral oration for Elizabeth, we are left with Samuel's last portrait of her in life. It is contained in the diary entry for 1 May 1669. The previous night Pepys had taken delivery of the coach that he and Elizabeth had promised to get for themselves if ever they made a success of their lives. That last May Day of their marriage was cold and rainy, and the varnish was barely dry on the coach doors, but Elizabeth was fiercely determined to go out and show off the new carriage at the traditional promenade in Hyde Park.

> Up betimes, called up by my tailor, and there first put on a summer suit this year – but it was not my fine old one of flowered vest and coloured camelott [ribbed woollen] tunic, because it was

too fine with the gold lace at the hands that I was afeared to be seen in – but put on the stuff-suit I made the last year, which is now repaired.; and so did go to the office in it and sat all the morning, the day looking as if it would be fowle.

At noon, home to dinner, and there find my wife extraordinary fine with her flowered tabby [watered silk] gown that she made two years ago, now laced exceeding pretty, and endeed was fine all over – and mighty earnest to go, though the day was very lowering, and she would have me put on my fine suit, which I did; and so anon we went alone through the town with our new Liverys of serge, and the horses' manes and tails tied with red ribbon and the standards thus gilt with varnish and all clean, and green raynes, that people did mightily look upon us; and the truth is, I did not see any coach more pretty or more gay than ours all day ... Expected to meet Sheres [Elizabeth's drawing teacher], which we did in the Pell Mell, and against my will I was forced to take him into the coach, but was sullen all day almost and a little complaisant; ... the park full of coaches; ... But here was W Batelier [the son of Pepys's wine merchant] and his sister in a borrowed coach by themselves, and I took them and we to the Lodge, and at the door did give them a sullabub [sweetened milk mixed with wine] and other things, cost me 12s, and pretty merry; and so back to the coaches and there till evening; and then home, leaving Mr Shere's at St James's gate, where he took his leave of us for altogether, he being this night to set out for Portsmouth post, in his way to Tanger – which troubled my wife mightily, who is mighty, though not I think too fond of him. But she was out of humour all the evening, and I vexed at her for it; and she did not rest almost all the night, so as in the night I was forced to take her and hug her to put her to rest.

The Venerable Mr Pepys

Pepys took refuge from grief in his work. The months after Elizabeth's death were a busy time for him professionally. A new round of recriminations was in the offing regarding the Navy's financial and administrative conduct of the Dutch war. Pepys was once again the only man in the Navy Office – the only man in England – with a good enough understanding of procedures and problems to answer the charges. This he did in a long and detailed written defence, the composition of which occupied his mind totally in the first months of bereavement. He was called before the Parliamentary Commission for Public Accounts in 1670, where he was treated like the defendant in a corruption trial. He fought his corner vigorously, cementing his reputation as an orator, and making a very good impression on King Charles, who was acting as judge. When it became clear that the commission was not going to be able to break Pepys down, the hearings were abandoned.

In 1672, Pepys narrowly missed out on a promotion to the job of secretary to the Duke of York. This turned out to be a blessing in disguise, because the following year anti-Papist feeling in the country at large forced Charles to reverse his tolerant policy towards Catholics and pass the so-called 'Test Act', which banned Roman Catholics from holding public office. The main target of the Act was the Duke of York himself, who had to stand down as Lord High Admiral. Had Pepys been in the Duke's direct employ at that moment, he would certainly have fallen with him. Instead he was appointed secretary of the Admiralty commission that was convened to carry out the Duke's functions. Pepys was now, in name as well as in fact, the man in charge of the Navy.

The same year, 1673, Pepys added to his establishment credentials by becoming a member of parliament. He became a governor of Christ's Hospital, a school which had just received a royal charter requiring it to teach its pupils mathematics and navigation: these boys were to be the naval officers of tomorrow. And he was appointed Master of Trinity House, the institution which was (and is) responsible for the maintenance of lighthouses and other aids to navigation in British waters. Pepys was arriving at the pinnacle of his career. And the betterment of his professional circumstances was accompanied by an accidental change in his personal life. Early in 1673 the house on Seething Lane, where Pepys had lived for over a decade, burned down.

Few of his precious possessions were lost, but the home he had shared with Elizabeth, and which had by some miracle survived the great conflagration of 1666, disappeared forever. He moved his home and his office to Derby House, a comfortable set of mansions on the river between the City of London and Westminster.

During the years at Derby House, Pepys began the reforms that make him a towering figure in naval history. For example, he created and defined official standards for junior officers, and did much to raise the appalling standards of discipline that crippled the hierarchy on board ship at every level. He used his position as an MP to justify his actions and the huge expenditure required to maintain a professional navy. In many ways he laid the foundations for the naval pre-eminence that Britain enjoyed in the 18th century and into the 19th. It is no exaggeration to say that without Samuel Pepys, there could have been no Horatio Nelson.

All that good work came to an abrupt end in 1679, when anti-French and anti-Catholic feeling erupted once again in the strange episode known to history as the Popish Plot. Two disaffected Anglican clergyman had manufactured a story that a Catholic uprising was about to occur. The king was to be murdered, and his Papist brother the Duke of York was to be installed in his place. The idea was an absurd fiction, but the story was widely believed and became a real political issue. Protestants began seeking out the sinister, undeclared Catholics in their midst. Parliament, carried away on wave of bigotry, demanded that the duke be removed from the king's presence. Pepys's long professional association with the Duke of York was well-known, and he was accused in the House of Commons of being a Catholic himself. It was noticed that he had illegally employed an Italian Catholic as his personal musician – Catholics were not permitted to reside in London – and this was taken as proof of his disloyal religious affiliations. Pepys's parliamentary enemies began to fabricate a case against him, dragging up for good measure the old stories about corruption at the Navy Office. One of his accusers, an MP named Bennett, conflated the charges of Catholicism and corruption by claiming that all the officers in the Navy were crypto-Catholics, put in place by Pepys and the Duke of York. Bennet and his fellows even made the outrageous assertion that Pepys had sold naval secrets to the French. 'I will prove Popery in the fleet at the bar!' Bennet shouted at Pepys across the floor of the House of Commons. Pepys told him he was welcome to try.

It all added up to a juicy political scandal, and the accusations against Pepys were a hot topic in the coffee houses. Almost inevitably, a satirical pamphlet appeared on the streets. It was entitled 'A Hue and Cry after P. and H.' The P in question was Pepys; the H was Will Hewer, Pepys's close friend and protégé, who had begun as Pepys's manservant, worked under him at the Navy Office and the Admiralty, and was now a wealthy and successful businessman in his own right.

These are to give notice to P. and H., began the pamphlet, **that if they will forthwith come forth with an humble submission and refund all the money they have unjustly taken by Permissions and Protections, to the merchants or owners of all such ships as were fitted out for the last Embargo, and also give satisfaction for the extraordinary gain made to yourselves, P. and H., in buying timber for building the new ships of war ...**

You must also refund those before-hand guineas or broad-pieces, and also the jars of oil and boxes of chocolate and chests of Greek wines and chests of Saracusa wines, and pots of anchovies and quarter-casks of old Malaga and butts of Sherry, and Westphalia hams and Bolonia sausages, and barrels of pickled oysters and jars of olives and jars of tent, and Parmesan cheeses and chests of Florence wine and boxes of orange flower water; and all those dried cods and lings, and hogsheads of claret, white wines and champagnes, and dozens of cider; and also of those mocos, parrots and parrakeets, Virginia nightingales and turtle-doves, and those fat turkies and pigs; and all those Turkish sheep, Barbary horses and lions and tigers and bears; and all those fine Spanish mats; all which were received from Sea-Captains, Consuls, Lieutenants, Masters, Boatswains, Gunners, Carpenters and Pursers, or from their wives or sons or daughters.

All this was pretty close to the bone, since (apart from the comic exaggerations about tigers and bears) Pepys had happily accepted gifts such as these all his working life. Having incisively made the point about Pepys's cupidity, the pamphlet goes on to attack his pomposity. It was an easy target.

P., there is one thing more you must be mightily sorry for with all speed – your Presumption in your coach in which you daily ride as if you had been son and heir to the great Emperor, Neptune; or, as if you had been infallibly to have succeeded in his Government of the Ocean. All which was Presumption in the highest degree.

First, you had upon the forepart of your chariot tempestuous waves and wracks of ships; on your left-hand forts and great guns and ships a'fighting; on your right-hand was a fair harbour and town, with ships and galleys riding with their flags and pennants spread, kindly saluting each other, just like P. and H. Behind it were high curled waves and ships a'sinking, and here and there an appearance of some bits of land.

And now really consider with yourself that you are but the son of tailor, and wipe out all this presumptuous painting, and new paint it with those things agreeable to your quality. In the first place, paint upon the fore-part as handsome a tailor's shop-board as you please, with Old Gentleman, your father, upon it at work and his journeymen sitting about him, each man with pint of ale and halfpenny loaf before him, and the good old Matron your mother and yourself and the rest of your brothers and sisters standing by: this will be agreeable to your qualities. Then behind your coach, paint all the evil deeds of P. and H. in particulars; also on your right hand, paint your Jesuit, M., [Morelli, Pepys's musician] playing upon his lute and singing a Holy Song: on your left hand paint two or three poor cripples, which P. reformed, and giving them his charity which he never was wont to do. All this will show P.'s great humility and reformation and reducement to his right station.

The remarks about his coach – to Pepys's mind, the very symbol of his success – also hit the bullseye, and suggest that the text was written by someone who knew him personally. Pepys always suspected the author was one of his own clerks, a man named Donluis. The pamphlet concludes with a paragraph even more scurrilous and personal than the remarks about his family – and once again it goes to the very heart of Pepys's character:

> For the better enabling this Hue and Cry, this is therefore to give notice to all persons whatsoever, that if they can apprehend P. and H., or either of them, or give notice of them to a Lady in Lincoln's-Inn-Fields, or to a Lady at her country-house in Chelsea; or to another at her house near the Exchequer, or to two merchants' daughters in London, they being both well-known to these two persons, especially P.; or to any of the Officers of Bridewell in Whitefriars [the reformatory for prostitutes] or to M.'s coffee-house in Westminster or to C.'s coffee-house in Westminster or to C.'s coffee-house by the Royal Exchange; before, or at, the next Session of Parliament, they shall have a great Reward.

Pepys shrugged off this libel, but he could not dodge the far more serious accusations being levelled at him in parliament. His enemies were deadly serious about bringing him down, and in due course he was formally presented with charges of 'piracy, popery and treachery'. But in the midst of the anti-Catholic witch-hunt, Pepys remained loyal to the Duke of York, the man who had been his superior for most of his career. He resigned the secretaryship of the Admiralty in disgust, and soon after was arrested and confined to the Tower of London, where he immediately began composing yet another cast-iron defence of his actions.

> But such is the incredulity of this unhappy age, he wrote at the time, that no accumulation of evidence can be too much to support the most obvious truth.

Pepys was released after six weeks in prison, but it was another year before the public hysteria had subsided to the point where the ridiculous charges against him could be dropped. In the meantime he was out of a job and, since his apartments came with the Admiralty position, he was obliged to move house again. He chose to go and live with Will Hewer in York Buildings, close to the Strand.

For several years, Pepys remained in the political wilderness. But in 1684 he was suddenly returned to office. The administration of the Navy had gone to ruin in the years since the Popish Plot, and the king decided that Pepys was the only person who could put things right. He created a new post specifically for him – Secretary for Admiralty Affairs – and made him answerable only to his royal self. Now Pepys was free from the interference of hostile elements in parliament, and invested with powers to do whatever he thought necessary to sort out the mess that had been made in his absence. He was, by royal appointment, de facto minister for the Navy. He continued in this role after Charles's death when, despite all the plots, the Duke of York came to the throne. As King James II, he was Pepys's boss once more. Pepys spent the next years repairing the damage done while he was unemployed, and pushing through yet more reforms. He was no longer merely the right hand of the navy; he was, as one contemporary described him, 'the oracle of the navy'.

This final burst of professional zeal came to an end with the overthrow of James II. The new king's pro-Catholic policies had inflamed the old religious enmities. He had installed Catholics in positions of power and, more worryingly for the Protestant masses, his wife had given birth to a son, ensuring a Catholic dynasty for decades to come. Until that event, the next in line to the throne was James's Protestant daughter Mary, who was married to her cousin William, Prince of Orange. Together, William and Mary plotted the downfall of the king. In the autumn of 1689, an invasion force was launched from Holland. It slipped past the naval ships waiting for them in the Channel and landed at Brixham in Devon. James at first considered leading his troops into battle against his son-in-law, but it rapidly became clear that he did not have the support of the nation. And so, for the second time in his life, James was forced to flee to France. In this letter, written as he made his way to the coast, James tries to pretend that his departure is a tactical retreat. But he knew that his reign was over: he took the Great Seal of England with him and threw it into the Thames as he ran away from the armies of his son-in-law.

> **My affairs are in so desperate a condition,** wrote King James, **that I have been obliged to send away the Queen and the Prince to secure them at least, whatsoever becomes of me that am resolved to venture all rather than consent to anything in the least prejudicial to the crown or my conscience. And having been basely deserted, could no longer resolve to expose myself to no purpose to what I might expect from the ambitious Prince of Orange and the associated rebellious lords, and therefore have resolved to withdraw till this violent storm is over, which will be in God's good time, and hope that there will still remain in this land seven thousand men who will not bow down the knee to Baal and keep themselves free from associations and such rebellious practices.**

In the wake of the crisis, Pepys was summoned to an audience with the new King William III. They had met once before – in Holland in 1660, when Pepys had described him as a 'very pretty boy'. Now the pretty boy asked Pepys to carry on doing his job for the time being, but Pepys must have known that his career would soon be over. Early in 1690 he pre-empted the inevitable by resigning.

This was not quite the end of it. Later that year Pepys was arrested once again, merely for having been an associate of King James. He was released after a few days, and the charges were put aside. Putting this last annoyance behind him, Pepys gently relaxed into retirement with his books, his music and his occasional fine dinners. His companion in these years was Mary Skinner, whom he had hired as his housekeeper soon after Elizabeth's death. Over the years she had come to be more to him than an employee. Though they never married, they were to all intents and purposes man and wife, in their own eyes and in the eyes of the world. Even a stickler for decorum such as John Evelyn referred to Mary as 'Mrs Pepys'.

It is surprising that Pepys was never awarded the knighthood that he dreamed of as a young man. He had certainly done enough to earn it. But one small civic honour did come his way late in life. In 1699, Samuel Pepys was granted the freedom of the City of London, an honour which – since he was a Londoner, born and bred in the Square Mile – would have pleased him mightily.

My Particular Friend

In 1700, Pepys moved out of London and went to live at Will Hewer's large country house in the rural village of Clapham, about six miles south of the Thames. The house and the village made a very suitable home for an old man such as Pepys. Here he was well looked after by Hewer and his household; there was plenty of room for his possessions; and he had a dutiful nephew, John Jackson, to help him with the grand and pleasurable task of refining and cataloguing his vast array of books and prints – which now constituted one of the finest collections in the land.

But Pepys was inevitably lonely. Most of his friends were long dead. The lone survivor among them was John Evelyn, but he was now in his 80s and cowed by many sorrows. Evelyn had outlived all but one of his eight children and his own health was failing. In 1694, he retired to Wooton in Surrey, and rented Sayes Court, the house and gardens that he had tended over the course of several decades. In 1698, the house was briefly sub-let to the Russian tsar, Peter the Great, for the duration of his visit to England. It was a grand enough billet for a king, and it was conveniently located right next to the dockyards in Deptford where Peter spent his days learning the shipbuilder's craft. But to Evelyn's great distress, the rumbustuous Prince of Muscovy and his courtiers completely trashed the place. During the weeks they lived at Sayes Court they used Evelyn's family portraits for target practice; they chopped up all the chairs for firewood; they spilt ink and grease on the carpets and prised the brass locks off the doors (presumably to see how they worked); they set off explosions in the house, blowing the polished floors apart; and they ripped all the mattresses to shreds. Worse still was the damage to the much-loved gardens. Every plant and shrub was trampled flat. The lawns were a sea of mud and the bowling green had been dug up. Evelyn's prized holly hedge – 400-feet long and five-feet thick – had been utterly destroyed. According to eyewitnesses, the Russians had invented a game that involved sitting a man in a wheelbarrow (on occasion the tsar himself) and charging with it at full tilt into the hedge. The damage was inspected by Christopher Wren in his capacity as Royal Surveyor, and Evelyn was awarded £350 as compensation – a large sum of money, but small recompense for the destruction of a lifetime's work. Yet he barely mentions the incident in his diary, and says nothing about it in his letters to Pepys.

Evelyn and Pepys had always corresponded regularly. It was their chief means of communication once they had both withdrawn from London. Their letters, while full of effusive praise for each other's qualities, have a crepuscular air about them. In the mid-summer of 1700 a servant of Evelyn's brought this note to Pepys at Clapham:

> I could no longer suffer this old servant of mine to passe and re-passe so neere Clapham without a particular account of your health, and all your happy family, wrote Evelyn. You will now inquire what I do here? Why! as the Patriarches of old, I passe the day in the fields, among the horses and oxen, sheep and cowes, bulls and sows, *et caetera pecora campi* ['and the other flocks of the field']. We have, I thanke God, finished our hay-harvest prosperously. I am sewing [draining] of ponds, looking after my hinds, providing carriage and tackle against reaping time and sowing. What shall I say more? *Venio ad voluptates agricolarum* ['I have discovered the pleasures of farming'], which Cicero, you know, reckons amongst the most becoming diversions of old-Age, and so I endeavor to render it.

Evelyn could barely write a paragraph without including some allusion to the classics or a quotation in Greek or Latin. His immense learning was one of the things that impressed the dilettante Pepys when they first made each other's acquaintance back in the 1660s. Books and reading were one of the main themes of the correspondence: it was something the men could share at a distance. Another common thread was the state of their respective constitutions; both men document their geriatric ailments, knowing each one is a milestone on the shortening road to death. In this letter Evelyn describes to Pepys some unpleasant symptoms he is experiencing as a result of a 'strangury', a blockage in his urinary tract. Pepys, who believed that he was something of an expert in this field, responded by imparting some homespun medical advice, having first given a tongue-in-cheek account of his own dull routine.

I have no herds to mind, nor will my Doctor allow me any books here. 'What then,' you will say too, 'are you a doing?' Why truly, nothing that will bear nameing, and yet am not (I think) idle; for who can, that has so much (of past and to come) to think on as I have? And thinking, I take it, is working; though many formes beneath what my Lady and you are a doing. But pray remember what a clock it is with you and me; and be not now (by over-stirring) too bold with your strangury any more than I dare be with my stone; which too has been no less kind to me, in giving me my warning, than the other to you, and to neither of us, I hope, and through God's mercy dare say, either unlooked-for or unwelcome.

I wish, nevertheless, with the same sincerity I do it for my self, that I were able to administer any thing towards the lengthening that precious rest of life which God has thus long blessed you (and you, mankind) with. But I have been alwayes too regardfull of my own health to be a prescriber to others. This onely I must not omit, with thanks to God Almighty, to tell you; that I am this day, and have been now longer together, under more ease in all things relateing to the passing and passages of my urine than I can remember my self to have been at all; and owe it onely to the leaving off malt-drink and betakeing my self wholly to barley-water, blanched with a few almonds and sweetened with a little sugar.

There is a postscript to this letter: 'My eyes force mee to use another's Hand to you which pray forgive.' Pepys weak eyesight had never ceased to bother him, but 30 years after ending the diary he had not gone blind. It was his kidneys that troubled him now: the old pain of the stone was back. But at the end of 1701 he was feeling better, and wrote to his friend to tell him so. Evelyn replied from his house on Dover Street in London.

> My deare, worthy, and constant Friend
> There could nothing have come to me a more gratefull present than what you lately sent me: the re-establishment of your health, and confirmation of the interest you still allow me in your friendship and kind thoughts. How accidents, and the vicissitudes of things in this life and world, puts Earth (as the Spainyard calls distance of place) betweene friends and neerest relations, and which interrupts their personal visites and conversations, no-body can be more sensible of and concerned for than myselfe; especialy since I am come to this smoaky, obstreperous Citty ...

Now they were discussing death as if it were just another one of their mutual interests. Later in this letter Evelyn, godly scientist that he is, makes a neat pun on the words 'Royal Society', which here denote not the scholarly institution to which they both belonged, but the assembly of departed souls in the kingly realm of heaven.

> The voyage which, through all these tempests and tossings here, shall (I trust) sete us safe on shore in those regions of peace and love and lasting friendships, and where those whose refined and exalted nature makes capable of the sublimest mysterys, and aspire after experimental knowledge (truly so called), shall be filled; and there without danger tast of the Fruite of the Tree (which cost our unhapy parents so deare); shall meete with no prohibition of what is desirable, no serpent to deceive, none to be deceived. This is, Sir, the state of that Royal Society above, and of those who shall be the worthy members of it.
> But how, deare Friend, am I fallen into a sermon instead of a letter!

In his reply Pepys invited Evelyn to visit him. They met face to face for the last time at Will Hewer's house in May 1703. Evelyn was recovering from a broken leg; Pepys was very weak. At the end of the month, Evelyn had a letter from Clapham – not from Pepys, but from his nephew, John Jackson.

'Tis no small addition to my Grief, to be obliged to interrupt the Quiet of your happy Recess with the afflicting Tidings of my Unkle Pepys's death; knowing how sensibly you will partake with me herein; but I should not be faithful to his Desires if I did not begg your doing the honour to his memory of accepting Mourning from him, as a small Instance of his most affectionate Respect and honour for you ... And I could most heartily wish that the Circumstances of your health and distance did not forbidd me to ask the favour of your assisting in the holding-up of the Pawle at his internment, which is intended to be on Thursday next.

I must not omit acquainting you, Sir, That upon Opening his Body (which the uncommonness of his Case required of us, for our own satisfaction as well as Publick Good) there was found in his Left Kidney a nest of no less than 7 stones, of the most irregular Figures your imagination can frame, and weighing together 4 1/2 ounces; but all fast linked together and adhering to his Back; whereby they solve his having felt no greater Pains upon motion, nor other of the Ordinary Symptoms of the Stone: The rest of that Kidney was nothing but a bagg full of Ulcerous matter; which, irritating his Bowels, caused an irresistible Flux, and that his Destruction. Some Other less Defects there also were in his Body, proceeding from the same Cause: But his stamina in general were merveillously strong, and not only supported him under the most exquisite Pains, Weeks beyond all Expectations, but, in the conclusion, contended for near 40 hours (unassisted by any Nourishment) with the very Agonies of Death, some few Minutes excepted before his Expiring, which were very calm.

After reading the letter, Evelyn made a slightly back-dated entry
in his journal.

> May 26th. This day died Mr. Sam. Pepys, a very worthy,
> industrious and curious person, none in England exceeding him
> in knowledge of the navy, in which he had passed thro' all the
> most considerable offices, Clerk of the Acts and Secretary of the
> Admiralty, all which he perform'd with great integrity. When K.
> James II went out of England, he laid down his office, and would
> serve no more, but withdrawing himselfe from all public affaires,
> he liv'd at Clapham with his partner Mr. Hewer, formerly his
> clerk, in a very noble house and sweete place, where he enjoy'd
> the fruite of his labours in greate prosperity. He was universally
> belov'd, hospitable, generous, learned in many things, skill'd in
> music, a very greate cherisher of learned men of whom he had
> the conversation. His library and collection of other curiosities
> were of the most considerable, the models of ships especially.
> Beside what he publish'd of an account of the Navy, as he found
> and left it, he had for divers yeares under his hand the History
> of the Navy, or *Navalia* as he call'd it; but how far advanc'd,
> and what will follow of his, is left, I suppose, to his sister's son
> Mr. Jackson, a young gentleman whom Mr. Pepys had educated
> in all sorts of usefull learning, sending him to travel abroad, from
> whence he return's with extraordinary accomplishments, and
> worthy to be heir. Mr. Pepys had been for neere 40 years so
> much my particular friend, that Mr. Jackson sent me compleat
> mourning, desiring me to be one to hold up the pall at his
> magnificent obsequies, but my indisposition hinder'd me from
> doing him this last office.

This encomium was a fine summing-up of Pepys's public life; and it is
somehow fitting that it was confided to the privy pages of a diary. John
Evelyn was too frail to go to St Olave's for Pepys's funeral. But he might
well still have been thinking of his old friend when he next opened his
diary – almost a month later – and wrote this single melancholy line:

Rains have ben greate and continual, and now, neere Midsummer,
cold and wet.

The Mind is the Man

Pepys left his library to his nephew, John Jackson. In a codicil to his
will, he stipulated that it should pass intact to Magdalen College on
Jackson's death. Jackson lived for another 20 years, during which time
the library and Pepys's impressive collection of model ships remained on
display in the house in Clapham. John Jackson died in 1723, and the
following year the books along with their tailor-made cases were duly
transported to Cambridge. The library was housed in the so-called 'New
Building', an elegant extension to the college which, in all probability,
was designed by Pepys curmudgeonly acquaintance Robert Hooke. To
advertise its presence, a Latin inscription was painted over the
colonnade of the new building: 'Bibliotheca Pepysiana 1724'. Next to
this was inscribed Pepys's motto: *Mens cujusque is est quisque* – a thought
that can be economically rendered in English as: 'The Mind
is the Man'.

In 1728, a shorthand enthusiast named Peter Leycester went to the
Magdalen library during a short visit to the city. Afterwards he wrote
this letter to a friend, John Byrom, who periodically taught shorthand
at the university.

I spent the last week at Cambridge. Whilst I was there I went to
see a curious collection of books bequeathed to Magdalen College
by the late Mr Pepys. In the catalogue I met with a book entitled
Shorthand Collection, and would gladly have seen it, but the
gentleman who showed us the library being a stranger, and
unacquainted with the method of the catalogue, we could not find
it. Mr Haderton [the University librarian] tells me it is a collection
of shorthand books containing above a hundred and fifty different
methods. In searching for this book we found five [actually, six]
large volumes quarto, being a journal of Mr Pepys; I did not
know the method, but they were writ very plain, and the proper

names in common characters. If you think it worth your while to make Cambridge in your way to London, you will meet with these and I doubt not several other shorthand curiosities in the Magdalen library. I had not time, and was loath to be troublesome to the library keeper, otherwise I would have deciphered some of the journal.

Leycester was handing his friend a fabulous historical scoop, but Byrom let it slip through his fingers. Though he was eminently qualified to decipher the diary, and though he was in Cambridge often over the course of the next 20 years, he seems never to have followed up on the lead.

Almost a century was to pass before the diaries were noticed again. In 1818 George Neville, master of Magdalen College, showed one or all of the volumes of Pepys's diaries to a relative who was a book collector. Neville may have known for some years of the existence of the diary, and it may have been the recent publication of Evelyn's diaries that prompted him to do something with it. A couple of expert opinions were enough to convince Neville that here was a journal at least as significant as Evelyn's.

Neville delegated the task of editing the diaries to his brother Richard, later Lord Braybrooke. A poor undergraduate named John Smith was employed for the mammoth undertaking of transcribing the hundreds of thousands of words of shorthand. No one had identified Pepys's method as Sheltonian, and nobody thought to point Smith in the direction of Pepys's large collection of shorthand primers. Smith learned the system by studying Pepys's account of King Charles's escape after the battle of Worcester, which existed in both a shorthand and longhand draft. Armed only with this Rosetta stone, he set to work. He laboured day and night for three years, at the end of which he was paid a flat fee of £200. Apart from that, his only thanks were a very condescending and grudging acknowledgment in Lord Braybrooke's first edition of the diaries: 'In justice to the Reverend John Smith (with whom I am not personally acquainted), it may be added that he appears to have performed the task allotted to him … with diligence and fidelity.' Smith, not surprisingly, was very bitter about his treatment at the hand of his editor, and remained so for years after.

As for Braybrooke's own contribution to the printed version of the diaries, it was neither diligent nor faithful. He cut three-quarters of the text, excising in the process all the erotic or lascivious passages (which, to be fair to him, would have been unpublishable in his day). He further bowdlerized the text by substituting words such as 'pox' with euphemistic alternatives. He precis'd or paraphrased passages that he had cut without giving any indication that these interpolations were not Pepys's own words; he 'corrected' Pepys's syntax where it struck him as faulty. The resulting book, published in 1825, was flat and anaemic compared to the ruddy, fleshly original, but it was well-received. It went through several editions and was favourably reviewed by Sir Walter Scott, who was nevertheless rather snobbish about Pepys's value as a historical source and about his gifts as a writer. The poet Samuel Taylor Coleridge also expressed a view on Pepys, but not in print. His thoughts were jotted in the margin of his own copy of the book. 'He was a pollard man, without the top,' wrote Coleridge, 'but on this account more broadly branching out from the upper trunk.' Coleridge seems to be saying that Pepys's energy, enthusiasm and breadth of interests derive from a mental inability to sift out what is important, and then to discard the chaff. It is Pepys's lack of discrimination, the total absence of a poetic sensibility, that make his diary interesting to the refined mind of Coleridge.

Braybrooke's edition was reprinted several times over the subsequent decades. It was superseded in 1875, when a fuller and better transcription was made by another Cambridge scholar named Mynors Bright. This edition was still far from being a complete verbatim transcription. 'It would have been tedious to the reader if I had copied from the Diary the account of his daily work at the office,' wrote Bright in the preface, and in the end he reproduced about 80 per cent of the text. His edition was a qualitative as well as a quantitive step forward. Many of the high-handed alterations of the Braybrooke edition were put right. And Bright finally identified that the shorthand system used by Pepys as Sheltonian.

A felicitous consequence of the new edition was that it prompted another professional writer to express an opinion about the amateur scribbler Samuel Pepys. Robert Louis Stevenson, author of the children's classic *Treasure Island*, published a long essay on Pepys in 1881. It is one of the most insightful things ever written about the man. He says, for example, that 'there never was a man nearer being an artist, who yet was not one.' This has the ring of truth, and is a kindlier way of expressing the same point as Coleridge was making: a true writer (or poet) has to pick and choose the things that seem emblematic or symbolic of the way of the world. Pepys simply and greedily devoured every experience that came his way. That is why he is not an artist, and why his diary is an almost accidental work of art.

A third edition of the diary appeared late in the 19th century. It was produced by Frank Wheatley, relying heavily on Mynors Bright, and it immediately became the standard version. Like all previous editions, Wheatley's Pepys was littered with errors and scholarly misjudgments – some inherited, some new-minted. Some of Pepys's accounts of his sexual adventures were published for the first time, even though they probed the Victorian boundaries of public decency, and the passages that were too explicit for print were honestly marked with ellipses.

A full, correct and unexpurgated edition was still a lifetime away. Two Cambridge men, the latest in a long line of Pepys scholars, began work on such an edition in the 1950s. They were Robert Latham and Professor William Matthews, and their text appeared in nine volumes over the course of the 1970s. The diary was supplemented by a companion volume and an index, and the whole was minutely researched and footnoted. The work of Latham and Matthews was immediately acknowledged a masterwork of textual scholarship, never to be surpassed. No student of Pepys or his times could be without it, nor could anyone who wished to read the diaries for sheer enjoyment.

But the last word on that endearing personality should go to his most perceptive and generous critic, Robert Louis Stevenson. Here he is speaking at quite some length about the childlike quality of Samuel Pepys, which is so much part of his personal charm, and of his writerly method:

Pepys was a young man for his age, came slowly to himself in the world, sowed his wild oats late, took late to industry, and preserved till nearly forty the headlong gusto of a boy. So, to come rightly at the spirit in which the Diary was written, we must recall a class of sentiments which with most of us are over and done before the age of twelve. In our tender years we still preserve a freshness of surprise at our prolonged existence; events make an impression out of all proportion to their consequence; we are unspeakably touched by our own past adventures; and look forward to our future personality with sentimental interest. It was something of this, I think, that clung to Pepys. Although not sentimental in the abstract, he was sweetly sentimental about himself. His own past clung about his heart, an evergreen. He was the slave of an association. He could not pass by Islington, where his father used to carry him to cakes and ale, but he must light at the 'King's Head' and eat and drink 'for remembrance of the old house sake'.

To be quite in sympathy with Pepys, we must return ... to the experience of children. I can remember to have written, in the fly-leaf of more than one book, the date and the place where I then was – if, for instance, I was ill in bed or sitting in a certain garden; these were jottings for my future self; if I should chance on such a note in after years, I thought it would cause me a particular thrill to recognize myself across the intervening distance. Indeed, I might come upon them now, and not be moved one tittle – which shows that I have comparatively failed in life, and grown older than Samuel Pepys. For in the Diary we can find more than one such note of perfect childish egotism; as when he explains that his candle is going out, 'which makes me write thus slobberingly'; or as in this incredible particularity, 'To my study, where I only wrote thus much of this day's passage to this,* and so out again'; or lastly, as here, with more of circumstance: 'I staid up till the bellman came by with his bell under my window, as I was writing of this very line, and cried, 'Past one of the clock, and a cold, frosty, windy morning.' Such passages are not to be misunderstood. The appeal to Samuel Pepys years hence is unmistakable. He desires that dear, though unknown, gentleman keenly to realize his predecessor; to remember why a passage was uncleanly written; to recall (let us fancy, with a sigh) the tones of the bellman, the chill of the early, windy morning, and the very line his own romantic self was scribing at the moment. The man, you will perceive, was making reminiscences – a sort of pleasure by ricochet, which comforts many in distress, and turns some others into sentimental libertines: and the whole book, if you will but look at it in that way, is seen to be a work of art to Pepys' own address.

Here, then, we have the key to that remarkable attitude preserved by him throughout his Diary, to that unflinching – I had almost said, that unintelligent – sincerity which makes it a miracle among human books. He was not unconscious of his errors – far from it; he was often startled into shame, often reformed, often made and broke his vows of change. But whether he did ill or well, he was still his own unequalled self; still that entrancing ego of whom alone he cared to write; and still sure of his own affectionate indulgence, when the parts should be changed, and the writer come to read what he had written. Whatever he did, or said, or thought, or suffered, it was still a trait of Pepys, a character of his career; and as, to himself, he was more interesting than Moses or than Alexander, so all should be faithfully set down ...

It is improbable that the Diary can have been carried on in the same single spirit in which it was begun. Pepys was not such an ass, but he must have perceived, as he went on, the extraordinary nature of the work he was producing. He was a great reader, and he knew what other books were like. It must, at least, have crossed his mind that some one might ultimately decipher the manuscript, and he himself, with all his pains and pleasures, be resuscitated in some later day; and the thought, although discouraged, must have warmed his heart.

Chronology

1633   Samuel Pepys is born in Salisbury Court, near Fleet Street, on 23 February. He is baptized at St Bride's Church.

1642   Civil war breaks out in England. About this time Samuel goes to live with his Uncle Robert in Cambridgeshire. He attends Huntingdon Grammar School.

c.1646   The king surrenders to the Scots at Newark, and is held at Hampton Court. Around this time Samuel returns to London and enrols at St Paul's School.

1647   The king escapes from Hampton Court and flees to the Isle of Wight.

1648   The Second Civil War takes place. The king is brought back to London, and in December MPs considered hostile to the army are forcibly removed.

1649   Pepys witnesses the execution of Charles I. In May England is declared a Commonwealth or Republic.

1650   Pepys goes to university at Magdalen College, Cambridge. He graduates in 1653.

1651   Charles II is crowned in Scotland, and attempts to overthrow the Republic in England. He is defeated in battle at Worcester, and escapes to France, where he lives in exile for the next nine years.

1652   The first coffee house opens for business in London.

1653   Parliament establishes the Protectorate, effectively a one-man dictatorship under Oliver Cromwell.

c.1654 Pepys is employed as an agent and steward by his cousin Edward Montagu.

1655 Jews are readmitted to England. In December, Pepys marries Elizabeth St Michel.

c.1657 Pepys takes on a second job as part-time clerk to George Downing at the Exchequer.

1658 Pepys is 'cut for the stone' on 26 March. Later that year he moves to Axe Yard in Westminster. Oliver Cromwell dies in September, having appointed his son Richard to the post of Lord Protector.

1659 Richard Cromwell resigns, and the Protectorate comes to an end. It is unclear what form of government will now prevail, but some leading Republicans, including Montagu, make contact with Charles Stuart in exile. Pepys sails to the Baltic to report to Montagu.

1660 Pepys begins writing his diary on 1 January. In the spring he joins the fleet as secretary to Montagu and sails to Holland to bring back the new king. In May the king enters London. In July, Pepys is appointed Clerk of the Acts to the Navy Office, and moves to new apartments on Seething Lane.

1661 Robert Boyle publishes *The Sceptical Chymist*.

1662 The Royal Society receives its charter from Charles II.

1663 Pepys begins his long affair with Mrs Bagwell.

1665 The Great Plague sweeps through London. Pepys remains at work in the city throughout. War with Holland breaks out in February. Nell Gwyn makes her debut on the London stage. Isaac Newton, working alone, develops the theory of gravitation and invents calculus. Robert Hooke publishes his *Micrographia*. Pepys is elected a Fellow of the Royal Society, and around this time he makes the acquaintance of John Evelyn.

1666 In June, a great sea-battle the Four Day Fight is waged between the English and Dutch fleets. The London theatres re-open after the ravages of the plague. In September the Great Fire of London destroys most of the City.

1667 The Dutch carry out a devastating raid on the Medway and burn the English fleet.

1668 Pepys successfully defends the Navy Office's conduct of the war in parliament. Nell Gwyn is installed as an official mistress of the king.

1669 In May Pepys, believing he is going blind, closes the diary. In the autumn he takes Elizabeth on a tour of the continent. She is taken ill on the trip and dies in London on 10 November.

1670 Work begins on demolishing the shell of the old St Paul's Cathedral. Pepys once again defends the naval administration, this time before a parliamentary enquiry.

1672 Outbreak of the Third Dutch War. Pepys's patron Lord Sandwich is killed in battle.

1673 The provisions of the Test Act force the Duke of York to resign as Lord High Admiral. Pepys is appointed secretary to the commission that replaces him – a big promotion. The house on Seething Lane burns down.

1675 Christopher Wren begins work on the new St Paul's Cathedral: it takes 33 years to complete.

1676 Pepys becomes Master of Trinity House and a Governor of Christ's Hospital.

1679   Pepys becomes MP for Harwich, but is forced to resign from
        the Admiralty. From May to July he is confined to the Tower,
        on suspicion of having sold secrets to the French.

1680   The charges against Pepys are dropped.

1684   The king appoints Pepys to a new and powerful position: Secretary
        for Admiralty Affairs. The same year, Pepys becomes President
        of the Royal Society.

1685   King Charles II dies, and is succeeded by his Catholic brother,
        King James II.

1686   Isaac Newton publishes his *Principia*, the foundation work of modern
        physics. Pepys's name, as President of the Royal Society, appears on
        the title page.

1688   William of Orange lands an invasion force in Devon, and King James
        flees to France.

1689   Pepys loses his seat in parliament, and then resigns all his official
        positions.

1690   Pepys is briefly imprisoned on suspicion of being sympathetic
        to the cause of King James II.

1699   Pepys becomes a Freeman of the City of London.

1700   Pepys retires to Clapham, where his lives with his old friend
        and protégé Will Hewer.

1703   Pepys dies on 26 May. He is buried at St Olave's on Seething Lane,
        next to Elizabeth.

Sources

Anonymous (1665) *Shutting up infected houses, as it is practised in England, soberly debated*, cited in Nicholson, Watson (1920) *The Historical Sources of Defoe's Journal of the Plague Year* Port Washington: Kennikat Press 144, 163

Anon. (1665) *Golgotha, or a Looking-Glass for London*, cited in slightly edited form in Bell, Walter, George (1924) *The Great Plague in London in 1665*, London: The Bodley Head 143

Aubrey, John (1949) *Brief Lives and Other Selected Writings*, London: Cresset Press 197, 217, 221–2, 227

Bacon, Francis (1926) *Essays*, London: Odhams Press 70

Baxter, Richard (1702) *Reliquiae Baxterianae: An Abridgment of Mr Baxter's History of His Life and Times* 170, 195, 202–3

Bell, Walter George (1924) *The Great Plague in London in 1665*, London: The Bodley Head 156, 189–90, 191, 201, 202

Boghurst, William (1894) *Loimographia: an account of the great plague in London in the year 1665*, reprinted (1984) for the Epidemiological Society of London, Shaw and Sons 145–6, 149

Boulton, W. (1901) *The Amusements of Old London* V2 London 129, 130

Boxer, Charles (1974) *Anglo-Dutch Wars of the 17th Century 1652–1674* London: HMSO 244–5

Bryant, Arthur (1948) *Samuel Pepys: The Years of Peril*, London: Collins 256, 257, 258

Bryant, Arthur (1979) *Pepys and the Revolution* London: Collins 39, 260

Burnet, Gilbert (Bishop of Salisbury) (1818) *History of His Own Time* V1, London 81–2, 90–91, 94–5

Byrom John (1854–7) *The private journal and literary remains of John Byrom* V.1 pt. 1 (Parkinson, R. Ed) Manchester: Chetham Society, cited in *Diary V.1*

Collier, Thomas (1655) *A brief answer to some of the Objections and Demurs made against the Coming of the Jews into this Commonwealth*, London 122

Defoe, Daniel (1722) *Journal of the plague year*, reprinted as Bell, George (1881) *History of the plague in London* 160–2

de la Bédoyère, Guy (1997) *Particular Friends: the Correspondence of Samuel Pepys and John Evelyn* Woodbridge: Boydell Press 251, 252, 262, 263, 264, 265

Diary Vol.1 36, 44, 45, 46, 47, 49, 50, 58, 64–5, 73, 79, 109, 113–4, 115, 135

Diary V.2 110, 114–5, 116, 135

Diary V.3 56, 66, 69, 71–2, 80, 81, 112–3

Diary V.4 60, 61–3, 65, 72, 81, 84–5, 85–6, 89, 96–7, 97, 98, 115, 128, 132–3

Diary V.5 72–3, 98, 99, 99–100, 100, 102, 118, 139

Diary V.6 69, 102–3, 103, 104, 105, 118, 143, 150, 150–1, 157, 162, 170, 226, 243–4

Diary V.7 73, 74, 105, 112, 116–7, 130, 152, 173, 176, 176–7, 180, 180–1, 181, 182, 182–3, 185, 186, 198, 199, 199–200, 218, 224–5, 225

Diary V.8 58, 59, 70–1, 71, , 72–3, 74, 74–5, 90, 95–6, 106, 100–1, 111, 117, 129, 249

Diary V.9 57, 74–5, 83, 106, 119, 218, 230, 247, 248–9, 250, 250–1, 252–3

Diary V.10 (Companion) 66–7

Dowsing, William (2001) *The Journal of William Dowsing* (Ed. Cooper, Trevor) Woodbridge: Boydell Press 30–1

Evelyn, John (1666) *Londinium Redivivum* or *London Restored*, reprinted in (1995) *The writings of John Evelyn*, (de la Bédoyère, Guy Ed.) Woodbridge: Boydell Press 207, 207–8, 208

Evelyn, John (1906) *The Diary of John Evelyn V.2* New York: Macmillan 35–6, 184, 184–5, 188, 195, 200, 266, 267,

Evelyn, John (1955) *The Diary of John Evelyn V3* (Ed De Beer, E.S.) Oxford: Clarendon 207, 210

Halifax, George Savile, (1989) *Marquis of The Works of George Savile, Marquis of Halifax V.2*, Oxford: Clarendon 77

Harrison, Michael (1951) *The Story of Christmas: its growth and development from earliest times* London: Odhams Press 32–3, 33–4

Henry, Philip (1882) *The Diaries and Letters of Philip Henry* (Ed. Lee, M.H) London: Kegan Paul & Trench 29

Hodges, Nathaniel (1720) *Loimologia, or, an historical account of the Plague in London in 1665* (Trans. Quincy, J) London 142, 158

Hodges, Nathaniel (1720) *Loimologia, or, an historical account of the Plague in London in 1665* (Trans. Quincy, J.) London, cited in Nicholson, Watson (1920) *The Historical Sources of Defoe's Journal of the Plague Year*, Port Washington: Kennikat Press 140–5, 142, 152

Hooke, Robert (1665) *Micrographia, or some physiological descriptions of minute bodies made by magnifying glasses, with observations and inquiries thereupon* London 219, 219–20

Huxley, Thomas Henry (1894) *Collected Essays V.4* London: Macmillan 220–1

Kemp, William, *A brief treatise of the nature, causes, signes, preservation from, and cure of the pestilence*, cited in Nicholson, Watson (1920) *The Historical Sources of Defoe's Journal of the Plague Year* Port Washington: Kennikat Press 141, 162

Leicester, H.M. and Klickstein, Herbert S. (1952) *A Source Book in Chemistry 1400–1900* New York: McGraw Hill 228–9

L'Estrange, Roger (1665) *The Intelligencer* October 23, cited in Bell, Walter George (1924) *The Great Plague in London in 1665* London: The Bodley Head 171

Life of Clarendon cited in Eye and Ear 16–17, 18, 19–20, 22, 22–3, 24, 25

Lyons, Henry (1944) *The Royal Society 1660–1940* Cambridge: CUP 223, 224

Magalotti, Lorenzo (1668) *Relazione d'Inghilterra*, Published as (1980) *Lorenzo Magalotti at the Court of Charles II* (Ed. and trans, Knowles Middleton, W.E) Ontario: Wilfrid Laurier University Press, 82–3, 130–2, 133–4

McKendry Maxime (1973) *Seven Hundred Years of English Cooking* London: Treasure Press 64, 67–8

Molyneux, T, (1841) cited in *Dublin Univ. Magazine* 18 216

Newton, Isaac (1687) *Principia Mathematica V.3* 240
Newton, Isaac (1686) *Principia Mathematica V.1* 240
Nicholson, Watson (1920) *The Historical Sources of Defoe's Journal of the Plague Year*, Port Washington: Kennikat Press 157

Notices of the Last Great Plague, 1665–6: from the letters of John Allin to Philip Fryth and Samuel Jeake, *Archaeologia Vol.XXXVII* (1856) 159

Oldenburg cited in Boyle, Robert (1999) *The Works of Robert Boyle* (Hunter, M and Davis E, Eds.) London: Pickering and Chatto 225–6

Pepys, Samuel (1932) *Letters and the Second Diary of Samuel Pepys* (Ed. Howarth, R.G) London: JM Dent 42

Prynne, W. (1665) *A short demurrer* London 121–22

Roth, Cecil (1938) *Anglo-Jewish Letters (1158–1917)* London: Soncino Press 123–4, 124–6, 126–7

Rushworth, *Historical Collections of Private Passages of State* cited in Adair 26–7, 27–9

Sévigné, Madame la marquise (1955) *de Letters from Madame La Marquise*, London: Secker &Warburg 92–3

Shelley, H. (1909) *Inns and Taverns of Old London* London: Pitman&Sons 136, 137, 138

Stevenson, Robert Louis (1988) *The Lantern-Bearers and other Essays*, London: Chatto & Windus 271–2

Taswell, William (1977) cited in *History Today* Vol.27 Issue 12 177, 178, 186, 194, 195

Thomas, WJ (1849) *Notes and Queries*, Oxford 51

(1852) *Notes and Queries* Vol. VI No.149 269

Thomson, George (1665) *Loimologia: a consolatory advice and some brief observations concerning the present pest* London 148

Tomalin, Claire (2003) *Samuel Pepys: the Unequalled Self* London: Penguin 39–40

Turnbull, HW, Scott, JF, Hall AR & Tilling L (1959) *The Correspondence of Isaac Newton V.1* Cambridge: CUP 232, 236, 236–7, 237–8

Verney, Ralph (1925) *Memoirs of the Verney Family* 14–15

Vincent, Thomas (1667) *God's Terrible Voice in the City*, Reprinted (1831) London: James Nisbet 88, 147–8, 153, 153–4, 154–5, 179, 183, 185, 187–8, 192, 194, 197–8

Waterhouse, Edward (1667) *A short narrative of the late dreadful fire in London* 174, 174–5, 175

Westfall, Richard (1983) *Never at Rest: a Biography of Isaac Newton*, Cambridge: CUP Cambridge 233–4

Wood, William (1842) *The Histories and Antiquities of Eyam*, Sheffield: Thomas 166–7, 167–8, 168–9

Wren, Christopher (1750) *Parentalia, or Memoirs of the Family of the Wrens*, London 212, 213–5, 215

Wood, Life and Times (Ed. Clark), cited in Adair 17–18

Young, *Marston Moor 1644* quoted by Scoutmaster-General Lion. Watson, to Henry Overton, a clerk at the House of Commons 20–21

Index

Picture Credits

Cover Illustration © Bettmann/CORBIS; Plate 1 © National Portrait Gallery, London/The Bridgeman Art Library; Plate 2 © The British Library, London; Plate 3 © The British Library, London/The Bridgeman Art Library; Plate 4 © Chateau de Versailles, France/The Bridgeman Library; Plate 5 © The British Museum, London/The Bridgeman Art Library; Plate 6 © The National Portrait Gallery; Plate 7 © Private Collection/The Bridgeman Art Library; Plate 8 © The Wellcome Institute; Plate 9 © Geffrye Museum, London/The Bridgeman Art Library; Plate 10 © Private Collection, Ken Welsh/The Bridgeman Art Library; Plate 11 © Private Collection, Phillip Mould Ltd, London/The Bridgeman Art Library; Plate 12 © Private Collection, Phillip Mould Ltd, London/The Bridgeman Art Library; Plate 13 © The British Library, London/ The Bridgeman Art Library; Plate 14 © Mary Evans Picture Library; Plate 15 © Private Collection/ The Bridgeman Art Library; Plate 16 © The Museum of London/The Bridgeman Art Library; Plate 17 © Royal Academy of Arts Library, London/The Bridgeman Art Library; Plate 18 © The Museum of London/The Bridgeman Art Library; Plate 20 © The British Library, London; Plate 21 © Private Collection/The Bridgeman Art Library; Plate 22 © The British Library, London; Plate 23 © Mary Evans Picture Library; Plate 24 © The British Library, London; Plate 25 © Private Collection, Phillip Mould Ltd, London/The Bridgeman Art Library; Plate 26 © Royal Society of Arts, London/The Bridgeman Art Library.